CROSSROADS OF EMPIRE

Regional Perspectives on Early America

JACK P. GREENE AND J. R. POLE, ADVISORS

Crossroads of Empire

THE MIDDLE COLONIES IN
BRITISH NORTH AMERICA

Ned C. Landsman

THE JOHNS HOPKINS UNIVERSITY PRESS
BALTIMORE

The Johns Hopkins University Press
2715 North Charles Street
Baltimore, Maryland 21218-4363
www.press.jhu.edu

LIBRARY OF CONGRESS CATALOGING-IN-PUBLICATION DATA
Landsman, Ned C., 1951–
Crossroads of empire : the middle colonies in British North America /
Ned C. Landsman.
     p. cm. — (Regional perspectives on early America)
Includes bibliographical references and index.
ISBN-13: 978-0-8018-9767-2 (hardcover : alk. paper)
ISBN-10: 0-8018-9767-X (hardcover : alk. paper)
ISBN-13: 978-0-8018-9768-9 (pbk. : alk. paper)
ISBN-10: 0-8018-9768-8 (pbk. : alk. paper)
   1. Middle Atlantic States—History—Colonial period, ca. 1600–1775.
2. United States—History—Colonial period, ca. 1600–1775. 3. Great
Britain—Colonies—America—History. I. Title.
E188.L36 2010
973.2—dc22   2010007502

A catalog record for this book is available from the British Library.

*Special discounts are available for bulk purchases of this book. For more information,
please contact Special Sales at 410-516-6936 or specialsales@press.jhu.edu.*

The Johns Hopkins University Press uses environmentally friendly book
materials, including recycled text paper that is composed of at least 30
percent postconsumer waste, whenever possible. All of our book papers
are acid-free, and our jackets and covers are printed on paper with
recycled content.

Contents

Acknowledgments

MANY YEARS HAVE passed since I was asked by Robert J. Brugger of the Johns Hopkins University Press, on behalf of the series advisors, Jack P. Greene and J. R. Pole, to undertake a volume on the Middle Colonies for a series on regional perspectives on early America. He has truly been the most patient editor imaginable. Life and work intervened, and it took far longer than I ever imagined, as well as the shedding of many responsibilities, until I was able to complete the volume. Over that time we have learned a great deal about a region that was still somewhat understudied when I began the project. We now understand the Middle Colonies much better than we did then. My view of the subject has changed, as has the whole idea of writing regional histories. Yet I am convinced that there is still something of value in both.

My debts over the years would be too numerous to list in full. I owe much to Richard S. Dunn and Michael Zuckerman, who as faculty advisors long ago insisted that the Middle Colonies were well worth studying. Jack P. Greene, series advisor, provided all the writers in the series with an important discussion of what a regional approach could do for early American history. John Murrin, in his own work and in countless discussions over the years, has given me more questions to think about in the history of the region than I can ever hope to answer. Special thanks go to a colleague at Stony Brook, Donna Rilling, for many conversations, and to the anonymous reader for the press. The greatest credit of all goes to my students at Stony Brook from whom I have learned and with whom I have conversed over the years. I submitted parts of the volume to the many, many fine scholars at the McNeil Center for Early American Studies and have benefited from their vast collected wisdom on the history of the region. There is really no institution like it.

Thanks to Blackwell Publishing for permission to adapt parts of chapter 4 from my essay in *A Companion to Colonial America*, edited by Daniel Vickers (2004). Thanks also to Daniel Richter of the McNeil Center for Early American Studies for permission to adapt chapter 5 from the Fall 2004 issue of *Early American Studies*.

I dedicate the book, as always, to Alison and to Emily.

CROSSROADS OF EMPIRE

Region and History

Every year, visitors from all over the United States flock to Philadelphia to view Independence Hall and the Liberty Bell, hoping to learn about the history of their nation's founding. The city where those places are located, in fact, had a much earlier history than the one the visitors are seeking, but most of those who travel to Philadelphia are far less interested in its origins than in the dramatic events that happened there during America's Revolutionary era. Indeed, those who are interested in exploring the beginnings of American society and of an American people rarely go to Philadelphia at all, looking instead to places such as Jamestown or Boston or Plymouth. In those earlier settlements, they believe, and not in what we have come to call the Middle Colony region, the foundations of American society first emerged.[1]

The neglect of that region, though understandable, may be unfortunate, for some important developments in the forming of early American society were more fully worked out in that region than elsewhere. That is not well known because it was, in many respects, a much messier and more contested story than Americans have been led to believe. It has long been observed that the Middle Colonies, with their diverse populations, extensive religious toleration, widespread commercial pursuits, and traditions of contentious and participatory politics, may have been the region that best represented the diversity of American society. That was not necessarily reflected in regional identity, which was undoubtedly less well formed among residents of the mid-Atlantic than among their New England neighbors to the north and east. In part for that very reason, it was all the more possible to extend the region's principal social characteristics beyond its borders.[2] Indeed, already by the second half of the eighteenth century, European observers and American writers were looking to the mid-Atlantic region for the answer to the question, "What is the American?"[3] It was the emergence of the Middle Colonies as a commercial and cultural crossroads at the center of imperial contest, more than the specific political activities of mid-Atlantic residents during the Revolutionary era, that gave Philadelphia the national importance for which it is celebrated.

Perhaps the first question we will have to answer is why we should focus on a single region at all. In fact, historians have long employed a regional approach to the study of Britain's North American colonies, viewing it as among the best ways to obtain a close-up view of some of the many varying lines of development in early America. Still, there were particular aspects of the Middle Colonies that make the question worth asking, once we come to recognize the growing interconnectedness that developed between those colonies and the other regions of British America.

In recent years, the regional focus in early American history has been challenged by several other popular approaches. One, called "Atlantic history," places Britain's American colonies within the context of an increasingly integrated world of commerce and culture that emerged all around the Atlantic rim from the sixteenth century onward. Such an approach often makes an exclusive focus on the history of any one region look rather disconnected from larger, often global developments. Another approach is a "continental history" that explores the development of early British America against the background of historical transformations that stretched all across the North American continent in the early modern era in a world of clashing and competing empires and peoples.

The Middle Colonies are well suited to combining those approaches. For one thing, the mid-Atlantic region was itself the creation of a series of contests for power and position in eastern North America, involving a succession of European and Indian nations and empires as well as powerful commercial companies.

As we shall see, the region was both defined and continually reshaped by those influences. For another, the emergence of the Middle Colonies as a central place in early America was both the result of, and an important development in, the coming together of an integrated British trading world encompassing a contest of commercial cultures as well.

It is important to recognize that what functioned as the boundaries of the Middle Colony region were neither fixed nor permanent. They were historical creations that could and did change over time in reaction to such matters as war and diplomacy, new trading opportunities, and political developments overseas. At various times the Middle Colonies saw the growth and decline of distinct subregions. Examples include the region along both shores of the Long Island Sound in the early years of the seventeenth century—at the center of a contest among English, Dutch, and Pequot Indians, and very much a part of the struggle to control the mid-Atlantic before mid-century—and the emergence of the Delaware Valley commercial hub toward the century's end.

The existence of such subregions leads us to another question: whether the Middle Colonies in fact represented a coherent region at all. The earliest references we find to "middle colonies" or "middle settlements" were meant to signify not a distinct region but rather simply those places located between the other clusters of early English settlement in eastern North America, in New England and the Chesapeake. Moreover, in important respects, the Middle Colonies can be divided into separate societies focused around the cities of New York and Philadelphia. Thus the economies of the Hudson Valley and northern New Jersey were tied closely to that of New York City, while those of southern New Jersey, Pennsylvania, and northern Delaware were linked to Philadelphia. Those areas grew at very different rates, and they possessed quite distinct characteristics. The proprietary plans for New York and East Jersey were among the most authoritarian in the colonies; those for West Jersey and Pennsylvania were among the most liberal. In religion, New York and northern New Jersey were largely Anglican, Dutch Reformed, and Congregationalist; Pennsylvania and southern and central New Jersey and Delaware were more often Quaker, Anglican, Presbyterian, Lutheran, and German Reformed.

Nonetheless, the Middle Colonies did share a number of things. One was their geography, a combination of climate and topography and setting, which determined some of the ways the land could be put to use, its accessibility to both intra-regional and international commerce, and its strategic importance in imperial competition. It was a region organized around extensive inland waterways, which gave merchants an almost unparalleled access to the American interior, building upon trade routes that pre-dated European settlement. They also placed the people of the mid-Atlantic in proximity to vast territories and many peoples and turned the whole region into a zone of interaction, where events happening in one corner had important ramifications at the opposite end. The wampum trade, in which native peoples along Long Island Sound employed European drills to manufacture the basic currency of the fur trade that extended far into the mid-Atlantic interior, is but one example.

Perhaps the most important argument for the coherence of the mid-Atlantic as a region is the extent to which those colonies shared a common history. The Middle Colonies emerged out of the competing claims staked by successive European powers and native peoples. The region was carved out as imperial space by a Dutch trading company building upon native trading networks, attempting to insert itself into a land contested by English, French, and several different native peoples. Their English successors employed a different but overlapping set of Indian alliances to establish their claims against New England, New France, and still other Indian nations. England's mid-Atlantic colonies were projects of England's Restoration era—a time of restoring the monarchy and a stable social order following the turbulence of civil war in England and its adjacent kingdoms. The Middle Colonies were all constructed with detailed efforts to produce orderly societies within an increasingly consolidated and ordered English colonial world.

The most often-noted characteristic of the region was the diversity of its peoples, a diversity that preceded European colonization. The society of the Middle Colonies surely was "America's first plural society."[4] New Netherland began as the most heterogeneous of colonies, with Dutch, German-speakers, Walloons, English, varied groups of Africans, and Swedes, among others, in its modest population, within a territory also inhabited by Mohawks, Montauks, Mohicans, and many more. Pennsylvania housed English, Welsh and Irish Quakers, German-speakers of the Lutheran and Reformed churches as well as sectarians, Scots and Irish Presbyterians, Anglicans, and a host of others, along with the peoples of several Indian nations—and the variety just seemed to grow over time. Culturally, as well as geographically, New Jersey fell somewhere in between.

There were two principal sources of the growing diversity of the European settlements. One was historical: New York, New Jersey, and Delaware were all conquered colonies, with Dutch, Swedish, Finnish, and many other populations already resident at the time of English conquest. The other was the consolidation that occurred as the colonies of six European nations along the Atlantic coast in the early seventeenth century were reduced to two by century's end, those of England and those of France. The result was that European Protestants heading for the New World were concentrated within English colonies, a situation that virtually mandated some form of toleration. At the same time, the native peoples of the region were brought into altogether new relationships with one another. Thus another set of questions that we will have to ask about the Middle Colonies is, how was all of that diversity accommodated within the region, and what were its effects on the society and culture? Did it influence the whole region uniformly? Toleration and pluralism, it turns out, were not based solely on enlightened benevolence but served varied and real social interests as well, prefiguring the varied forms of pluralism that would manifest themselves throughout American history.

From the beginning, the Middle Colonies filled a distinct niche within a world of empires. As such it was closely connected to imperial diplomacy, to an emerging network of Atlantic commerce, and to the principal currents of transatlantic culture. The mid-Atlantic colonies shipped a multitude of goods to neighboring colonies, to the West Indies, and across the Atlantic. They imported ever-increasing quantities of refined products. They relied upon a wide-ranging transatlantic immigrant trade to build their populations and supply much-needed labor. They were active participants in an Atlantic slave trade that moved Africans in bondage across the ocean and from colony to colony. And they imported books and pamphlets to supply the needs of an expansive network of schools, colleges, and readers. Still another set of questions we will ask, then, is how were the society and culture of the region affected by the abundant commercial opportunities and by their connection to the often conflicting cultural trends of the day? Those included the intellectual movement known as the Enlightenment; the rise of evangelical religion as well as religious toleration; the growth of popular, participatory politics; and an increasing interest in the doctrines of constitutionalism. One answer, as we have noted, was that their central location and their extensive outward contacts would place the mid-Atlantic at the heart of an emerging American polity in the Revolutionary era.

The Middle Colonies thus were linked in both their origins and their histories. Even before the English conquest, the influence of the Iroquois Five Nations redounded throughout the mid-Atlantic, from the Hudson Valley to the Great Lakes and far to the south, and would continue to do so thereafter. The Dutch colony of New Netherland, established to trade with the Iroquois and other native peoples, extended from the Great Lakes to the mouth of the Delaware Bay, including or bordering most of what would become the Middle Colonies. The English conquerors of 1664 built upon that earlier Dutch dominion, administering a territorial unit largely established by New Netherland and working within trading networks created by the Dutch, both with up-river native inhabitants and with overseas Atlantic ports.

The further development of the colonies of the region was interconnected as well. Pennsylvania's period of peace, prosperity, and commercial progress depended to a significant degree on military and diplomatic power emanating from New York. Moreover, the rapid growth of Pennsylvania's population was in part a product of New York's conservative land policy, which lessened its attractiveness to potential migrants, as did the presence of powerful Indian nations. Conversely, not until Pennsylvania's borders were threatened by Indian attacks in the middle of the eighteenth century and its frontiers experienced crowding did the settler population of New York really begin to grow.

The mid-Atlantic colonies were dynamic societies with sharply defined networks of interchange that extended throughout and beyond the bounds of the Middle Colonies. Indeed, so extensive would those connections become that by the end of the colonial period it was becoming more difficult to identify a separate mid-Atlantic region at all. In diplomacy, the Middle Colonies stood at the center of the contest for empire in America, involving both European and native peoples through much of eastern North America. In commerce, the mid-Atlantic sat at the nexus of an extended commercial web linking the merchants of its port cities to small producers and traders throughout the region, to neighboring colonies to the north and south, and to overseas contacts in the West Indies, Europe, and beyond. And culturally, the Middle Colonies experienced a mixing of populations unprecedented in the British colonial world, where those populations worked out the very contours of what would come to be American pluralism. All of these factors put the mid-Atlantic colonies right at the heart of the western extension of the emerging British Atlantic empire. More than any other region of American settlement, the Middle Colonies would help draw together its diverse and far-flung parts.

ONE

The Origins of the Middle Colonies

In 1609, when the English-born navigator Henry Hudson sailed the *Half Moon* up the river that was to bear his name, he staked a claim to the land on behalf of his new Dutch employers. Hudson had not intended to venture into the mid-Atlantic at all; his original quest was for an Arctic passage to the Indies, and only his inability to navigate through the northern ice led him to turn his ship in the direction of America's warmer climes. Hudson was neither the first nor the last to arrive in the mid-Atlantic by circumstance more than by design, as he and others entered a region that was emerging against a background of ever-shifting imperial allegiances. Indeed, nearly a century earlier Giovanni de Verrazzano, a native of Florence, had been the first European to visit much of the region while sailing along the Atlantic coast in the employ of France. And thirty years after Hudson, Peter Minuit, a former director-general of the Dutch colony of New Netherland, would lead an expedition into the Delaware Valley on behalf of the new rival colony of New Sweden.

Nor was it only Europeans who shifted their affiliations amid swirling patterns of diplomacy and empire. Along the northern reaches of the Susquehanna Valley, within what is today central Pennsylvania, lived a powerful Iroquoian-speaking people called the Susquehannocks. Some time around the beginning of our period they began to move southward, possibly to avoid conflict with another Iroquoian power, their northern neighbors of the Five Nations, or Iroquois League. In their new home in the southern Susquehanna Valley region, they would align themselves with the new English colonies of Virginia and Maryland in order to defend themselves against their Indian adversaries. By the late seventeenth century, they had fallen into conflict with westward-moving settlers from those colonies. Still seeking refuge, the Susquehannocks now accepted the protection of the Five Nations and of their allies, the even newer province of New York, and moved back to the north. In the process they would lose some of their members to the Five Nations and others to that group's rivals, the Lenape, or Delaware Indians, in the valley of the same name. There the remainder resided until they were surrounded and eventually displaced by settlers from the still newer colony of Pennsylvania.

Such complicated relocations of position and place typify the story of many of the peoples of the mid-Atlantic both before and after the beginning of European colonization. It was a region where many paths crossed, and a multitude of peoples traversed and fought over its potential trade routes and strategic spots. The Middle Colonies emerged as a region less from the individual aspirations of those who settled than from its geographical position and the competing claims of a succession of Indian and European nations and empires. For colonial powers, the early importance of the region resulted less from *what* it was than *where* it was, while native inhabitants found themselves inhabiting contested territories at the central crossroads of imperial claims. The result would be a region of conflicts and seeming contradictions.

THE MID-ATLANTIC REGION

The area commonly referred to as the Middle Colonies encompasses the three-colony region of New York, New Jersey, and Pennsylvania—and sometimes Delaware, which was initially included in the Duke of York's charter for New York and in William Penn's Pennsylvania proprietary. It would be a middle region principally from an English or British colonial perspective, lying between the older, more established settlements of New England to the northeast and the Chesapeake settlements to the southwest. Those were not its only borders. To the north and west lay territories claimed by France until their surrender to Britain in 1763 in the Treaty of Paris, which concluded the Seven

Years' War. They were home as well to powerful Indian nations, some of whom would align with New France, some with Britain and its colonies. To the east lay the Atlantic Ocean, which, far from constituting a barrier in the maritime world of the seventeenth and eighteenth centuries, represented an opening to the far-off homelands of European settlers, to other American settlements, and to trading partners among the northern Indians. In the days of sailing vessels, the Atlantic constituted the principal communications link not only to Europe but to Africa and the Caribbean as well as to the rest of the British colonial world.

The topography of the mid-Atlantic region would play a major role in the way the Middle Colonies evolved. Along the coast and inland through the extensive river valleys, much of the land within the region is low-lying and arable. Rainfall in the region is sufficient and often ample, but cold winter temperatures, especially during the "little ice age" of the early modern era, precluded significant production of the most profitable plantation crops of the seventeenth and eighteenth centuries such as sugar, rice, coffee, indigo, or—except for the southernmost reaches of the region—tobacco. The land would prove much more suitable for the cultivation of grains such as corn and wheat, typically raised on single-family farms, although those crops were less sought-after at the outset of European colonization.

The region also contained excellent natural harbors, not only at what would become New York and Philadelphia but for a series of lesser ports extending from New Castle in Delaware, to Perth Amboy in New Jersey, to Long Island's Sag Harbor. Their presence would promote considerable commercial activity before and after European settlement, ranging from large-scale transatlantic trading that would emerge after settlement to the smaller coastal trafficking that individual traders—Indian as well as European—often undertook in an effort to benefit from whatever commercial opportunities local conditions might provide.

Beyond several of those harbors lay broad and navigable rivers that cut their way northward from the coast well into the interior, including the Hudson, the Delaware, and—farther inland, but winding its way through the mid-Atlantic backcountry—the Susquehanna. There were also a number of important secondary rivers, such as the Lehigh, the Schuylkill, and the Raritan. Farther north, the St. Lawrence waterway extended its

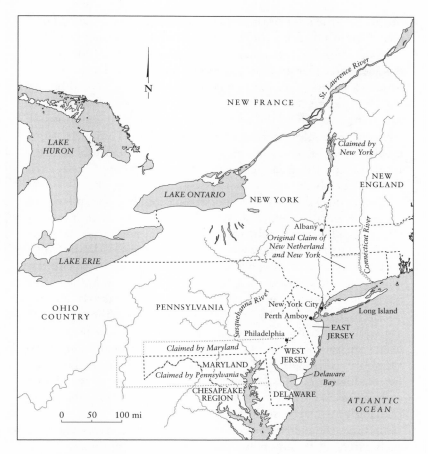

The Middle Settlements of British America. The map shows the many contested boundaries of the Middle Colonies. Adapted from *A general map of the middle British colonies in America*, published by Lewis Evans and corrected by Thomas Jefferys, 1758.

reach all along northern New York from the Great Lakes, its tributaries extending southward to Lake George. To the east, the Connecticut River—the initial boundary claimed by successive Middle Colony governments—offered a path to upper New York. To the west and south, the Ohio River would provide access to the Mississippi Valley and beyond. No other region of British America had so extensive a series of rivers that cut so deeply into the interior or branched so widely along the Atlantic coast: the route from the St. Lawrence south to Lake George reached within a few miles of the valley of the Hudson; the Susquehanna near its source approached both the Delaware and Mohawk Rivers while extending southward to the broad bay of the Chesapeake. The mid-Atlantic was a veritable crossroads of early America, where the commercial and imperial ambitions of a variety of peoples intersected, Indian as well as European, from Quebec, the Great Lakes and Mississippi Valley, southern New England, and the Atlantic coast as far south as the Chesapeake and the Caribbean.

If the mid-Atlantic was a middle region only from an English or British perspective, it possessed many of the attributes of a region well before that. Its topography, combined with the aspirations of its peoples, gave what would become the Middle Colonies an element of integration and coherence even before the coming of the Europeans. The network of natural harbors and navigable rivers permitted commercial dealings across and beyond the region as well as from the coast well into the interior of the American continent. Indian inhabitants of the region established far-flung systems of commercial exchange extending from the shores of Long Island and the Delaware Bay to the banks of the St. Lawrence. Those waterways gave European merchants early access to a vast fur-trading network from the mouths of the Hudson and Delaware Rivers to their upland sources. At the same time, the ability to access the interior, the involvement in such extensive trading networks, and the opportunity for European merchants to establish trading links to inland farms would long involve Europeans and Indians together in a world of commercial rivalries, imperial conflicts, and military contests.

NATIVE PEOPLES

Well before the advent of English settlement, the mid-Atlantic already was a land of many peoples. The native inhabitants included a variety of Algonquian speakers in coastal areas from Long Island through the Delaware Valley; the Five Nations, or Iroquois League across the Mohawk Valley through much of what would become upper New York; their Iroquoian adversaries, the Susquehannocks, along the rivers to the south and west, as well as numerous smaller groups. Native cultures, languages, and lifestyles were both varied and ever-changing. Along the coast, Indians engaged in a variable mix of farming and fishing as well as the hunting and gathering of both animal and vegetable products from the shores and the woods. They also traded regularly with their inland neighbors, exchanging corn, fish, shells, and beads for meat, skins, and furs as well as any products that they or their trading partners might happen to procure from other inland Indians or Europeans.

The Indians along the shores of Long Island Sound produced what would become a particularly valuable trading commodity: wampum, made from shell beads, which would serve as an important medium of exchange between the native peoples and the later Dutch and English inhabitants. Actually, wampum was not produced in significant quantities by Indian inhabitants until the arrival of metal European tools and the intensive involvement of the Dutch in regional exchange. But then it became a widely recognized marker of value in the fur trade, one that was utilized as far as the northern reaches of the region and beyond. Through the control of wampum production, the Pequot Indians of southern Connecticut came to dominate both shores of the Long Island Sound in the early seventeenth century, until a bloody Puritan campaign of eradication in the 1630s, fought with the assistance of rival Indian nations, eliminated at once Pequot dominance and the local influence of their Dutch trading partners.

Among the Algonkian speakers in the southern part of the region were several large groups whom the later European inhabitants would come to call Delawares. How closely related they were to one another at the beginning of the period is not altogether clear. They were divided into many nationalities. Those to the north, from about the Raritan River in central New Jersey through the lower Hudson Valley, largely spoke a Munsee dialect. To the south and east, through what would become southern New Jersey, eastern Pennsylvania, and Delaware, they were more often Unami speakers and used the name Lenape, which outsiders sometimes applied to both groups.

The Delaware peoples shared many things with other woodland inhabitants throughout the northeast. They lived in villages governed by their own chiefs. It was once thought that the powers of the chieftains lay as much in persuasion as in raw power, yet nearly everywhere the authority of the chiefs was expanding in the seventeenth century. Native villages were the centers of agricultural life, which was quite developed and was largely the domain of Lenape women, although men participated in the clearing of the fields and other important activities. This was often accomplished by setting small fires to the brush that cleared out the tangled undergrowth of the forests while leaving the taller trees unharmed—a common method of improving soil fertility and facilitating the agriculture, hunting, and food gathering practiced by many woodland peoples. These were productive economies: their mixed agriculture of corn, beans, and other crops often far out-produced what their European successors would achieve. Women were the central figures in the households of most woodland Indians, which were both matrilineal—with kinship and descent passing through the female line—and matrilocal, with couples usually residing in the wife's village.

Lenape villages often remained in fixed locations, but their communities were anything but static. At the end of the agricultural season many would disperse to winter residences, where they often relied upon fishing or hunting for much of their sustenance. Those activities were largely the work of men. Indian women provided vital parts of the winter diet in the form of ground grain and nuts and dried foods preserved from their summer stores. In spring, the Lenape would often return to summer residences to begin the work of clearing the fields once again, although fields that were farmed too long lost their fertility and were replaced by new fields—and often new villages.

Another major block of Indian peoples in the region were the Five Nations, or Iroquois League, who spread out from the eastern Mohawk River Valley, where Mohawks held sway, as far west as the Genesee Valley settlements of the Seneca. (A sixth nation, the Tuscarora, would migrate northward from Carolina and join the League in the eighteenth century.) In between were found Oneidas, Onondagas, and Cayugas. The League dated from about the fifteenth century, its origins celebrated in the legend of Hiawatha, who, after losing all of his daughters during a period of persistent warfare, encountered and then spread the message of Deganawidah, the Peacemaker, throughout the region.

The Iroquois League was far from a government, since individual nations retained authority over most decisions, including many concerning warfare. At a later date writers would call their form of government "confederacy," a European term that does not quite fit the realities of the Iroquois alliance but that gives some indication of the independent decision making the nations asserted even after the League adopted enlarged powers. The alliance did minimize troubles among the Iroquois nations. It was essentially a league of peace among themselves, which strengthened their hand in their regular battles with various Algonkian peoples to the south and east, Hurons to the North, Sioux and Miamis to the west, and a variety of weaker nations often caught within the conflicts among their stronger neighbors.

The importance of the League came largely from its extensive geographical reach, which surpassed that of any other group in eastern North America. That was the result of geography as well as politics. To the north, Lake Ontario and Lake George provided water access to the St. Lawrence seaway. To the south, the three principal rivers of the mid-Atlantic—the Hudson, the Delaware, and the Susquehanna—extended to the Atlantic and the Delaware and Chesapeake Bays. To the west lay the interiors of the Great Lakes and trade connections to the Mississippi. Thus the people of the Iroquois League were usually well situated for travel and for trade. That the St. Lawrence, Hudson, Delaware, and Susquehanna Valleys would all initially house settlements of rival European nations added to the potential opportunities of the League as well as the dangers it confronted. The Five Nations were truly a people at the crossroads.

The Iroquois were noted for their abodes, called longhouses, within each of which might reside twenty or more families. In these long, narrow structures, often a hundred or more feet long, the families shared fires and other elements of domestic experience. Each house, ideally, represented a female lineage, reflecting the matrilineal structure of Iroquois society. That partly reflected the division of labor within Iroquois society, in which women assumed the primary role near the house in cultivating crops, while men were often away from home for long periods, engaged in hunting or warfare. Iroquois society was divided into three clans—the turtle, the bear, and the wolf—and the Iroquois were expected to marry outside of their clans. Each house was inhabited by husbands from the other clans.

Iroquois women held considerable power within their vil-

Native Peoples of the Mid-Atlantic. Adapted from the map in Cadwallader Colden, *History of the Five Indian Nations Depending on the Province of New-York,* 1747.

lages. They were the holders of most of the property, including the housing, and they represented the most permanent members of house and town. Women had the power to demand wars of retribution against their enemies whenever they lost members of their families and communities, a vital diplomatic power in Iroquois society, as we shall see. Women also played the main role in child rearing. Iroquois marriages were often impermanent, and the principal male figure in a child's life was likely to be not the father but one of the mother's relations.

The longhouses were clustered into towns, which contained thirty or more houses inhabited by as many as two thousand people, constituting one of the largest densities of population in eastern North America during the early years of the seventeenth century. These were not permanent places, however, but were moved periodically as the fields surrounding the towns became exhausted and as the structures within them began to deteriorate. The Iroquois inhabited at least ten such towns in the early years of the seventeenth century, along with many smaller hamlets. Much of the purpose of the towns was defensive; most were located away from the riverbanks, on or near hilltops, and surrounded by wooden palisades several rows thick.

While the Iroquois League maintained a measure of peace among its members, its existence did not inhibit hostilities with their rivals. The Five Nations and several of their neighbors often engaged in a form of warfare known as the "mourning war," which—unlike most western warfare—was designed to add to rather than reduce population. In the typical mourning war, villages or nations that had lost inhabitants through wars or other tragedies attacked their enemies for the purpose of taking captives from them. These would either be tortured to death by relatives of the deceased or adopted into their villages and families, filling important roles in family and community and maintaining population. Unlike European nations, the native peoples of the region feared the loss of population; thus, they rarely went to battle unless circumstances assured that there would be little loss of life.

European observers had little appreciation for these aspects of Iroquoian culture, which struck them as paradoxical, both cowardly and shockingly brutal. They found the rituals of torture that preceded the adoption or execution of captives appalling to European sensibilities. Yet at the same time they were contemptuous of those features of Indian warfare that mitigated its brutality and limited the loss of life, as compared to European tactics that they considered "manly," such as shunning the ambush and fighting to the death.

The arrival of the first European settlers only aggravated those conflicts. As the French, English, and Dutch established settlements near to the Atlantic coast, they aligned themselves initially with nations who were potential rivals and enemies of the Five Nations: Hurons, Susquehannocks, and Mahicans, among others, who inhabited the territories closest to the principal European trading posts established by the French in the St. Lawrence River Valley, the English in the Chesapeake region and in coastal New England, and the Dutch in the valleys of the Hudson and Delaware Rivers. Moreover, the Iroquois lacked direct access to the most valuable trade commodity: furs, or at least the best-quality furs, which came from colder and more northerly areas than the Five Nations controlled. They made up for this shortfall principally by raiding their enemies to intercept recently obtained European goods or, more often, to hijack shipments of the better Canadian furs heading for European markets at Montreal or Quebec.

During the middle years of the seventeenth century, the Five Nations battled their rivals in what came to be known as the Beaver Wars, both for access to the European markets and for the possession of furs. By mid-century, they had defeated the Hurons in the north; the Susquehannocks had removed far to the south; and, perhaps most importantly, the Mahicans were driven eastward beyond the Hudson River, opening the path to the Dutch traders around Fort Orange in the Upper Hudson Valley. Iroquoia was now directly surrounded by competing European powers on all sides.

The Indian wars of the seventeenth century were aggravated by another factor: the loss of population among the peoples of the region due to warfare and, especially, to disease. In the mid-Atlantic as elsewhere in the Americas, one of the first and most dramatic consequences of the arrival of the first European visitors was the introduction of epidemic diseases such as smallpox, to which the native peoples had no natural immunity. Even before Europeans arrived to settle, European traders inadvertently passed microbes onto their trading partners that could decimate coastal populations by as much as 90 percent. The costs of such epidemics were not felt equally everywhere, however. Coastal inhabitants bore the brunt of the first contacts, while inland peoples such as the Five Nations, with less direct contact with Europeans, suffered far less. The result was to alter the balance of power among Indian populations dramatically—in favor of inland populations at the expense of their down-river adversaries.

As conflicts grew during the Beaver Wars, and as the diseases brought by European settlers ravaged native populations, the demand for captives to replace lost members of the populations grew. In a series of aggressive actions, the Five Nations attacked first their Huron adversaries and then a variety of other Indian nations to whom Huron refugees fled, destroying those peoples and taking countless hostages in an effort not only to secure their access to furs but also to maintain their population level. By that time, the majority of Iroquois were very likely adoptees rather than persons born into the Five Nations. Thus, even as European settlers were diversifying the mid-Atlantic population, the warring native peoples were also becoming increasingly intermixed and intermingled.

EUROPEAN EMPIRES AND SETTLEMENT

From an early date the mid-Atlantic also housed a variety of European groups. Unlike the neighboring regions to the north and to the south, the area was never the preserve of a single European power. That was partly because exploration itself came relatively late to the mid-Atlantic, since the region lay outside of the natural flow of winds and currents that took European ships southward to the Caribbean, where Columbus and several other early explorers first landed, and northward from there toward Florida and Carolina. Nor did Europeans easily reach the mid-Atlantic via the northern route pioneered by John Cabot, sailing for England, toward Newfoundland and New England. Cabot visited the Canadian coast as early as 1497, European fisherman probably a decade or more before that, and Norsemen many centuries before. By contrast, the first recorded European voyage to the mid-Atlantic did not happen until 1524, and visits thereafter remained sparse. Thus explorers from a number of European nations had visited the region well before colonization began in earnest. The lack of obvious riches of the sort the Spanish found in the Indies discouraged those powers from aggressively attempting to assert their control at the outset. Thus Verrazzano, Cartier, and Champlain all laid the basis for French title to parts of the mid-Atlantic over many years; Hudson and Arnout Vogels did the same for the Dutch. Some of those voyages occurred in the seventeenth century, a very late date for the establishment of European claims along the Atlantic coast.

Early European settlement reflected that checkered history,

and the mid-Atlantic was home to a succession of European colonizing ventures. At New Amsterdam, the Dutch West India Company established a colony as early as 1624, along with numerous other small settlements in the valleys of the Hudson and Delaware Rivers. By 1664, the city on the Hudson contained perhaps fifteen-hundred persons; the European population of the colony was five or six times that number. Long Island held Dutch settlements in the west and migrants from New England in the east, some of the latter claiming allegiance to the government of Connecticut. The boundaries were never well established or generally acknowledged in any case. The Swedish outpost in the Delaware Valley reached four-hundred strong before it was conquered by the Dutch in 1655.

Each of those colonies was a good deal more diverse than their labels suggest. Most of the early colonizing ventures were really extensions of trading voyages. European nations typically drew sailors and other participants from across national borders. To populate their expeditions as well as their settlements, the fledgling mid-Atlantic colonial ventures accepted migrants of varied backgrounds, resulting in de facto policies of toleration. New Netherland, sponsored by one of the most heterogeneous national states in Europe, contained a mixed population of Dutch and German-speakers, French-speaking Protestants from the Low Countries known as Walloons, Swedes, Danes, Africans from many lands, English, Scots, and Jews, among others. The largest element in the population of New Sweden was probably Finnish. Long Island, with portions claimed by New England and New Netherland, housed significant settlements of Dutch Reformed, New English Congregationalists, English Quakers, Baptists, and other sectarian groups.

All of those settlements were intended primarily as commercial ventures, efforts to tap into the region's extended trading networks. New Netherland, under the sponsorship of the Dutch West India Company, was an outpost of a far-flung Dutch commercial empire in the seventeenth century, with New Amsterdam and Fort Orange well situated to promote Dutch interests within the northeastern fur trade. It was to be an empire not of territory but of trade, a preserve of private merchants with few aspirations for the land except as a base for commerce and as means to service the needs of the more aggressive Caribbean ventures. New Sweden was established as a set of trading posts on the Delaware, also with commercial aims. Even the New English settlements on eastern Long Island were sited principally along the coast, where maritime occupations would long constitute one of the area's principal employments.

The combination of a central location and commercial pursuit involved the mid-Atlantic region early on within the intricate web of international trade and diplomacy. Already before 1660, Fort Orange and the adjoining hamlet of Rensselaerswyck, in the vicinity of what would become Albany, constituted the principal sites of Dutch commerce and negotiation with the Five Nations. New Amsterdam had already garnered an important place within the West Indian provisioning trade. Dutch merchants led a coasting trade between English and Dutch colonies and with Indian nations. New Sweden found itself entangled in triangular diplomacy among the Delaware and the Dutch. Dutch involvement in the wampum trade extended from the shores of Long Island Sound to the far north of the region.

NEW AMSTERDAM AND NEW NETHERLAND

The most important of the early seventeenth-century settlers were the Dutch, or, more accurately, persons of diverse nationalities who settled within the bounds of the Dutch colony. Dutch involvement was a product of European rivalries and that nation's eighty-year war for independence from Spain (1568–1648). In an effort to augment its wealth and power and to preserve its independence, the Dutch Republic began chartering trading companies to commandeer profitable products in far-off corners of the globe and funnel them through Dutch ports. The largest and most important was the Dutch East India Company, dominated by leading merchants from Amsterdam, which set out to break the Portuguese monopoly on East Indian trade. Soon competition within the Dutch commercial community would lead to additional opportunities.

In response to the East India Company monopoly, a group of Lutheran merchants in Amsterdam in 1615 secured a charter for a "New Netherland Company," with exclusive trading privileges in the Americas. In 1621, after changing political fortunes in the Netherlands brought Calvinists to the fore, the New Netherland Company was succeeded by a newly created Dutch West India

Company, a national joint-stock effort dominated by Calvinist traders, including many smaller merchants from outside of Amsterdam, especially the province of Zeeland. Its primary purpose was not to settle territory but to fight and to trade. Its principal focus was the plantation colony of Brazil, which it wrested from Portugal in 1630. Raiding Spanish shipping was another primary goal.

In 1624, the West India Company sponsored its first North American settlement, consisting of about thirty families of French-speaking Walloons, Protestant refugees from southern Belgium. They were scattered at strategic trading spots throughout the company's claim, from the Delaware River north to Fort Orange on the Hudson. Others soon followed, settling chiefly on Manhattan Island at a place they called New Amsterdam. By 1630 the colony contained perhaps three hundred settlers, mostly Walloons. Over the next thirty years the population grew to perhaps nine thousand, extending from Fort Orange to the Delaware Valley to western Long Island. By the time of its demise, the Walloon population was augmented by Dutch speakers, German speakers, and French-speaking Huguenot refugees from France, along with a smattering of Norwegians, Swedes, Danes, Africans, English, Scots, and Jewish refugees from Brazil.

The diversity of the population of the colony largely mirrored that of the Netherlands, which served as home to Protestant refugees from many European nations in an age of intense religious warfare, as well as impoverished job-seekers from the German territories to the east. The Netherlands was a complex and cosmopolitan society in the seventeenth century. The relative toleration it provided as well as the safety it secured for Protestant refugees helped turn it into a center of foreign trade; indeed, the wealth produced by Dutch trading during its "Golden Age" would make the economy of the small Dutch Republic into the wonder of seventeenth-century Europe.

In important respects, the Dutch were the ideal people to settle the mid-Atlantic. In the Netherlands, Dutch merchants developed the landscape in a manner suited to their commercial prowess, with a system of rivers and canals linking the major ports and cities. They approached the mid-Atlantic in similar fashion, creating a system of interconnected commercial sites on Manhattan Island at the mouth of the Hudson, along the Long

Island Sound, and at various stages up the Hudson: at Esopus, later Kingston, and Fort Orange, near where the city of Albany would later be situated. Territory itself was of minor interest to the Dutch company, and they made little effort to colonize beyond those trading stations. On the Delaware also, on a smaller scale, Dutch colonists established a connected series of commercial stops.[1]

The principal settlement in New Netherland was New Amsterdam, located at the southern tip of Manhattan Island, the key to the colony's involvement in overseas trade. From there commercial activity extended in several directions. Looking northward, New Amsterdam merchants bought furs from traders upriver near Fort Orange, by the junction of the Hudson and Mohawk Rivers. There Dutch settlers had established the trading town of Beverwyck (Beaver-town), which would be renamed Albany after the English conquest. To the south and east, merchants worked to supply the Dutch plantation colonies of the Caribbean and Brazil with foodstuffs and slaves, although from early on the development of the local economy was inhibited by the desire of so many inhabitants to devote their energies to the fur trade.

The web of the Dutch commercial network is well illustrated in the career of Teuntje Straatmans, a woman from the Netherlands who probably followed her husband, a soldier, to the Dutch colony of New Holland in Brazil. With her husband dead and Dutch control of the colony ebbing, Straatmans left for the Caribbean, staying for a time at Guadeloupe and possibly other Dutch settlements. From there she moved on to New Netherland, settling in Brooklyn. She left a husband behind in the Caribbean, but in New York had him declared dead and then remarried. He was not dead after all, and after her demise he turned up in the colony.[2]

Links between New Netherland and the rest of the Dutch Atlantic empire led to the early appearance of another colonial inhabitant: the African slave. Dutch plantations in both the West Indies and Brazil used Africans from an early date. Even more, the Dutch West India Company was one of the largest in the African slave trade in the early seventeenth century; it was Dutch merchants who brought the first slave cargoes to Virginia and other English colonies. Most of the early slaves had belonged to

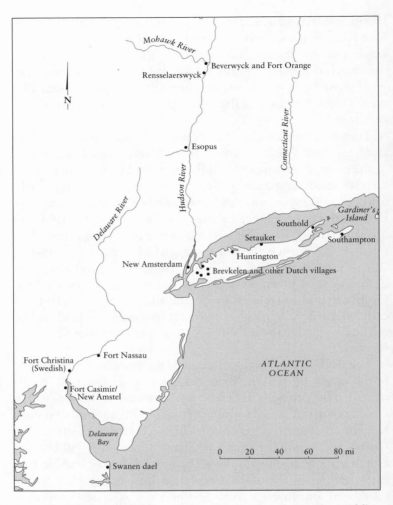

Some Early Dutch, English, and Swedish Settlements in the Middle Colonies.

the Company, who provided the opportunity for long-serving slaves to attain a measure of freedom. By 1664, New Netherland housed several hundred Africans, mostly in New Amsterdam. The largest number of them had been brought in during the previous decade, since the loss of Brazil. By then, Africans in the colony could be slaves, free people of çolor, or in a position of partial freedom granted to some of the first slaves in their later years.

Dutch commercial interests in New Netherland put them in direct competition with the French as Fort Orange became the principal rival to Montreal in the fur trade. The French had the advantage here, since their Huron and Algonkian allies in the north country had access to a better and more plentiful supply of furs than did New Netherland's partners among the Five Nations, who instead took to hijacking the furs that Huron traders were carrying to market. French ties to the Huron and Algonkians led them to attack the Five Nations, who turned to the Dutch at Fort Orange for help. The presence of rival trading networks in what would become Albany and Montreal would shape imperial contests in the mid-Atlantic for many years.

Common hostility to the French traders at Montreal put the Dutch and Five Nations into a tentative alliance. That was especially true while Arent van Curler served as trading agent for his patron, Nicholas van Rensselaer, and as principal Dutch negotiator with the Five Nations. Van Curler established generally good relations with the Mohawk, or so the people of the region would remember it. He died in 1667, shortly after the English conquest, but the Five Nations would subsequently apply the name "Corlaer" to all of the colony's English governors.

Elsewhere, Dutch relations with their native neighbors were not so positive. Although the acquisition of territory was never a prime goal of the colony, the growth of New Netherland was stunted by frequent hostilities with Indian neighbors. In 1639 the colony under Governor Willem Kieft tried to levy taxes upon a Lenape village. When they refused, it turned into a protracted war that proved to be a bloodbath. Enlisting the aid of several veteran soldiers from New England with experience in Indian-fighting from the Pequot War, the Dutch launched a series of attacks in which they slaughtered more than one hundred villagers in what would become New Jersey and Westchester County. In one village the soldiers massacred everyone they found. For their part, the villagers and their allies laid siege to the walled city of New Amsterdam and drove Dutch colonists out from most of the surrounding outposts. By the time hostilities ended in 1645, the damage to the colony was considerable.

The slow growth of the colony, exacerbated by Indian wars

and imperial rivalries, eventually persuaded some of the Dutch West India Company to attempt to bolster settlement. To do that, the Company promised active promoters huge landed estates called *patroonships,* which they could control and govern if their colonizing efforts were successful. For each sixty colonists the patroons brought over, they were promised four miles of frontage in the Hudson Valley, with lands as far inland as the inhabitants cared to settle. The patroonships had a troubled early history, in part because Dutch merchants had little interest either in land or settlement, and only the Hudson Valley property of Rensselaerswyck, chartered to company supporter Kiliaen van Rensselaer, would have a long and significant existence. Still, the patroonships would set an important model for the later history of the colony.

Whatever difficulties New Netherland had in peopling the land, what finally destroyed the colony was not internal squabbling but imperial rivalry, in this case with their other regional rivals, the English, who had pushed Dutch traders back from their Connecticut River claims several decades before. The two nations were competing globally in several arenas: in West Africa, where the Royal African Company challenged Dutch primacy in the slave trade, and in the North American fur trade. The outbreak of war between England and the Netherlands in 1663 provided an opening for English action against New Netherland, and in 1664 the Duke of York organized an invasion force under the command of Richard Nicolls. For several years Governor Stuyvesant had warned his superiors in the Netherlands of the threat of invasion, but they provided no additional soldiers or supplies. New Amsterdam, with fewer than 150 soldiers in its garrison, was poorly prepared to resist.

MID-ATLANTIC PERIPHERIES:
DUTCH, SWEDES, AND NEW ENGLISH

The Dutch were not the only European power to lay claim to lands and trading privileges within the mid-Atlantic region. With New Netherland's trade firmly in the hands of the Dutch West India Company, a rival merchant group from the Netherlands took their cause to Sweden, nominally allied with the Netherlands in the Thirty Years War, and a nation whose military prowess under Gustavus Adolphus (1611–32) and later Charles X

(1654–60) had not been matched by accomplishments in trade. With the investment of Dutch merchants and the guidance of such veterans of New Netherland as Peter Minuet, the former director-general, Sweden fitted out a small fleet to establish an outpost in the Delaware Valley at a place they called Fort Christina, in the vicinity of modern-day Wilmington, Delaware. There they established trade with the natives, chiefly for furs brought south along the river from the back reaches of New Netherland. The Swedes, like the Dutch, were essentially middlemen, seeking to divert commerce previously funneled through New Netherland into their own colonial post.

Like most of the other early colonial efforts, New Sweden attracted only a small population, no more than about four hundred settlers at the time of its demise. The largest number were Dutch at the outset. Later they were probably Finns, who constituted a class of poor laborers within a Sweden that included their homeland. The colony continued to expand slowly, extending its settlements thinly along both banks of the Delaware and into what would become New Jersey.

For more than fifteen years Dutch and Swedes coexisted uneasily in settlements that faced one another across the Delaware Bay. Owing to their nominal alliance in Europe, they were under orders not to attack one another, but settlers on both sides maneuvered for commercial advantage, confident that the trade of the valley would not easily accommodate them both. The Dutch, catching the Swedes at a moment of weakness and seeking the advantage, challenged the Swedes with a fort on the western bank of the Delaware at a place they called Fort Casimir, by the harbor that would become Newcastle. For a time in 1654 the situation seemed to favor the Swedes, when the arrival of two hundred settlers tripled the colony's population, and they set out to conquer the Dutch fort. A year later a Dutch force led by Peter Stuyvesant retaliated and drove the Swedes from Fort Christina, incorporating the whole colony into New Netherland. Some Swedish settlers remained under Dutch rule, where they were allowed to keep their homes and to worship in the Swedish manner. That leniency was in part because of the shortage of inhabitants and because New Netherland had once again gone to war against its Lenape neighbors. But the Swedish colony was no more.

Dutch rule did not last much longer. Populating the Delaware region was never a priority of the New Netherland colony, and in the unsettled times of the 1650s the concerns of the Fort in the valley ranked low in Stuyvesant's priorities as well. With the collapse of New Netherland in 1664, the lower Delaware Valley also passed into English hands. The principal legacy of the era of Continental European settlement in the valley would be a small residue of Swedish and Finnish farmers located within the bounds of New Jersey and Delaware. They were occasionally restive—there was a brief uprising known as the Revolt of the Long Swede in 1669 and occasional later efforts to resist Quaker oversight—but for the most part they did their best to avoid confrontation or overt control.[3]

Migrants from New England who moved across the Sound to Long Island comprised the other main group of Europeans who settled within the mid-Atlantic before the English conquest. In the early years of the century, the area was dominated by the Pequot confederacy of southern Connecticut, which controlled the wampum trade on both shores of the Long Island Sound, until a Puritan war of extermination destroyed Pequot power. That opened the territory to new settlement, and in 1640, Puritans from Lynn, Massachusetts, sailed southward to the south fork of eastern Long Island, where they established a New England-style township at Southampton, complete with town meetings and Congregational churches. At about the same time, another New England group settled on the north fork of the island at a place they called Southold. Over the next two decades other New Englanders settled at Easthampton, Oyster Bay, Huntington, and Newtown, the last of those located near Dutch settlements on the west of the island. By 1664, eastern Long Island resembled New England in its emerging landscape and social order.

There were several differences between the Long Island settlements and those north of the Sound. The religious order on eastern Long Island did not replicate that of New England. In its first decades the Massachusetts Bay Colony had worked assiduously to try to establish Puritan orthodoxy within its settlements. The result was that many of those who deviated from that colony's standards looked for other places to go. The town of Lynn, Massachusetts, was known early on as a place where religious sentiment often deviated from Puritan orthodoxy; thus, Lynn was the source of some of the first settlers of Southampton. Other Puritans from religiously radical backgrounds ended up in Oyster Bay. In the ensuing years, the Long Island Sound would be traversed repeatedly by those who interpreted Puritan religion differently, including Quakers, religious separatists, and Baptists. In the Middle Colonies, there was ample room for such diverse ideas and practices to take hold.

Another difference that separated Long Island from New England was the presence south of the Sound of a number of prominent individuals who deliberately separated themselves from the Puritan authorities to the north. One such individual was Lion Gardiner, an Englishman with considerable military experience gained during Europe's religious wars. Gardiner had served in the Netherlands as a builder of military fortifications and had married a Dutch woman. He was recruited to New England in the 1630s to help the colony build fortifications prior to the Pequot War. Gardiner disagreed with several aspects of the conduct of the war, including both their readiness to go to war and the level of brutality inflicted. When he was subsequently courted by Montauk Indians from eastern Long Island who were seeking to avoid their own conflict with the English, Gardiner negotiated. In 1639, as part of his new alliance, he obtained from them an island off Long Island's eastern shore. The property, which became Gardiner's Island, has remained in the family into the twenty-first century. In addition to his Indian deed, Gardiner secured an English patent for the island from the estate of a Scottish nobleman. Still, it remained a private manor outside of the jurisdiction of existing colonies.

Another important individual was John Underhill, an early settler of Puritan Massachusetts who, like Gardiner, had military experience in the Netherlands and a Dutch wife. He also fought in the Pequot War. Underhill was a follower of Anne Hutchinson, the Boston woman who was exiled from the Massachusetts Bay colony for her radical and unorthodox views. Upon his return from the war, Underhill, like other of Hutchinson's followers, was disfranchised and disarmed.

Disenchanted with Massachusetts, Underhill responded to an invitation from New Netherland to assist in the military campaign of Kieft's War and moved in 1643 to that colony, where he was later accused of turning Dutch warfare in the brutal direction it went. In 1652, with the outbreak of war between the Netherlands and Cromwell's England, Underhill sided with England and raised its flag on Long Island. He subsequently fled to Rhode Island, where upon the death of his first wife he married a Quaker woman. He then returned to Long Island, settling in Setauket, where he signed a petition in favor of uniting Long Island to Connecticut. Underhill later moved to Oyster Bay, where he became a powerful supporter of the local Quaker meeting, although there is no record that he actually joined the Society of Friends. In 1664, with the impending English invasion of New Netherland, Underhill aligned himself with the invaders and the new government of New York, to the chagrin of both his former Dutch employers and his Connecticut allies, the latter still hoping to attach Long Island to their colony.[4]

The ability of men such as Gardiner and Underhill to shift their loyalties and move between cultures made them fitting inhabitants for a mid-Atlantic region, where the contest for dominion was central, where a succession of empires asserted their claims, and where diverse populations were the norm rather than the exception. Those individuals with the ability to negotiate those boundaries—and the valuable military skills that allowed them to enforce their interests and their often grandiose claims —found themselves with almost unlimited opportunities.

The situation within the region was always volatile, and it took only small incidents to set off much larger conflicts. Thus a Dutch assault on a village of Raritan Indians in 1640 would lead to a Raritan attack on a farm on Staten Island the following year, followed by later missions by the Dutch and their Indian friends against the Raritans. As more and more groups pressed in upon the region, their interests came ever more frequently into conflict. For that reason the Iroquois drove the Susquehannocks southward into the lands that Maryland claimed, Mohawks pushed Mahicans east of the Hudson, the Dutch removed the Swedes from the Delaware, and, in 1664, the English would force the Dutch from New Netherland.

Those small European beginnings in the mid-Atlantic left a large legacy. New Netherland's foundation as a commercial colony gave it an increasingly central position within the Atlantic coastal areas of North America, helping to extend and solidify a region that had emerged out of complex Indian and European claims. The most concrete legacy was a diverse population of up to ten thousand European migrants, who would comprise the bulk of the settler populations of New York and of the lower Delaware region for the rest of the century. They established population centers at what would become New York and Albany, along with diverse collections of outliers inhabiting Long Island and the lower Delaware. They built upon Indian trade routes to trade across the region and to develop international commercial networks from the fur trading capital at Albany and the Mohawk Valley south to New York City, the Long Island Sound, the Delaware forts, and on across the Atlantic. They initiated an important trading relationship with the Mohawk and a fierce rivalry with French settlements to the north. They established a foothold in the important West Indian provisioning trade and the beginnings of African slavery in the mid-Atlantic. Those would all have long-lasting significance in the region.

TWO

The Duke's Dominions

ALTHOUGH INDIVIDUAL Englishmen had been involved in the mid-Atlantic since Henry Hudson's initial 1609 voyage and scattered groups of English colonists were to be found within New Netherland and New Sweden as well as on Long Island, England itself only entered into the colonization of the region in 1664. In that year a small fleet under the command of Richard Nicolls arrived at Gravesend Bay on Long Island, within striking distance of New Amsterdam, and demanded its surrender. The city had no more than 150 soldiers at their command and thus was in poor shape to resist, a fact quickly recognized by most of its leading citizens. The conquest was accomplished without a shot being fired, much to the dismay of then-governor Peter Stuyvesant, who had tried to persuade his countrymen to fight. Both the city and the colony were renamed "New York," the province extending in theory from the Connecticut River—the same boundary initially claimed by New Netherland—to the southern reaches of Delaware Bay, with additional territories that included Long Island and other offshore islands as far north as Maine. In short, it included the whole of New Netherland and more.

The name attached to the new colony was no idle compliment. The moving force behind the conquest was James Stuart, Duke of York, Lord High Admiral of England, brother of Charles II, and heir to the crowns of England and Scotland, which he would assume upon his brother's death two decades later. In the world of Restoration politics, James cut a substantial figure. Unlike his elder brother, the duke was no trimmer in either religion or politics. While during Charles's reign rumors circulated of the king's secret conversion to the Church of Rome, James would boldly proclaim his Catholic allegiance. That, combined with an aggressive employment of the king's prerogative, which his brother had asserted more often than he exercised, and the granting of toleration to Catholics in both his kingdom and his colony, would make James a widely feared figure within Britain's Protestant and Parliamentary communities.[1]

James was certainly not the prototypical proprietor, and his legacy in North America is far less remembered than that of his Pennsylvania counterpart, William Penn. He consistently built upon foundations laid by native peoples and by his Dutch predecessors in establishing the region, its alliances, and its trading patterns. Nonetheless, the duke would be among the most influential figures in the history of the Middle Colonies, bringing New York under English dominion, extending its boundaries, institutionalizing a system of alliance with Indian nations in the northeast, and controlling the colony for more than two decades, first as proprietor and then as king. In the process, he would link those territories to the turbulent politics of England's Restoration years and to a larger world of power politics and imperial rivalry across western Europe.

James organized his colony in a distinctive manner, creating an authoritarian political system, establishing a centralized imperial diplomacy, and imposing religious toleration upon an often unwilling populace. Where the two came into conflict, James preferred dominion to development. Paradoxically, in creating such formal structures of authority, the duke created space as well for some altogether different colonial forms to emerge within the region, under the administration of other powerful proprietary authorities with quite distinct political and religious goals. Indeed, James's association with William Penn was one of the key factors in the Quaker acquisition of Pennsylvania, which, like New York, was a proprietary colony founded on principles of toleration, diplomacy, and central authority.

THE DUKE AND HIS COLONY

In important respects the involvement of James with New York was itself a product of that colony's Dutch background. In his role as Lord High Admiral, the Duke of York was a leader of the faction within the government that favored an aggressive military posture toward the Dutch, whose extensive commercial interests conflicted with English mercantile aspirations in several parts of the world. Those included Africa, where the Company of Royal Adventurers Trading to Africa, also led by James, competed with well-entrenched Dutch slave traders, and the East Indies, where James also played a significant role. Like his colony, James himself had extensive and complex ties to the Dutch. His Protestant daughter and heir, Mary, was married to the Dutch prince William of Orange. It would be William who would remove James from the throne and succeed to the crown along with his wife.

James's career owed much to his upbringing. Son of the deposed (and beheaded) King Charles I, James spent his formative years in Catholic France. Ever after, he displayed many attitudes that would have been recognizable in that kingdom. One of these was the claim of unfettered royal authority, something expressed with far greater freedom by Louis XIV than James was ever able to assert. Another was his support for a limited religious toleration, which was state policy in France under the Edict of Nantes (1598) until its revocation in 1685. The motive behind toleration in France was not necessarily benevolent: allowing Protestants to worship safely within their own fortified cities in that Catholic kingdom assured their loyalty to the Crown and lessened the threat of political strife and a Protestant challenge to royal authority.

In Britain, James was known for his aggressive defense of the royal prerogative, and he displayed some of that same assertiveness in New York. The seizure of New Netherland, in fact, contributed to another of James's ambitions: to unify the administration of England's American colonies, which the Dutch province had divided in half, while at the same time controlling his Protestant adversaries there. To establish a centralized American authority would allow England to wrest power from the Puritan colony at Massachusetts, which was decidedly hostile to the Restoration government. Indeed, Massachusetts provided shelter for two Puritan leaders implicated in the execution of Charles I, father of both James and Charles. The grant James obtained gave him title to territories that would surround New England on the

King James II of England, by Sir Godfrey Kneller, Bt., 1684. James far outranked any other figure active in the life of the Middle Colonies. Courtesy of National Portrait Gallery, London.

north, south, east, and west, including Maine, Long Island, Martha's Vineyard, and Nantucket, with New York's boundary extending as far east as the Connecticut River. It established English sovereignty over virtually the whole of the Atlantic coast from Maine to Virginia.

The duke's grant for his province contained fewer restrictions on proprietary authority than that of almost any other colony. It did not require that James create a representative assembly in New York, as did those of other Restoration colonies; instead, the proprietor was free to establish laws and control trade by himself. In 1665 Richard Nicolls, acting as James's deputy, issued what became known as the "Duke's Laws," which established a governor's council for the colony in the place of a legislature and offered few political concessions to the inhabitants. As Nicolls commented, "Our new Lawes are not contrived soe Democratically" as were those of the other colonies.[2] Of elected assemblies, James wrote, "I cannot but suspect they would be of dangerous consequence," such bodies being apt "to assume to themselves such priviledges wch provfe destructive to, or very oft disturbe, the peace of the governmt wherein they are allowed."[3] Not until two decades later, in the midst of intensive political squabbling on both sides of the Atlantic, would the New York government seek to placate aggrieved settlers by announcing a more expansive "Charter of Libertyes and Priviledges" for New Yorkers. However, James succeeded to the throne shortly thereafter and quietly shelved the new charter.

The duke's government took special care to limit the power of local authorities. On eastern Long Island were several towns that had borrowed their local form of government from New England, from which most of the settlers there had come; many in that region maintained their allegiance to Connecticut until placed under York's jurisdiction by his patent. But the Duke's Laws gave no authority to that prized New England institution, the town meeting, and the towns were subsumed under the new county of Yorkshire, which extended from Westchester to Montauk Point.

The principal concession the proprietor did offer New Yorkers was religious toleration, which was partly a carryover from the Dutch period and was amenable to the needs of the old inhabitants, many of whom adhered either to the Dutch Reformed Church or to the various radical Puritan persuasions that Long Islanders had brought with them from New England. In fact, James considerably broadened the reach of toleration in New York, extending it at least in part to groups such as Lutherans, Quakers, Catholics, and Jews, who had been tolerated only grudgingly, if at all, by his New Netherland predecessors. Toleration was very much in keeping with James's prior experience of exile in France. For James, toleration had the practical advantage both at home and abroad of legitimizing Catholic forms of worship and the holding of political office by adherents of the Church of Rome in a predominantly Protestant kingdom and colony.

The toleration established in the colony was not the same as religious freedom. Officially, it extended only to Christians, although Jews, who were already living in New Amsterdam, did begin to hold public worship without negative repercussions, which they had not been permitted to do under Stuyvesant. More important, perhaps, toleration did not mean religious equality. The various towns were authorized to collect taxes to support a minister and a meetinghouse, and religious minorities, where they existed, were not exempt from the tax. Thus toleration within the duke's province was more about religious autonomy for strong local churches than about spiritual liberty for individuals (see chapter 5).

For decades, New York displayed characteristics of a conquered society. The majority of the European inhabitants were still holdovers from the Dutch period, but their allegiance was considerably divided. At the upper levels of society, especially in New York City, some leading Dutch merchants began to seek an accommodation with the conquerors. The privileged Anglo-Dutch commercial elite that emerged would long hold prominent places in New York's local and overseas trade. Lesser merchants spread their trading networks across the region. Elsewhere, Dutch-speaking families often retreated into local enclaves, maintaining a considerable degree of isolation from the newcomers. The town of Albany, for example, whose name had been changed in recognition of one of the duke's titles, would long retain a decidedly Dutch character and a notoriously independent attitude that came to be known as the "Albany Spirit."

Contributing to that isolation was the peculiar topography of the colony. North of New York City the bulk of cultivatable land was confined to the broad expanse of the Hudson Valley; settlement farther west was impeded by the Catskill Mountain range. Moreover, some of the upper valley had already been distributed in the form of the vast patroonships that the Dutch West India Company had granted to its most aggressive or politic promoters. Only Rensselaerswyck, a huge parcel extending for miles along both sides of the Hudson below what would become Albany, persisted. Rather than abandoning that system, the English government chose to further it, granting many more large manors to favorites of its own, from the Livingston and Cortland Manors in the north country to the Sagtikos and St. George Manors on southern Long Island.

Nor was English rule so firmly established in 1664 as three hundred years of hindsight would suggest. New Netherland had been conquered by a small English fleet, and for several years rumors circulated of the approach of Dutch vessels planning to take it back. In fact, such a takeover was never out of the question; and in 1665 and again in 1667, New Yorkers were warned of Dutch ships prowling in the vicinity. The third Anglo-Dutch war in 1673 did result in the reconquest of New Netherland, but it was returned to New York as part of the peace treaty at the end of the following year. It is little wonder that Dutch settlers did not uniformly transfer their allegiance upon first conquest.

Another source of tension in New York was located in the Long Island towns of Suffolk County that owed their origins to New England. Those settlers had little affection for the Dutch and even less desire to subordinate their interests to that of the New York merchant community. Nor did their Puritan origins leave them inclined to favor the rule of the Catholic James. Those settlements were accustomed to local governance through their town meetings, and they did their best to maintain that form of administration, even after the New York government quashed their efforts to align with Connecticut and subordinated the rule of the towns to county government.

James's policies helped to enforce another division. The duke granted the city of Albany, dominated by Dutch merchants, a monopoly on the fur trade, and granted a similarly exclusive control on overseas trade to the merchants of New York. Of course, most of the furs were destined for foreign points, which necessitated uncomfortable dealings between those long-autonomous communities. In fact, there was considerable resentment against the New York City merchants from all of the river towns. Beyond that, James's government granted monopolies to leading merchants in several trades, which caused considerable dissatisfaction among many of the smaller and less-connected merchants in the colony.

A special source of tension for all of those groups was New York's central position within the English colonial world. From the beginning, New York was the only colony with a garrison to defend it against both the Dutch and hostile Indians allied with New France to the North. Armies cost money, and James had never intended to subsidize New York out of his own pocket. On the contrary, the possibility of drawing a revenue from an already-settled colony was one of his principal motives in taking on the proprietary. But the taxes New York imposed upon its inhabitants did not sit well with a citizenry denied the right of representation within a colonial assembly. Especially troublesome were the Long Islanders, with their traditions of strong local government, whose resistance prompted Nicolls to complain that "democracy hath taken so deep a Roote in these parts," and that it was his task to lay "the foundations of Kingly government . . . which truely is grievous to some Republicans."[4]

The work of turning the duke's plans into actions fell upon the governors he appointed, who were firm Stuart loyalists with a decided propensity for military force. The first, Richard Nicolls, generally sought to implement James's goals through conciliation, offering the inhabitants security of property and other subtle concessions—but few formal rights—in exchange for the recognition of proprietary authority and peaceable conduct. That did not appease all of the inhabitants, but they had little choice other than to accept the conditions.

Others employed a different style. In 1674, following the return of New York to English rule after the third Anglo-Dutch war, James sent Sir Edmond Andros, a career soldier and long-time Stuart associate, to settle affairs in the newly reacquired colony. Andros's methods were far from subtle. When the three eastern Long Island towns of Southold, Southampton, and Easthampton announced their intention to maintain the allegiance to Connecticut that they had resumed during the Dutch reconquest, Andros declared the town leaders to be rebels and promised the same treatment for their whole populations if they did not submit. Andros appeared in person with a band of soldiers to persuade the reluctant townsmen. They got the message. Andros also traveled to Delaware to enforce the duke's claim to territory there that was claimed by Lord Baltimore. And when the Quaker John Fenwick planted a colony in West Jersey and challenged Andros's authority in the region, Andros sent soldiers to capture Fenwick and bring him to New York for trial and punishment, which included fines and a term in a New York jail.

The tensions that divided groups in the colony offered some dramatic possibilities for those positioned to bridge the gaps. One such individual was Robert Livingston, the son of a renowned Presbyterian minister in Scotland. Following the restoration of monarchy and episcopacy in that kingdom in 1660, the Livingston family sought refuge in Rotterdam, an important commercial city in the Netherlands with a large community of Protestant refugees, many of them Scottish merchants and ministers. There the young man learned the arts of commerce and of personal connection, along with the Dutch language. In 1673 he embarked for Massachusetts, where his father had once been offered a pulpit. But the newer colony to the west seemed to hold prospects better suited to Livingston's commercial training and linguistic skills, and the following year he moved on to Albany.

From small beginnings, Livingston utilized his varied experience and connections to put himself at the center of a vast commercial web. Like such earlier figures as Lion Gardiner and John Underhill, Livingston was able to trade on what he had learned in the cosmopolitan world of the Netherlands. As one of the few English-speakers in Albany, he became clerk of the town and English secretary to Nicholas van Rensselaer of Rensselaerswyck Manor, whose wealthy widow he married upon the death of his patron. His religious background as the son of a pious minister led to a trading partnership with the Puritan merchant John Hull in Boston, while his Scottish connections provided a tie to the merchant James Graham in the city of New York. He used his facility with language and negotiating skills to get himself appointed Secretary to the Board of Indian Affairs. In the process, Livingston became one of the principal conduits

of the fur trade and one of the few individuals who could negotiate simultaneously with the tightly knit Dutch traders of his
adopted city and the rival English or Anglicized merchants of
New York. His ability to work within that trade and to mobilize
resources would make the Scotsman indispensable to the func-
tioning of government and commerce. That he could communi-
cate both in Dutch and in English made him a vital negotiator of
Indian policy.

THE COVENANT CHAIN

One area of particular interest to the duke's government was
Indian affairs. Part of James's plan for establishing order in the
region and projecting English authority was to create working
alliances with powerful Indian neighbors who could simultaneously help balance rival European interests, control lesser Indian
peoples, and check the aggressiveness of the New Englanders.
During the two-and-a-half decades that James ruled New York,
his government and the Five Nations established a basic framework for regional diplomacy that would be important for much
of the next century. They built upon earlier relations, to be sure,
including the establishment of Fort Orange and the adjacent
settlement as New Netherland's center of the fur trade, attracting the commerce of the Iroquois as an alternative to French-
sponsored trade with Huron and Algonkian Indians through
Montreal and Quebec. Under the duke, New York secured a
central position in Anglo-Indian relations, creating a diplomatic
structure that encompassed the entire northeast.

Much of that structure was worked out by Sir Edmund Andros in a sequence of activities in and about the year 1675. In that
year much of New England was nearly wiped out by a series of
Indian attacks in what came to be known as King Philip's War,
named after the Wampanoag Grand Sachem Philip, or Metacom,
who led the attacks. Andros was no friend to the Puritan governments of the region, but he was committed to defending the
king's empire overseas, and he saw as well an opportunity to
augment the authority of New York within the region. Andros
recruited Mohawk warriors in eastern New York, traditional enemies of the Algonkian supporters of Philip, to attack the latter's
army from the west, saving New England from further devasta-

tion. Andros then invited some of the survivors of Philip's revolt to move peaceably into New York territory under the dominion of the Five Nations.

At almost the same time, events far to the southward further reinforced the significance of the bond between New York and the Five Nations. That was largely the result of the movements to the south of the Susquehannock Indians of what would become Pennsylvania, in reaction to hostilities with the Five Nations. It was also an effort to attain a better trade position by moving closer to their principal source of European goods, the plantations of the Chesapeake. Soon thereafter, they suffered attacks from Virginia frontiersman, who were supporting the uprising in that colony led by Nathaniel Bacon. Andros offered the Susquehannocks refuge in their old territories and in western New York under the protection of the Five Nations. In the process, the governor increased the numbers of his Iroquois allies while reducing their enemies, at the same time establishing the primacy of New York in Indian diplomacy.

Those events were the foundation of a flexible alliance that emerged between the English and the Five Nations known as the Covenant Chain. The chain is hard to describe with precision, in part because it was interpreted variously by different groups. It was less than a formal alliance in that it was neither fully comprehensive nor precise. Thus specific agreements negotiated between the parties could never be fully binding on all of their allies. For example, a pact of non-aggression between the government of English New York and the Mohawks could not guarantee the peaceable conduct of far-flung bands of Seneca Indians or rampaging colonists from Maryland or Virginia. Moreover, the terms of the Covenant Chain were almost always left to interpretation by peoples possessing very different cultural assumptions.

The Covenant Chain was more than just a treaty of alliance. It was not restricted to a specific set of terms but was intended to signify an ongoing relationship of mutual accord. It was as much about the repeated ritual of treaty making as it was about particular terms of agreement. In that, it followed forms derived more from Five Nations traditions than those of the Europeans, employing some of the patterns that had been initiated in the Iroquois league of peace. The very terms used, and the regular and very structured patterns that diplomatic encounters were compelled to follow, all originated in the customs of the Five Nations, which European negotiators had to learn. They also had to learn to reinforce their oral agreements with gifts of wampum. Gift-giving became an important part of diplomatic ritual as well as providing local Indians with a regular source of trade items. For many years New Yorkers would maintain the peace through the regular giving of gifts.[5]

The very lack of precision allowed the Covenant Chain to survive occasional infringements: if neither the Five Nations nor the English government could control the actions of all of their allies, they could also disclaim responsibility for individual violations and maintain at least a process for negotiation. During the latter part of the seventeenth century, Middle Colony settlers as a whole established more peaceful relations with their Indian neighbors than did those of the other principal mainland regions, relations that continued for more than half a century. Indeed, the existence of the Covenant Chain was one of the principal reasons that William Penn was able to establish a colony nearby on the principle of peace.

In some respects, the Covenant Chain was more of a metaphor than a precise agreement. When relations between its adherents were strained, Iroquois spokesmen might refer to the chain as tarnished; when they improved, they would call the chain bright. As such, it was useful for mediating between the needs of English and Iroquois when the two sides did not share a common frame of reference. The two peoples could attach different meanings to their relationship. Following Iroquois tradition, they often used the language of kinship. Thus, for example, the English might refer to the Iroquois as their children, signifying a relation of authority and dependency. The Five Nations insisted instead that the relationship was one of brothers. Still, the language of parentage could have its uses, as Indian groups also would at times refer to the French king as "father," but only for the purpose of insisting that he owed his "children" protection, assistance, and gifts.

The Covenant Chain had many advantages for New York. Among the most important was the power it gave Andros and his successors in Indian diplomacy. When governors of other English provinces had negotiations to conduct with the Five

Nations, they often had to do so in New York, under the auspices of the governor of that colony. Not only did that give him considerable sway over other provinces, but it insured the continuing primacy of Albany as the seat of diplomacy and deterred the creation of competing trade centers.

The Covenant Chain benefited the Five Nations as well. It secured trading relations for those Indians who otherwise risked being shut out of commerce by Algonkian domination of the connection to New France, especially since the Iroquois had long since used up the best fur-capturing territories in their vicinity. It provided a bulwark against the threat of attack from rival Indians with French support. It also gave the Five Nations considerable leverage in negotiating with smaller Indian nations in their vicinity: they could promise protection and access to trade for those who would make their peace. In essence, the chain allowed the Five Nations to speak for other nations under their umbrella. In the process, the Iroquois were able to partially replenish a population that was consistently under pressure from fatalities suffered through warfare and disease.

COLONIAL OFFSHOOTS

New Jersey began as an offshoot of New York. In June of 1664, even before the conquest of New Netherland was complete, James severed New Jersey from the rest of his colony and granted it to two close associates, Lord John Berkeley and Sir George Carteret, both prominent Restoration figures and Stuart loyalists. They devoted little effort to developing their colony, instead issuing "Concessions and Agreements" designed primarily to attract settlers to New Jersey from New England and Long Island. Their efforts quickly bore fruit, and over the next several years several hundred settlers moved to New Jersey, principally to a cluster of six New England–style townships that they established at Newark, Elizabethtown, Woodbridge, Shrewsbury, Middletown, and Piscataway. Like the New England offshoots that grew up on Long Island, these were a varied set of communities, ranging from the rigidly orthodox and relatively homogeneous Puritan settlement at Newark to the diverse mixing of Puritans, Quakers, and Baptists that developed in the last three towns. Together with Dutch settlers living principally in the vicinity of Bergen, they gave the Jerseys a total population of about three thousand persons.

James's rather hasty action sowed the seeds of later conflict. While the duke was conveying the Jerseys to Berkeley and Carteret, Governor Nicolls, not knowing of James's gift, had granted extended patents to two groups of settlers at Elizabethtown and a tract in what would become Monmouth County. The new proprietors ordered the Nicolls patentees to renew their titles to the lands, but they refused, and the proprietors lacked the means to enforce their order. The status of those properties would constitute the greatest source of conflict in the Jerseys throughout the colonial era, as we shall see.

All of those early settlements were located in the eastern half of the colony. In 1676 the proprietors divided the province, Berkeley already having sold his share, which became the western half. The leading figure in the West Jersey purchase was Edward Byllinge, an English Quaker merchant who hoped to use the acquisition to improve his troubled finances. Byllinge arranged the purchase through his agent, John Fenwick, also a Quaker; and Fenwick insisted on a ten percent share of the colony. While the two proprietors disputed Fenwick's entitlement, he went ahead and lodged a settlement of his own. In 1675 he transported about a hundred settlers to "Fenwick's Colony," to a place they called Salem in the far southern ranges of the colony. Over a period of five years Byllinge sent about 1,400 more, who settled in the vicinity of Burlington. When Byllinge's finances did not improve, several prominent Quakers, hoping to avoid scandal, stepped in to superintend the property. That marked William Penn's first involvement with the colonies. They soon divided the colony into small proprietary shares, attracting investments from a wide range of English Quakers. West Jersey would have little connection to the duke or his plans thereafter.

East Jersey followed a very different course of development. Carteret held onto his share for another six years, but in 1682 he sold his interest to another group of Quaker proprietors. That colony was of secondary interest to the English Quaker community, however, which was already invested in West Jersey and Pennsylvania, and the twelve original Quaker proprietors took on an additional twelve partners, six of whom were Scots. Those six encouraged more than a hundred of their countrymen to invest in East Jersey, purchasing about half of the proprietary interest, and Scots quickly became the most active force in colonization.

The Scottish effort was substantially influenced by the divisions of the Restoration. The proprietary group was closely connected to James and to the upper reaches of Scottish society. During the Exclusion Crisis of 1679, James had removed himself from England and sought refuge in Edinburgh among prominent courtiers in that city. The most active proprietor was the Quaker Robert Barclay, author of the famous *Apology for the True Christian Divinity of the People Called Quakers* (1676), who also had close ties to the Duke of York. Barclay was joined by two high-ranking members of the aristocracy: James Drummond, Earl of Perth, and his brother, John Lord Melfort, both important Restoration politicians related to Barclay and to the duke. On the other side, a few prominent purchasers were Presbyterian dissenters, who found themselves fined, imprisoned, and exiled from Scotland by James's friends during the height of the "killing times" of the 1680s.

The Scots plan for the colony was ambitious and distinct. Over the next several years proprietors from that nation organized four expeditions to East Jersey and sent about seven hundred settlers. Rather than interspersing their settlements among their English neighbors, the proprietors arranged to have their lands allocated together within separate Scottish settlements, creating a colony within a colony. Those they organized into neighborhoods of large estates of two thousand acres or more, modeled on the large properties found in much of rural Scotland. At the same time, those proprietors discouraged land sales in units of less than five hundred acres. They also set out to challenge the land patents of several of the older English towns in the colony. Thus East Jersey was to share with New York a society sharply divided between large properties and much smaller holdings. The two colonies would remain closely linked thereafter.

More than most colonial governing groups, the Scots proprietors maintained substantial influence over their subordinates. Many of them were actively recruited by the proprietors and often hailed from regions where the proprietary families were prominent. Although proprietary servants were entitled to acquire land upon the expiration of their indentures, many of them did not immediately take up those lands but instead sold them back to the proprietors and continued working on the now-enlarged proprietary properties. The manor called "Rariton River," near Bound Brook and Piscataway, patented to Lord Neil Campbell, employed tenants and servants from among the original settlers for decades thereafter. The vast territories the proprietors patented would form the basis both for proprietary authority and for the conflicts that ensued with other settlers through much of the next century.

THE FALL OF YORK

In the decade and a half that followed the reconquest of New York in 1674, the nature of James's rule varied in accordance with fluctuations in Restoration politics. Under the active and aggressive government of the former military officer and dedicated Stuart loyalist Edmund Andros, James's authority appeared to be on the rise. But by the end of that decade, James was forced into exile by the anti-Catholic hysteria in England surrounding the "Popish plot," in which a man named Titus Oates claimed to have discovered a Catholic conspiracy to murder Charles and put James on the throne. During that period the New York government came under such pressure both from the English towns on Long Island and from city merchants resistant to the proprietor's taxes that his administration agreed for the first time to the calling of an elected assembly in 1683. That body met and drafted a "Charter of Libertyes and Priviledges" that included a permanent representative assembly for the colony. In fact, the charter was rather moderate compared to the constitutions of West Jersey and Pennsylvania, but for New York it was without precedent. The duke's government probably had little choice, since the recent drafting of a similar document in Pennsylvania and the more liberal plans for East and West Jersey threatened to deplete New York of its English merchant population, leaving only a somewhat hostile Dutch populace.

By the time the document reached James, his star had risen again, and he had returned from exile and was back in England. The duke ignored the charter, instructing his governor to disallow the acts of assembly. Instead, James succeeded to the throne upon his brother's death in 1685 and, as king, dissolved his proprietary into a royal colony. More controversially, he announced plans to integrate New York and New Jersey into an enlarged Dominion of New England, along with Massachusetts, Connecticut, and Rhode Island. That did not sit well with New York's merchants, already unhappy with James's commercial restrictions, who feared the impact on their trade of moving the colony's capital to Boston. Nor was it popular among ardent Protestants in either place, who rightly viewed the Dominion as an effort by James to reduce the autonomy of colonists in general and Protestants in particular. It was especially unpopular among radical Protestant settlers in New England and on Long Island, who had favored the Commonwealth during the English Civil War and had never supported the Stuart Restoration.

New York's affairs were now tied not only to Restoration politics but to royal matters, where James's aggressive style caused him far more trouble than it ever did in his role as proprietor. Part of the opposition derived from James's high-handed, imperial style and part from his Catholic allegiance, but as long as he had no Catholic heirs, most of the English political community tolerated his reign. That changed with the birth of a son. In 1688, with James having alienated important interests in church and state, English political leaders invited James's daughter Mary, along with her husband, William of Orange, to come to England and displace James. William landed with an army, James fled, and William and Mary were proclaimed joint monarchs, replacing James, who, according to the English Protestant version of events, had abdicated the throne.

The "Glorious Revolution," as that movement came to be called, set off a chain reaction in the colonies. The disruptions began in Boston, where loyal Protestant groups proclaimed William and Mary, imprisoned Andros, and took back control of the colony. Their actions would be replicated in several other provinces, where Protestant groups seized their governments from regimes loyal to James, professing allegiance to William and Mary and to the Protestant succession.

No colony experienced a greater disruption than New York, where the conflict was exaggerated by several circumstances: the general level of contention between some Dutch and English groups within the colony, commercial rivalries between the merchants of Albany and New York, the restlessness of the English towns on Long Island, and the fact that James, the deposed monarch, had also been proprietor of the colony. Religious divisions were particularly acute, since James's government had included prominent Catholics. Adding to the complications was the fact that William of Orange, who succeeded James, was a Dutch prince as well as James's son-in-law. Thus the fault lines of provincial politics in New York everywhere overlapped imperial divisions.

The conflict in New York began in 1689, after New Yorkers received word of the Revolution in England and of the rebellion against the Dominion's governor, Edmund Andros, in Boston. A succession of towns began to rebel against the Dominion and were joined soon after by the New York militia, which came under the leadership of the wealthy Calvinist merchant Jacobus Leisler, proclaiming William and Mary and the Protestant religion. Leisler, of German origin, was a veteran of the Dutch colony with wide-ranging commercial connections. With a group of supporters among whom ardent Protestants and Dutch-speakers played large roles, Leisler controlled the province for most of two years. He attacked his adversaries as Papists who had betrayed the Protestant cause. Some of those, such as Thomas Dongan, were indeed adherents to the Church of Rome, while others, such as Andros's deputy, Francis Nicholson, a strong supporter of the Protestant Church of England, were wrongly accused of Catholic leanings.

Much of what occurred in New York reflected the heated religious and political conflicts of late seventeenth-century Europe. Leisler's Rebellion followed by just a few years the revocation of the Edict of Nantes in France, which led to the persecution and dispersal of that nation's Huguenot community, flooding Europe with more than 100,000 Protestant refugees. Britain was also suffering intense religious conflict, especially in Scotland, where Stuart loyalists imprisoned, exiled, or executed Presbyterians who refused to take the required loyalty oaths. Refugees from all of those places flocked to the Netherlands, especially to Rotterdam. Included among them would be several of Leisler's leading supporters (and one prominent opponent). It is little wonder that devout Protestants such as Leisler feared Catholic plots and Catholic rule and distrusted the duke's commitment to toleration, especially since some of the most important officials in James's regime worshipped in the Church of Rome.

The rebellion divided the colony, creating fractures even within religious and national groups. The Dutch population split. Among the merchant families that had established the closest connections to the English rulers, Leisler's rule posed a severe threat. The city of Albany also resisted Leisler and his band of New York merchants, their trade rivals. Among the leaders of the opposition was Robert Livingston, the Scotsman who mediated between English- and Dutch-speakers in that town and who, like several of Leisler's prominent supporters, had lived among the refugee community in Rotterdam. A good indication of the intensifying radicalism of Leisler's movement is that Livingston sought refuge in the staunchly Protestant colony of Massachusetts to avoid Leisler's wrath.

English settlers were also divided. Many of the leading families had ties to James's government and were fearful of Leisler. Several Long Island towns had followed the New England example and were among the first in New York to abandon James and proclaim William and Mary. Yet they were also suspicious of Leisler and his Continental ways; moreover, they also feared the domination of New York City merchants, against whose control they had struggled for two decades.

As tempers rose, so did the rhetoric of the Leislerians. Leisler himself threatened his opponents, calling them "Popish Doggs" and "Divells" (devils). On his arrival in Albany, Leisler's deputy, Jacob Milborne, a former New Englander, declared that the people there had it "in there power to free Themselfs from that Yoke of arbitrary Power and Government under which they had byen so long in the Reign of that Illegal king James, who was a Papist." He continued, saying that "now the Power was in the People to choose new Civill and Military officers as they Pleased."[6] Leisler subsequently alienated most of the colony's elites, including many firm Protestants and Whigs.

Leisler's demise came swiftly. Early in 1691, Captain Richard Ingoldsby arrived in New York from England and demanded the surrender of the fort on behalf of the newly appointed governor, Henry Sloughter. Leisler refused to give way until he had seen the captain's commission, which Ingoldsby did not have in his possession. When Sloughter himself arrived late one March day, Leisler still delayed until the following morning. For those offences, he was arrested and, with the backing of those whose power he had threatened, was quickly tried for treason. Both Leisler and Milborne were subjected to a gruesome traitor's execution.

The hanging of Leisler did nothing to end the contention. Some of Leisler's Dutch supporters retreated to New Jersey, away from the dominion of powerful anti-Leislerian forces in the Dutch leadership, or into local communities in the Hudson Valley. Others joined forces in opposition to the government and, over the next several decades, helped fuel a persistently factious politics. The actual revenge extracted by the Leislerians when they took power was modest, consisting chiefly of the exhuming of Leisler and Milborne in 1695 for proper burial, and the trial and condemnation of one of their principal Dutch adversaries, whom they then pardoned.

The divisions spawned by Leisler's Rebellion continued to fuel New York politics for several decades thereafter. The new governor, Sloughter, and his successor, Benjamin Fletcher, allied with British Tories, promoted the interests of the anti-Leislerians. By the end of the 1690s, England's Whigs were in the ascendant, and Fletcher was replaced by Lord Bellomont, who aligned himself with the former Leislerians and the Protestant interest. For decades thereafter, New York would experience a persistent and distinct factional politics related to ethnic, religious, geographic, and class divisions.

Political turmoil also disrupted the elaborate diplomatic structures Andros had created. The relations of the Covenant Chain pitted the interests of the Five Nations more directly against those of New France and its allies. With England more concerned with imperial concerns on the European Continent, the Iroquois were largely left to fend for themselves. Seriously outnumbered, they finally surrendered to New France in 1701. The always resourceful Five Nations negotiated a new treaty with England at the same time, leaving them officially neutral between European empires with the ability to play the forces of one against the power of the other. That would be the principal diplomatic strategy of the Iroquois for much of the next century.

THE END OF PROPRIETARY GOVERNMENT

Conflict also reached the Jerseys. Because James had devolved the proprietorships of those colonies to others, they did not become royal colonies when James ascended to the throne, and thus their governments did not change with the events of 1688. Nonetheless, the revolution of that year unleashed conflicts within the colonies that persisted long after James's removal, which followed the principal lines of social division in each. In the words of imperial official Colonel Robert Quarry in a 1703 letter to the Board of Trade: "The Contests of West Jersey have always been betwixt the Quakers and her majesty's subjects that are no Quakers. . . . The contest in East Jersey is of a different nature, whether the country shall be a Scotch settlement or an English settlement."[7]

The conflict was most acute in the eastern section, where many of the proprietors had close ties to James. With the advent of the Revolution in Britain, two leading proprietors—the Earl of Perth and Lord Melfort—fled Scotland for the European Continent, and many of their colleagues abandoned their efforts on behalf of East Jersey. Instead, power devolved upon a local group of resident proprietors, most of whom were Scots. Those proprietors were committed to the same kind of hierarchical plan for East Jersey that the Duke's supporters promoted in New York. For decades their position within the colony would be challenged by local townsmen seeking security for their land titles and less-authoritarian forms of government and society.

Their principal adversaries in East Jersey were the inhabitants of the older English towns in the colony, along with a few men who held claims derived from the dormant English proprietary group in London. Not only did the townspeople have little desire to defer to the authority of the proprietors, but the proprietary claims to extensive lands surrounding their towns threatened the security of their land titles as well. In response, they made common cause with a succession of ambitious office-seekers of various sorts who were willing to take an anti-proprietary stance in return for popular support.

The most important such official was the sometime Anabaptist minister, Jeremiah Basse, a staunch opponent of the Scottish proprietors. When the passage of the Navigation Act of 1696 threw into question the legitimacy of Scottish office-holding in the colonies, the proprietors chose Basse to replace the Scotsman Andrew Hamilton as governor of the colony. They soon realized their mistake when Basse set out to curb the power of the proprietors by accusing the Scots of smuggling and piracy. When the proprietors removed Basse from office, he enlisted the townspeople of Elizabethtown in an anti-proprietary campaign to free the colony of its "Scotch yoak."[8] By 1700, Middlesex County had descended to riots and jailbreaks, leading the proprietors to petition the Crown to take over the government of the colony as the only means to restore order. In April of 1702, the proprietors formally surrendered East Jersey to the Crown. In return, they were able to keep their hold on valuable proprietary property throughout the province. Proprietary rule, though not proprietary influence or ownership of the land, was at an end.

Anti-proprietary sentiment in West Jersey was less widespread but no less aggressive. There also Basse managed to put himself at the center of contention, first as agent for the West Jersey Society, a London-based organization of non-Quaker investors, then as governor, and, after that, as a principal member of an emerging anti-Quaker faction. The largely Quaker colony maintained the peace longer than its eastern neighbor, but with Basse fomenting opposition, that colony too descended into disorder and riot. As in East Jersey, the surrender of the government to the Crown seemed the only remedy.

By 1703 proprietary government within the bounds of the duke's patent had come to an end. New York had been a royal colony for nearly two decades and was now joined in that state by the newly reunited colony of New Jersey. Maine and western Connecticut had been returned to New England, and Delaware was now within the bounds of Penn's proprietary. Yet the effects of James's proprietorship were great, not least in his attempt to bring the colony into the orbit of the English political world and impose order on a diverse population. That resulted in the continuation in New York and the Jerseys of a factious politics, pitting the duke's former allies against communities of ardent Protestant settlers. The latter group challenged not only the politics of their leaders but also their continuing ownership of the land. Nonetheless, James's allies remained a powerful conservative force in each colony, with a strong influence upon their respective governments.

An even more important legacy lay in the framework for diplomatic relations James's government established. Imperial diplomacy within the region was still influenced by the Covenant Chain, with imperial officials in Albany negotiating with representatives of the Five Nations—officially neutralized by the "Grand Settlement of 1701"—over the status of territories that extended across much of eastern North America. The ability of the Five Nations to play one power against the other left them in firm control of their own territories. At the same time, the preoccupation of New York officials with such concerns freed colonials elsewhere in the mid-Atlantic from the need to confront matters of defense and security and allowed them to concentrate instead on settlement, expansion, and trade.

Still another legacy would be toleration, albeit of a top-down variety. Whatever the duke's motives, he laid the groundwork in New York for expanding the limited toleration of New Netherland to a greater variety of religious groups. The Jersey colonies would permit both toleration and something close to full tolerance almost from the beginning. And in neighboring Pennsylvania, as we shall see, James would accede to the development of a colony whose founding principle was religious freedom.

Ironically, even the duke's attempts to combine and consolidate the colonies, which had provoked so much opposition, substantially survived his overthrow. While the grand Dominion of New England was abandoned, separating the Middle Colonies from their northeastern neighbors, a surprising number of links among those colonies would be recreated under the new regime. From 1692 onward, the two Jersey colonies employed the same governor, Hamilton, and the surrender of the proprietaries in 1703 returned them to the status of a single colony. Even links outside the region reappeared in 1699, with the appointment of the Earl of Bellomont as governor of both New York and Massachusetts. And beginning in 1703, New York and New Jersey shared governors until 1738. Thus New York would remain a center of imperial influence for the whole of the northeast, and the duke's former provinces remained closely tied to the politics of the larger imperial world.

THREE

Penn's Proprietary

ALTHOUGH JAMES'S PATENT secured him control over a large
territory in North America extending from the Maine coast to
the Delaware River, once it was placed under his dominion he
was content to convey considerable portions to political friends
and allies. The first had been New Jersey, to Berkeley and Carteret. Later, in 1664, he agreed with Connecticut leaders to settle
his eastern boundary at a point well to the west of the Connecticut River, the limit set in his charter. Maine and the islands beyond Long Island he never pursued. James would subsequently
divest himself of the "lower counties" along the Delaware, which
had formed part of New Sweden and New Netherland. Those
would be incorporated into the patent of still another Stuart
friend, a Quaker gentleman named William Penn. Penn's father,
Admiral Penn, had been a member of James's inner circle, and
James had approved the son's charter. That patent would extend
England's Middle Colony region west of the Delaware into the
new colony of Pennsylvania and would further English involvement with diverse Indian nations and rival empires.

At first sight, there would seem to have been little to connect Penn or his province to the duke and his strategic designs.
Whereas James was an avowed Catholic, Penn was a Quaker, a
member of the Society of Friends, a radically spiritualist sect that
had sprung out of the most anti-ritualistic and anti-authoritarian
elements of English Protestantism. Quakers were thus about as
far removed from James within the spectrum of English eccle-

siastical practice as it was possible to go. Whereas the duke's plan promoted hierarchy in a colony closely controlled by his appointees, Penn provided a far more liberal design, with much more widespread opportunity for both landowning and political participation. Whereas the duke's colonial domain was intended to fence in the claims of his Protestant opponents, Penn promoted expansion and integration. And whereas the duke's colony housed the only garrison in the English provinces and served as the center of imperial power in North America, Penn envisioned a proprietary based on the testimony of peace. Pennsylvania was built upon peace over power and commerce over coercion, although as we shall see, those were not always as contradictory as they might seem.

Yet in several respects the plans of the proprietors were quite complementary. Theirs were the largest and most powerful individual proprietaries granted in English America. Although Quakers derived from a strain of radical Protestantism, by Penn's day many of the sect had abandoned political activism and anti-Catholicism for toleration and an emphasis on inner devotion—"Quietism," in the language of the day. Penn shared James's hostility toward aggressive and powerful Protestant churches, especially of the Puritan or Reformed Protestant variety, such as those found in New Netherland and New England. The two proprietors shared as well the goal of limiting conflict with the local native populations, if not necessarily for the same reasons. Indeed, the power that New York projected through its military and diplomatic projects spared Pennsylvania the early experience of warfare that nearly every other colony confronted and provided Penn with much of the space he needed to conduct his experiment in peace.

Penn's own ties to the duke, his natural support for proprietary authority in general, his opposition to strong Protestant establishments and willingness to tolerate Catholics, and his predilection for peace all made the Quaker colony far less threatening to James and his province than almost any other Protestant settlement would have been. Indeed, while New York's authoritarian government was taken by many to be a model for the polity the duke would have liked to impose in Britain had he had the power to do so, the pluralistic religious settlement that developed in Pennsylvania, with an empowered proprietor and no established church to challenge his authority, was also not far removed from Stuart designs.

Thus in a number of respects the two colonies were not the polar opposites they would at first appear to be. Rather, they represent alternate possibilities that emerged within the Restoration empire at a time when neither the haphazard settlement schemes of the Chesapeake region nor the strict religious uniformity of New England were viable colonial options and when colonial constitutional arrangements were carefully considered in the name of order, balance, toleration, and—increasingly—trade. In supporting Penn's province, James was extending the reach of Restoration politics into a greatly expanded Middle Colony region.

PENN AND THE SOCIETY OF FRIENDS

The prime mover behind the new colony, William Penn, was a devout Quaker and the most renowned member of that despised sect. Although Penn was the son of a Presbyterian who later conformed to the Anglican Church, the younger Penn had broken with his father in the matter of religion. Penn was raised as a gentleman in the vicinity of London and attended Oxford and the Inns of Court, where he studied law. He became a Quaker some time in the late 1660s and was imprisoned several times for disorderly behavior and for violating the Conventicle Act of 1670 against unlawful gatherings, a common offence charged against Friends.

The Society of Friends had originated in Civil War England as one of a number of radical groups that sprang up in those troubled times. Most of the early Quakers had been people of marginal status, many from remote areas of northern and western England. Friends made a point of defying status and hierarchy, refusing to doff their hats toward their social superiors or otherwise display the outward signs of respect that English society traditionally demanded. One recognized a Quaker by his or her speech—the use of the familiar "thee" and "thou" rather than "you," which still signified social superiority and respect in the seventeenth century. Early Quakers were disorderly in the extreme, and deliberately so, one of the principal reasons for their persecution by authorities.

At the heart of those Quaker attitudes was the concept of the "inner light"—the internal voice of God. In that belief, Friends differed markedly from their Puritan predecessors, who held fast to the notion that truth was revealed in Scripture and that true godliness was confined to an elected few. By contrast, in Quaker doctrine the inner light existed in everyone. Not everyone attended to that voice, of course, and Quakers worked to spread the message, or "convince," those around them. Such ideas led to an opposition to priests and church hierarchies as authoritarian and repressive, distracting attention from the inner light. They led also to a belief in spiritual equality. Quakers emphasized persuasion, or what they called "tender dealing," rather than the force of law, as the best means to convince others to follow the light.

What distinguished Friends from other radical spiritualist groups that grew up during England of the Civil War era was the supreme emphasis that Quakers placed on organization. Under the leadership of George Fox, Friends created an ordered system of meetings, ranging from local meetings of worship, to the larger and supervisory monthly meetings, to the still-larger yearly meetings encompassing representatives of the Quaker population across whole regions. Fox also moved Quakers away from the violent resistance of radical groups in Civil War England to embrace the testimony of peace.

By Penn's generation, the character of the Society of Friends had begun to change. With the advent of persons of greater standing, such as Penn, some of the radicalism of their attitudes was muted. Penn—like his East Jersey counterpart Robert Barclay—was well born and well connected at court. The younger Penn's conversion to the Quaker faith subdued some of his courtly attitudes, but not all: he continued to spend his income as lavishly as a courtier, and, as events in Pennsylvania would show, he continued to believe in his own entitlement to rule. He also maintained his relations with James and his extremely hierarchical attitudes. Penn's life thus required an extraordinary effort to reconcile seemingly contradictory impulses, as would appear in his efforts to plan and promote the colony.

Before his involvement with Pennsylvania, Penn had established himself as a leading Quaker spokesman. A decade before, he had been imprisoned for his beliefs. There he wrote significant tracts against persecution, including *No Cross, No Crown*

(1669) and *The Great Case of Liberty of Conscience* (1670). His belief in tolerance was not yet as great as it would become later, as evidenced by his 1670 *Seasonable Caveat Against Popery*; he would abandon his anti-Catholic position after his alliance with the Duke of York. His writings did make him an important representative not only of the Society of Friends but of the interests of Protestant dissenters within England generally, and Penn was soon deeply involved in English political affairs in turbulent times.

QUAKERS AND THE AMERICAN COLONIES

For a small sect originating in remote regions of England, Quakers early on developed an unusual attraction to the American colonies. In 1656, at a very early point in Quaker history, two Quaker women turned up in Massachusetts Bay, having arrived in Barbados the year before. Puritan authorities were not pleased to see them and had them imprisoned and then sent out of the colony. But they were soon followed by others. Despite constant threats, whippings, and eventually several hangings of those who refused to stay away, Quakers kept returning as a testimony against persecution. Friends also turned up in more tolerant Rhode Island, where they lived peaceably.

From there, the first Quakers spread into the mid-Atlantic. In fact, Long Island, having received radical dissenters from New England orthodoxy for several decades, would prove an exceptionally fertile ground for Quakers. One Lady Deborah Moody, an English woman who had left Lynn, Massachusetts, after her conversion to Anabaptist beliefs, set up a religious meeting in Gravesend in 1654, which gravitated towards the Society of Friends. She was joined by a number of others from Lynn. Another meeting grew up in Flushing, within the bounds of Dutch settlement. It was led by John Bowne, who was deported to Amsterdam by Peter Stuyvesant. There the directors of the West India Company listened to his plea and ordered the governor to end his harassment. Richard Smith, founder of Smithtown, was converted to Quakerism on a visit to England as early as 1654. Three years later, Quaker missionaries headed for New England also began to arrive in New Amsterdam and its surroundings. While they found little welcome in the city, they met a much warmer reception on Long Island.

Those small, indigenous groups of Friends were soon strongly outnumbered by the influx of migrants heading for the new Quaker colonies. Their first organized foray into the Americas was West Jersey, where Friends began to settle in 1675 at "Fenwick's Colony." A larger movement to the rest of West Jersey, under Edward Byllinge's control, began two years later, promoted by Penn and others. Within five years more than 1,400 Quakers had migrated to West Jersey. Another 360 followed in 1682, but that was the high-water mark for West Jersey for some time, since the founding of Pennsylvania that same year diverted the attention of Penn and most potential Quaker migrants. The largest threat to West Jersey came from New York, where the duke's representatives maintained that the proprietor had sold only the land and not the government of the Jerseys to Berkeley and Carteret, a position Penn's *Case of New Jersey Stated* (1676) explicitly attempted to refute.

West Jersey represented one of the most liberal political and economic regimes in England's colonial empire. The West Jersey Concessions of 1677, drawn up by the Quaker proprietors, provided for an elected assembly with wide powers and nearly universal suffrage for adult white males, as broad a suffrage as any to be found in early America. The West Jersey Concessions created no governor but only a body of ten elected "commissioners" to serve during the adjournment of the assembly. They guaranteed due process of law and jury trials, along with an almost unprecedented measure of religious freedom, ensuring that "every person might freely enjoy his own judgment and the exercise of conscience in matters of worship." The system of land distribution led to the division of West Jersey proprietary shares into smaller and smaller units, so that not only the very wealthy but merchants, craftsmen, and farmers would eventually take up portions. By 1685, the hundred proprietary shares were selling in fractions as small as one-sixteenth.

THE PENNSYLVANIA CHARTER

Quaker settlement in the mid-Atlantic was thus well under way before the founding of Pennsylvania. That venture built upon the earlier settlements: William Penn's first American involvement had been a modest engagement with West Jersey, where he had first noticed the interest that an American colony attracted among Friends. Moreover, he, like other proprietors before him, thought of using colonial investment to fortify his own unsettled fortune

Thus Penn had varied and sometimes conflicting motives in planning his colony. On the one hand, his own finances were in need of repair, and his experience with West Jersey had led him to believe that there was potential interest within the Quaker community. On the other hand, he was also desirous of helping his persecuted co-religionists and offering them a place where they could raise families away from either the corruptions of English society or the pressures that economic necessity might put upon their adherence to their faith. That created a number of tensions within Penn's plan.

Less clear than Penn's motives were those of Charles and his court, which agreed to grant him a charter. Why they did so may never be definitively established. Certainly, the king was in debt to Penn's father, but that was not the only debt Charles owed and would not automatically have entitled the son to so vast a colony. Some have thought that Charles was pleased to rid the kingdom of a troublesome group, although the increasingly peaceable Quakers surely formed less of a challenge to royal authority than did more formidable groups of dissenters, such as Presbyterians or Independents.

Before Penn's charter was granted, it went first for review to the King's Privy Council and from there to the Commissioners on Trade. They, in turn, forwarded it to James, upon whose territory the new colony would border. One of James's goals had been to rein in the independence of his Puritan neighbors in New England, so it seems unlikely he would have accepted additional colonists on his borders if he viewed them as troublemakers. The duke further bequeathed to Penn his title to the so-called lower counties along the Delaware, which would eventually become a colony of their own. James was probably more influenced by his own good relationship with Penn and that individual's conservative instincts. In addition, the government was then embroiled in a difficult political contest in England involving the effort by those called "Whigs" to exclude the Catholic James from the succession. Penn served as liaison with two groups who undoubtedly were of significant interest to both James and Charles: the Quaker portion of the London merchant community—who were certainly pleased at the opportunity to invest in a new Atlantic colony—and the dissenting interest at large. On the fourth of March, 1681, the king issued a patent, amounting to some 45,000 square miles, to William Penn for Pennsylvania. The name was a tribute to Penn's father, Admiral Penn. William Penn at first resisted the choice, fearing it would be regarded as a sign of vanity by those thinking it referred to the proprietor rather than to the admiral.

THE FRAMING OF GOVERNMENT IN PENNSYLVANIA

After securing his charter, Penn went to work to create a government for his colony, attempting to balance the privileges of the proprietor with the liberties of his subjects. This he set out to accomplish through the careful construction of a constitution, an interest he shared with many leading thinkers of the day. Indeed, all of the Restoration colonies except New York would have detailed constitutional plans. A properly balanced constitution seemed essential to attracting the support of potential settlers and investors while still ensuring the maintenance of social order, and it was only James's high position that allowed him to believe he could achieve those same goals on his own authority. Penn and several associates devoted an enormous effort to drafting a constitution for his colony. Among the surviving Penn Papers are to be found twelve full or fragmentary drafts of what became *The Frame of Government of the Province of Pennsylvania in America*, three outlines, two drafts of a variant plan, the "Fundamentall Constitutions of Pensilvania," and three written commentaries upon those plans by friends and advisers.[1]

The *Frame of Government* suggests some of the balancing that Penn attempted. Compared to the Duke's Laws or the Scottish Proprietors' plan for East Jersey, the *Frame* was liberal in its promise of an elected assembly, its allocation of suffrage, and its unusually strong guarantee of religious liberty, which was the first principle both of the "Fundamentall Constitutions" and of the "Laws Agreed Upon in England" that accompanied the first *Frame*. Yet in reality that was not so far removed from established practice within the region, where considerable de facto toleration existed almost everywhere, and where an almost complete freedom of conscience had been enacted in West Jersey. Moreover, the *Frame of Government* was clearly less liberal in its political structure than the corresponding Concessions and Agreements of West Jersey, which had consolidated legislative powers in a powerful and elected one-house legislature. In Pennsylvania, by contrast, most lawmaking authority was located in an elite upper house, which served also as a governor's council, while the popularly elected lower house was intended to do little but assent to the laws drafted by the governor and council.

The differences were deliberate. During the drafting of the *Frame of Government*, Penn and his lawyers worked gradually away from their first, more liberal plans of government, which had included a one-house or "unicameral" legislature, toward a final version intended to secure the positions of the prominent and powerful. The purpose was partly to attract the participation of wealthy purchasers, which was necessary both for the success of the venture and for the repair of Penn's fortune. It may also have been that Penn was simply more comfortable with a constitution that protected the powers of the proprietor. Nonetheless, the changes drew sharp criticism from some of the more liberal colleagues in Penn's circle such as Benjamin Furley, a Quaker residing in Rotterdam, who asked the proprietor who it was who had persuaded Penn to abandon the liberal early plans for the "unjust" later versions. Another political figure, probably the political radical Algernon Sidney or his brother Henry, was reported to have described Penn's laws as "the basest in the world" and more absolute than those of the Turks—the usual example eighteenth-century Englishmen cited to represent despotic government.[2]

In order to attract settlers to the colony, Penn adopted a land policy that was far more liberal than that of his fellow proprietors in New York and East Jersey, although not so generous as that of his West Jersey neighbors. Pennsylvania was not without manors and other large properties, and Penn's plan certainly envisioned extensive holdings for himself and other leading gentlemen, but he did not attempt to restrict landholding in the manner of East Jersey's Scots proprietors. He encouraged the sale of small farming units as well as large. That would make Pennsylvania more appealing than its northeastern neighbors to many prospective settlers.

Penn's plan also included a capital city, which he called "Philadelphia," the city of "brotherly love." Penn was determined that it not be crowded and diseased like London or even Boston or New York; instead, he envisioned each house residing in the center of a larger property along the river, to make a "green country town." Each house was to be surrounded by gardens and free from the risks of fire and disease. Penn instructed his surveyors to locate lands along the Delaware suitable for a harbor and a town, extending some fifteen miles in Penn's original plan. It was to be an orderly town, with houses set as near to a straight line as possible and with roads laid out in a rectangular grid. Penn intended the town lands to serve as an incentive for first purchasers; each buyer of 5,000 acres in the initial allotment was to receive a one-acre house lot in the town.

Penn's plan for the capital city proved impossible to carry out. Much of the land along the Delaware was already settled by Dutch, English, or Swedish colonists who had arrived earlier. Penn instructed his agents to try to arrange exchanges or purchases from these settlers, even offering an abatement of "quit-rents," an annual fee purchasers would continue to owe even after purchasing their lands. Once again, the proprietor's general stinginess left little incentive for cooperation. Penn suggested reducing those rents by half, even exclaiming, "Yea, make them as free as purchasers, rather than disappoint my mind in this township." But rather than make that a general offer, he cautioned his agents to be "as sparing as ever you can" in the matter.[3]

In fact, Penn's agents were only able to secure 300 acres along the riverfront rather than the 10,000 he had hoped for. Instead, they acquired an equal frontage along the Schuylkill River running parallel to the Delaware lands. With the land in between, that amounted to some 1,200 acres for the new city. But it meant that many of the first purchasers did not receive their expected allotments of riverfront lands. In order to get the city built rapidly, Penn allocated back lots along the Schuylkill to those who did not emigrate right away. In fact, everyone received less that they had been led to anticipate, which would be another source of discontent in the colony.

THE QUAKER MIGRATION

Not since the "Great Migration" of Puritans to Massachusetts Bay half a century before had English America experienced an organized migration on the scale of the Quaker move into the

Delaware Valley. In fact, the movement to Pennsylvania and its neighbors was larger, exceeding eight thousand within the first four years, and perhaps twice that number over the next decade. Another two thousand or so Friends migrated to the Jerseys.[4]

Penn recruited widely. In addition to English Friends, he engaged Quakers from Ireland, Wales, and Holland in the venture, and he attempted to involve Scottish Friends before their decision to pursue a separate settlement in East Jersey. Yet although the proprietor was planning a Quaker colony, he wanted it to be profitable and populous as well, so Pennsylvania promoters advertised on the European Continent in the Netherlands and among German-speaking sectarian groups as well. The colony also obtained African slaves, a boatload of whom arrived in Philadelphia as early as 1684. From an early date Pennsylvania, like East Jersey and New York, had separate national groups inhabiting distinct areas of settlement in such places as Germantown and the Welsh Tract, although as in New York there was also considerable intermixing.

For a fairly small religious movement, Friends sent an unusually large number of colonists to America; their numbers among the migrants far surpassed their proportion in the British population. Part of the reason had to do with Quaker antipathy to the social hierarchies that characterized rural English society. Rather than holding property under powerful landlords, Friends preferred the more lateral social relationships inherent in the world of trade.

Quaker migration was also promoted by the universalist implications of their belief in the inner light. Since Friends believed that the light resided in everyone, the task of Quaker preachers and parents was to persuade hearers to pay attention wherever they could; "convincement" was the term Quakers used to describe conversions. Early Friends thus devoted considerable effort to proselytizing, and an unusual number of Quaker missionaries traveled through the American colonies.

The belief in the inner light also inspired migration in another way. Unlike orthodox Calvinists, who often sought to gain converts by preaching the terrors of the law and inspiring the fear of eternal punishment, Quakers emphasized persuasion and "tender dealings." Those beliefs extended to Quaker children, who required a nurturing environment at home in order to develop their convictions. That was in sharp contrast to prevailing notions of child rearing in the seventeenth century, which emphasized the evils of human nature, requiring discipline and the breaking of the child's will. Quakers have been called the originators of the modern affectionate family.

Thus it was important to Quaker families that they raise their own children at home, rather than sending them out at an early age to serve in other households, which was a common practice among other seventeenth-century English families. Since most Quakers came from lower and middling families from some of the least-prosperous areas of Britain, that was not always an easy matter. The opportunity to migrate to a land of ample resources where they could raise their families at home had great appeal.

How many of the early migrants to Pennsylvania were Quakers at the outset is not easy to determine. In Pennsylvania itself, it seems that most of the early settlers attached themselves to Quaker communities. Yet surprisingly, only a minority of those settlers can actually be traced back to Quaker meetings in their homelands. Part of the reason is the incompleteness of the records; part also appears to be that many who came to the Quaker colony were sympathetic to Quaker beliefs but had not been active members of their meetings. It may be that some among the migrants had belonged to other spiritualist groups in England or elsewhere and had only joined the Society actively when the creation of Pennsylvania provided an opportunity to live easily among like-minded religious folk. It was not uncommon for seventeenth-century English men and women to move among different spiritualist sects. In the New World as well, Quaker communities would also interact quite regularly with Baptists and other sectarians. The result was that Pennsylvania Quakers turned out to be quite a different group from Friends in England or in other American colonies.

DIVERSITY AND DISRUPTION

Like James, his proprietary counterpart, Penn would face strong challenges to his authority. As had happened in its mid-Atlantic neighbors, the conflicts of Restoration Britain manifested themselves strongly in Pennsylvania. In fact, Pennsylvania's larger size led to a compounding of those difficulties. Like the East Jersey proprietors, Penn laid claim to a territory already inhabited by several groups of Europeans. Those included the remnants of the New Sweden settlements in the lower counties along the Delaware River in what is now Delaware, as well as English settlers who had come into the region with patents either from the Duke of York or, more threateningly, from Lord Baltimore's colony to the south. One of the greatest difficulties Penn confronted was that the bounds of Baltimore's patent greatly overlapped Penn's charter. In fact, had the Maryland patent been enforced, it would have subsumed Philadelphia itself, while Penn's interpretation of his charter would have given him most of Maryland. The two proprietors would contest the boundaries for many years.

In his eagerness to establish government by consent in Pennsylvania, Penn allowed the settlers of the lower counties to have representation in the assembly, where they held nearly half of the seats at the outset. At best those settlers tolerated Quaker domination but rarely supported it. Their votes contributed to the rejection by the assembly of the first *Frame of Government,* along with other measures designed for a Quaker colony. When the Glorious Revolution in England severed the proprietor's ties to the English Court, the lower counties, aided and abetted by agents of Lord Baltimore, who held a competing claim to the territory, began to move toward outright rebellion.

Not all of the opposition to Penn's government came from non-Quakers. The independent spirit that characterized members of the Society of Friends, coupled with their persistent drive for land and independence, soon pushed them into conflict with the proprietor. Well before the end of the century, Pennsylvania Friends would experience unforeseen contentions both within the government and within the meeting.

Part of that conflict arose from an inherent tension within the proprietor's vision for the colony: Pennsylvania was to provide an international homeland for Quakers, but it was to do so in a way that would profit the proprietor. "Though I desire to extend religious freedom," Penn wrote, "yet I want some recompense for my trouble."[5] It was partly the relatively high prices Penn set for Pennsylvania lands that persuaded the Scottish Quaker proprietors to choose East Jersey instead. As the leader, Robert

Barclay, remarked to Penn at the time: "Thou has land enough," he remarked, "so need not be a churle iff thou intend to advance thy plantation."[6]

Once in Pennsylvania, some investors thought that Penn had reserved too much for himself. While "First Purchasers" had been promised a dividend of land in the capital as an inducement to buy shares, they soon discovered that they were not receiving the choicest waterfront lots, but rather lands on the outskirts of the city. They were even less pleased when, just two years after the founding, the proprietor began to pursue his claims for the payment of quitrents.

Another source of contention arose from within Quakerism itself, in the principles and personal styles that characterized the Society of Friends. The Quaker insistence upon liberty within the spiritual realm carried over into the political. Friends in Pennsylvania, like their fellows elsewhere, were sensitive to any-thing that suggested an infringement of their liberties, even at the hands of a Quaker proprietor. Thus some of them challenged the spirit of the *Frame of Government* from the beginning, and it was voted down in the Pennsylvania Assembly by a combination of Quaker assemblymen and representatives of the lower counties. Over the succeeding decade and a half, a faction of leading Friends continually challenged proprietary authority, promoting the cause of provincial autonomy. That led Penn to plead with his co-religionists to "be not so governmentish."[7]

Toward the end of the century, Pennsylvania politics took a different turn. Where political opposition during the first decade had sprung largely from prominent Friends dissatisfied with pro-prietary greed, by the later years the principal source of dissent would be less-affluent Quakers, who would coalesce within the assembly under the leadership of David Lloyd. Lloyd had gone to Pennsylvania originally to serve as Penn's attorney general, but once in the colony, he took to opposing the powers of pro-prietors and governors. Lloyd appealed for support to country delegates—those representing areas outside of the capital city—and to persons of middling position, while attacking the powers of proprietors and elites. The result would be a gradual populari-zation of political proceedings in Pennsylvania (see chapter 7).

Factionalism within the political realm was amplified by re-ligious conflict. In the last decade of the century, the Society of

Friends divided, in a dispute that reverberated throughout the region. At the center of controversy was the Quaker George Keith, a Scotsman and an associate of Robert Barclay and other East Jersey leaders. Keith moved to that colony in 1685 to work as surveyor for the Scottish proprietors. From there he moved on to Philadelphia, where he soon began to quarrel with that city's Quaker establishment.

At the heart of the dispute were changes then taking place within the Society of Friends. Where the first generation of Quakers had been noted for a radical spiritualism that made them seem among the most disruptive groups in mid-seventeenth-century England, with the conversion of such prominent individuals as Penn and Barclay, the Society began to change. Under the leadership of George Fox, some of the radically individualist aspects of Quakerism were muted by the countervailing emphasis on organization. Fox initiated the hierarchy of local, monthly, quarterly, and yearly meetings, dominated by ever more selective groups of Friends. If Quakers still looked to the inner light, that light was increasingly coming to be identified with the sense of the meeting and the authority of its weighty Friends.

In Pennsylvania, where Friends were in actual possession of a colony, the drive toward organization was particularly acute. The most prominent Quakers in Pennsylvania worked to solidify their supervisory authority within the meeting in their role as traveling ministers or Public Friends. The result was that the practices of their meetings came to differ considerably from those of most of the meetings on Long Island and New Jersey, which were founded before the Philadelphia meeting and lay outside of its immediate influence. Quakers in those outlying regions remained considerably closer to the spiritual egalitarianism of the early Quakers than did their co-religionists in Pennsylvania.

Into that division stepped George Keith, who brought with him a reputation as one of the most learned members of the Society of Friends. Keith hailed from Aberdeen, a university town and the primary home of Scottish Quakerism. Scottish Quakers in general were known for a greater concern for both Christian theology and secular learning than were other Friends, and Keith was no exception. After arriving in Philadelphia and listening to the pronouncements of leading Quakers in that city, Keith decided that Friends there needed to pay closer attention to the Bible and Christian doctrine rather than relying so heavily on the authority of the leadership through their Quarterly and Yearly meetings. That suggestion proved unacceptable to Pennsylvania's Quaker leaders.

The Keithian schism divided the Society of Friends. On the whole, the Scotsman's appeal was greatest among marginal members of the Society of Friends. In Philadelphia, the majority of Quakers remained with the meeting, especially among the more prominent Friends. Keith did gain considerable support among the tradesmen and the middling sorts, who seemed to share his concerns about the authority of more highly placed Quakers. A critical follower was William Bradford, the city's only printer, who helped to publicize Keith's cause.

Keith found greater support outside of Philadelphia, often from groups who had little desire to subordinate their decisions to the authority of that city's meeting. In East Jersey most of the Scottish Quakers joined with Keith, a former resident of the colony and a neighbor of some in Scotland, and they were joined by other East Jersey residents. Whole local meetings severed their connection with the Philadelphia meeting. On Long Island, some joined with Keith, while others, adhering to the individualist tendencies initially prevalent among Friends, steered in still more radical directions. Some allied themselves with the highly egalitarian Rhode Island meeting; others would further subdivide into such radical branches as the Singing Quakers or would abandon the Society to become Baptists.

Keith himself drifted for a number of years. He moved on to England to take his criticism of Quaker heterodoxy to the London Yearly Meeting. That meeting, angered by Keith's positions and his attacks on leading Friends, disowned him. Eventually, Keith decided that the Church of England, with its prayer book, its ritual, and its authority backed up by the state, best suited his positions; and in 1702 he was ordained by that church. His choice was not really surprising. Keith, in fact, had been educated at the universities in Aberdeen, where Episcopalian sentiment had always been strong, so that the move to the Episcopal Church of England was rather like returning home. Keith was then recruited by the new Society for the Propagation of the Gospel, the evangelizing branch of the Anglican Church, to return to the mid-Atlantic and proselytize among his former associates. In New Jersey and on Long Island, he met with considerable success.[8]

The Keithian dispute overlapped several other issues of spirituality and authority among Friends. One of those was slavery. The same well-to-do merchants who claimed authority within the Quarterly and Yearly Meetings were also among the leading Quaker slaveholders. Yet from the very beginning some Friends, mostly among those of lesser social standing and removed from the center of Quaker authority, questioned the morality of that trade. As early as 1676, the English Quaker William Edmundson, then in Newport, Rhode Island, recorded the first such attack on slavery, among the very first antislavery statements to appear in English America. The first such pronouncement in Pennsylvania appeared in 1688, signed by four Germantown Friends, on the grounds that slavery violated the Golden Rule, encouraged sinful rather than Christian behavior, and was founded upon violence. That was followed by another in 1693, issued by a group of Keithians who had recently separated from the meeting. Another Keithian, John Hepburn of East Jersey, published an extended antislavery tract in the second decade of the eighteenth century. The leadership of the Society had little reaction to those publications, and Quaker merchants continued to trade in slaves unimpeded for many decades, causing tensions between Friends of higher and lesser rank.

Another spiritual issue that affected Pennsylvanians was their desire to maintain peace with their Indian neighbors. Their relative success in that effort occurred partly because New York's involvement in the Covenant Chain had cleared the way for peaceable relations with the local Lenape, or Delawares, who had been weakened by years of warfare and shifting power relationships. Pennsylvania was able to provide a measure of shelter for those Indians against threats from the Five Nations.

Penn's desire for peace was undoubtedly sincere; however, in the long run, sincerity did not impede the force of greed. In 1686, according to a deed produced only years later whose authenticity has never been proved, Penn purchased from the Delaware Indians a territory located inland from the Forks of the Delaware "back into the woods as far as a man can go in a day and a half." This later became famous as the "walking purchase." The deed lay dormant for nearly half a century, until by 1735 settlers and speculators had taken up lands through the region. One of the most aggressive of those speculators was Penn's former secretary, James Logan, an active investor in lands, furs, and an ironworks in the vicinity, who was desirous of removing the Indians as far as possible. When they balked at the request, Logan enlisted the Five Nations to assist in pressuring the Delaware to remove. The rest is well known: Logan staked out three athletic runners, cleared the woods ahead of them, and set them loose on their "walk." They covered more than sixty miles, fully double what one would have expected, and Logan then drew the boundaries of the territory still more in his favor than the original deed had implied. Whatever the reality, the legend of the Walking Purchase would influence Indian affairs long afterward.

Nonetheless, Indian relations in Pennsylvania over its first half-century remained more peaceful than those of almost any other colony, most of which had experienced major conflicts in their early years. Not until conflict with New France heated up on the colonial frontiers after 1740 in the series of wars known as King George's War, did frontier hostilities in Pennsylvania reach the level experienced early by most other colonies. For the remainder of the colonial period, Pennsylvania would find itself at the very center of imperial conflict, and in that regard, any positive legacy of Quaker rule nearly disappeared.

By the beginning of the eighteenth century, proprietary authority throughout the Middle Colonies was in a shambles. The Duke of York, now James II, sat in exile in France, his province, like his kingdom, under the dominion of the House of Orange. The Jerseys were in turmoil, on the verge of a royal takeover promoted by the proprietors as their only hope of restoring authority and establishing secure control over their lands. William Penn had returned to England in 1684 in an effort to put his strained finances aright and to fight off a challenge to his proprietary claims from Lord Baltimore, whose charter conflicted with his own. Penn remained there to try to influence matters at Court during James's reign, and the conflict that followed the overthrow of the king forced Penn to retreat from public view, with many suspecting him of Jacobite—or pro-Stuart—sympathies in opposition to the Protestant rule of William and Mary. Penn's charter was revoked in 1692 and not returned to him until he made peace with the new monarchs two years later. Thus he did not return to Pennsylvania until 1699, and he left again two years later when his charter again fell under attack.

For a time Penn actually lost his province to his own steward, Philip Ford. Ford had long had the management of Penn's Irish estates, and he kept his accounts in such a way that soon it appeared that Penn owed him money. As security, Penn gave Ford a deed for Pennsylvania to guarantee the debt. On Ford's death in 1702, his wife went public with the deed and claimed title to Pennsylvania. Penn was imprisoned for debt in 1708 and would not clear his title to Pennsylvania until October of that year.

In the course of defending his title in 1701, Penn left one of his most important legacies for the colony: a new *Frame of Government*. Facing the threat of royal takeover, Penn sought to protect his commonwealth by vesting power in an elected assembly. For the remainder of the colonial period authority in Pennsylvania was sharply divided between governor and assembly, with no legislative role for a council, in contrast to the three-way division of power found in the British system and in nearly every other colonial government.

Penn was the only mid-Atlantic proprietor to retain his colony beyond 1702, and he and his family would face continuous threats to their control. His death in 1718 left the government of the province very much in doubt, with competing claims from the heirs of William Penn Jr., son of his first wife, Gulielma Springett, and Penn's children by his second wife, Hannah Callowhill. Not until long after his death would English courts grant the colony to Hannah Penn's children. As in the other colonies, Pennsylvania's rulers confronted a continuing legacy of conflict between proprietors and colonists, one that would only intensify after control of the province fell to Penn's son Thomas, a lapsed Quaker. The Quaker proprietary no longer had a Friend as proprietor.

Yet Penn's departure from the scene did not signify the end of his influence. On the proprietor's second trip to Pennsylvania in 1699, he brought with him the young, educated Scottish Quaker schoolmaster, James Logan, to serve as his secretary. When Penn returned to England the following year, Logan stayed on to serve his employer's interest. That he would continue to do for most of the ensuing half-century, holding a variety of public offices, contributing greatly to the intellectual life of the colony, and repeatedly defending the interests of the proprietors against whoever threatened them—including Native Americans in the Walking Purchase.

Other legacies of the seventeenth century were no less important. Among those were diversity and toleration: Penn's contacts with Quakers and sectarian groups in Ireland, in Holland, and in Germany would all send settlers to Pennsylvania during the early years. Perhaps more importantly, those early migrants would show the way for much larger groups of their countrymen later on, many of whom were neither Friends nor sympathetic to Friends. German-speakers would comprise as much as a third of the Pennsylvania population by the middle of the eighteenth century, most of it Lutheran or Reformed rather than sectarian, and only intermittently allied with the Quakers. Irish Presbyterians would represent nearly as large a group and would come to be the Friends' principal rivals.

Another legacy was the continuing colonization of Pennsylvania by families seeking to raise their children in the sort of comfortable circumstances that would tie them to their homes rather than forcing them to seek their sustenance outside. That allowed Quaker children to remain under the nurturing influence of parents wanting to instill in their children proper morals, godliness, and humanity. Such affectionate and relatively egalitarian families allowed women a greater voice in family affairs than was common among other groups, and that voice extended into greater authority within Quaker meetings and in public expression.

Quaker morals would continue to influence the colony in other ways. One of those was the testimony of peace, which kept Pennsylvania largely away from the theater of war for more than half a century. Pennsylvania thus extended a new kind of influence upon the region's continuing imperial competition, for Native Americans as well as for Europeans. Another legacy would be early Quaker antislavery. At a time when antislavery voices were almost entirely lacking from British North America, Quakers were almost the only ones to articulate such notions in public conversation. They met with limited success at the outset, even among Friends, and more aggressive antislavery advocates were disowned by the meeting. But well before the middle of the eighteenth century the issue of slavery would be irrevocably on the Quaker agenda, even as leading merchants continued to participate in the trade.

The combination of Quaker trading connections, religious tolerance, and the opportunity to raise families in peaceful and prosperous surroundings led to economic and demographic growth in Pennsylvania that far exceeded that of its neighbors to the north and east. By 1700, less than twenty years after its founding, the population of Pennsylvania was approaching 20,000 persons and would soon surpass that of New York. Philadelphia by 1720 had grown to 10,000 souls and would soon pass Boston as the largest city in British America. The colony's economy grew just as rapidly, setting the pace for the provinces around it. The involvement of Quaker merchants turned the newest of the Middle Colonies into a major commercial hub of the British Atlantic trading world.

Perhaps Penn's greatest legacy was the model of an orderly and prosperous Quaker society, a society founded on spiritual values that would not descend into individualism, anarchy, or conflict. Pennsylvania Quakers were less egalitarian than their counterparts in the Jerseys and on Long Island, but the colony's appeal to aspiring and well-to-do Quaker merchants and prominent Friends, as well as others inclined to follow their lead, allowed Pennsylvania to thrive beyond all expectations. In Pennsylvania, it seemed for a time, one could maintain Christian morals, spiritual values, expanding families, and a prospering economy all at the same time. In thus promoting the values of economic life, in the relative freedom it gave individuals to pursue it, and in the general idea of tolerance with which it was combined, Pennsylvania would set an important example for the entire region.

FOUR

The Commercial Crossroads of the British Atlantic

IN OR AROUND THE YEAR 1661, even before the Duke of York had launched England's entrance into the world of the mid-Atlantic, a former New Englander named Samuel Maverick wrote to a member of the duke's inner circle offering some economic reasons why English forces should seek to oust the Dutch from New Netherland. The region was full of possibilities, according to Maverick. The land itself was good, and it was well served by large and navigable inland waterways, which would facilitate trade. The territory was especially rich in beaver, and Maverick estimated that Dutch traders had obtained more than one hundred thousand skins from local Indians. Moreover, the mid-Atlantic was "most Commodious for commerce from and wth all pts of the West Indies," providing the promise of an outlet for whatever the region could produce. Thus even before the English conquest, Maverick anticipated a commercial future for Europeans in the mid-Atlantic, organized initially around two foundational trades: the shipment of local produce to distant markets—especially markets in the Caribbean—and the fur trade.[1]

Those trades, and others that followed, required the development of extensive commercial networks both within and beyond the region. Already Maverick foresaw that if there were to be an economically viable English colony within the mid-Atlantic, it would rest not on the plantation system found to the south, in the Chesapeake region and the Caribbean, nor on the largely village-based farm regimen found in much of New England to the north and east. Rather, it would be a producer of staples and an Atlantic trading hub. It would rely on the geography of the region—its location, its soil and climate, and the topography of land and water—as well as trading connections established within and beyond its bounds. The fur trade required obtaining skins collected over a wide area extending as far as the Great Lakes region and what would be Upper Canada over the region's network of inland waterways, using trading connections that Dutch merchants had already developed both with their Indian neighbors and across the ocean. The provisioning trade involved gathering produce from farms within the region and transporting it over established commercial routes to the plantation colonies, a link also pioneered by the Dutch. Over time, it would also require the development of regular internal trading links and an ever-increasing level of productivity on the part of mid-Atlantic households. The development of the Middle Colonies, established rather late in the history of the European colonization of the Americas, depended in part on the emergence of an increasingly specialized and intricately interconnected Atlantic commercial sector, along with the employment of force where necessary to secure it.

As a major commercial hub in the emerging British Atlantic, the Middle Colonies linked together places housing diverse economic activities, with the result that the regional economy itself was uncommonly varied compared to those to the north and the south. It incorporated competing commercial cultures originating in varied imperial ambitions. It contained both the trading capital and the agricultural breadbasket of the colonies; increasingly, it would produce a variety of other goods as well. Its merchants traded over local commercial networks and with distant markets. It had major foci in the valleys of the Hudson, the Delaware, and—by the mid-eighteenth century—the Susquehanna. Its labor force included some of the freest workers in North America, along with a substantial complement of African slaves. It possessed a class of powerful landed families, but at times it provided openings for seemingly powerless groups to take action for themselves, including some Africans, Indians, and women.

The physical imprint of the economy on the landscape was similarly diverse; Middle Colony settlers pursued varied occupations within a number of different forms of settlement. The most conspicuous was an open-country landscape of enclosed, single-family farms, where families could both provide for themselves and aspire to profit from the fruits of their labors. Passing through the region, one would have met with other forms of settlement as well. Scattered throughout could be found small crossroads hamlets similar to those found in Britain's poorer upland communities as well as the larger urban landscapes of cities and towns. In other places were large agricultural villages established by migrants from New England, who clustered in northern New Jersey in Elizabethtown, Newark, and the Monmouth Patent, and on eastern Long Island. Nor were manors and plantations wholly lacking; they could be found along the upper reaches of the Hudson and on Long Island's southern shore, in the iron plantations of New York and New Jersey, and in the most extensive planter's holdings in New Jersey and Pennsylvania. All of those mixed free laborers and tenant farmers with servants and slaves.

Throughout the period the territories of the Middle Colonies also retained a substantial non-European landscape, although its extent was continually shifting and diminishing. Those lands housed a mixed-use economy of hunting, planting, fishing, and gathering, with a diverse array of often-impermanent settlements situated to utilize each of those activities. Although European observers regarded those parts as "natural" and "unimproved" country, they were far from it. In earlier days, native peoples regularly improved the quality and suitability of their hunting and planting grounds through techniques such as the controlled use of fires and the application of natural fertilizers. As European involvement grew, Indian peoples would merge their agricultural traditions with imported methods, employing European materials while adapting them for their own purposes and undertaking new activities designed specifically for commerce in their new trading world.

The diversity of the social geography of the region should not be surprising: England's initial involvement in the mid-Atlantic was designed simply to claim and control the space between the earlier-settled regions of coastal North America to the north and to the south and, at the same time, to supply some of their needs. The Middle Colonies would funnel furs and later foodstuffs to European markets, produce flour and grain for the plantation colonies, employ both free and bound labor from Europe and Africa—this in spite of the first antislavery movement in the British Atlantic—and transport goods and people across colonial and racial frontiers and through the whole range of Britain's Atlantic possessions. Increasingly, they would serve as an active market for England's industrial products while beginning to produce for both internal and external markets themselves.

Like much else within the region, economic activity seemed to cluster around competing poles in Philadelphia and New York. For most of the period, the former would see faster commercial growth, denser European population, more intensive land use, and a more rapid decline in the native landscape. Over time those differences would diminish, as a growing European population in both areas would promote a narrowing of economic activity, with a relative decline in the fur trade and the extension of European land use over greater portions of the region. Moreover, within an environment of commerce and growth, the region as a whole would develop a distinct combination of prosperity and poverty, which grew up nearly simultaneously.

In its commercial basis, its diversity of products and populations, and its forms of labor as well as in the overall integrating functions that it served for Britain's American colonies, the economy of the Middle Colonies was in several respects the most fully *British* economy on the North American mainland. It was British it its reach, extending to British trading partners all around the Atlantic rim. Moreover, at a time of political union and imperial expansion, the creation of the British Atlantic itself involved the incorporation of varied peoples, interests, and trading styles into an increasingly complex commercial empire both at home and abroad. The emergence of the Middle Colonies on the western shore of that Atlantic economy brought together a diversity of peoples within a dynamic commercial space, pushing the very boundaries of the region as it did.

That there were no British colonies in the mid-Atlantic before 1660 was in large part because there was little reason for there to be any. The Dutch had carved out a set of trading outposts in the region designed to further the interests of commercial empire, but neither English nor Scots had yet made a serious attempt at settlement. Even the English conquest of 1664 was intended as much to further political and strategic interests as to produce immediate tangible benefits. James was at least as concerned about combating Dutch competition from the West Indies to West Africa and reigning in the ambitions of his Puritan adversaries in New England as he was to possess the territory, a large part of which he was content to give away almost as soon as he obtained it.

The Dutch West India Company never planned extensive settlement within the mid-Atlantic; it was not land they were after. Theirs was to be an empire more of trade than of territory. New Netherland was intended as an outpost of a Dutch commercial empire, one that would tap the products of the Indian trade and service the larger commercial needs of the Dutch plantation colonies. The mid-Atlantic colony was only one site in a developing Dutch trading interest in the Atlantic that would extend from the Netherlands and New Netherland to Africa, the Caribbean, and—for a quarter of a century after 1630—Brazil. Dutch merchants became nearly ubiquitous figures in Atlantic commerce, extending their reach to English, Spanish, and Portuguese as well as to Dutch colonies. Dutch traders, in fact, showed up regularly at nearly every colonial port.

The settlements established in New Netherland fit into the broad pattern of Dutch trading. Although the company encouraged small groups of migrants to establish working agricultural communities, such as that of the French-speaking Walloons north of New Amsterdam, the shape of most of their settlements was determined by their commercial ends. Thus New Amsterdam was located at the natural harbor at the mouth of the Hudson, from which goods garnered along the inland waterways could be transferred to coasting or ocean-going vessels. From there settlement extended northward along the Hudson Valley through a series of inland trading posts established at regular intervals. Among the largest was Esopus, now Kingston, some one hundred miles north of New Amsterdam. Still farther north lay Fort Orange, near the junction of the Hudson and Mohawk Rivers, New Netherlands' principal outpost of the fur trade, surrounded by the trading town of Beverwyck (Beaver-town).[2] Other commercial settlements appeared along both coasts of the Long Island Sound and on the Delaware River. The latter included Forth Nassau, which sat opposite Fort Christiana, established by settlers from New Sweden in 1638, with similar trading goals.

The commercial nature of the colony thus shaped its geography, as settlements everywhere hugged the coastline or the shores of navigable rivers in what have been called "alongshore" settlements.[3] They made little attempt to settle inland beyond the up-river trading posts. That led to the early development of the geographical distinction that would later emerge as an upstate/downstate rivalry in New York. The main centers were New Amsterdam, home of the principal overseas merchants, and Beverwyck and Fort Orange, their upriver contacts and rivals in the fur trade. The towns were centers of commercial activity, where not only merchants but common tradesmen sought to set up their own small fur trading enterprises. Tradesmen there sought the traditional protection of Dutch burgher status, which entitled them to exclusive rights to conduct their businesses. The limited agricultural settlements that grew up around them were located to serve the needs of those trading centers. For example, Schenectady was founded in 1661 on rich farmland in the Mohawk Valley; its inhabitants were expressly forbidden from trading with the natives in competition with the people of nearby Beverwyck.

The one exception to Dutch West India Company land policy took place outside of regular channels. In 1628, a small group of Company members led by Kiliaen Van Rensselaer pushed through a new plan in the Amsterdam Chamber—over the objections of leading merchants—granting large tracts of land called "patroonships" to those who would invest private capital in the colony and attract migrants. The grants extended as far as sixteen miles along the Hudson River waterfront. Even that did not generate much interest either in promoting settlement or

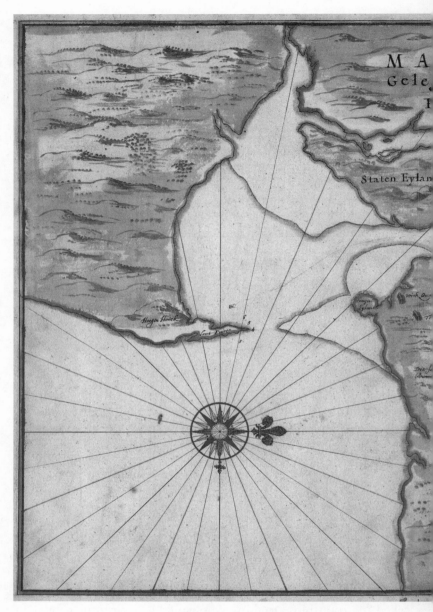

An early Dutch map of Manhattan by Joan Vinckeboons, 1639, showing the prominence of waterways in the perceptions of Dutch settlers. Courtesy of the Library of Congress.

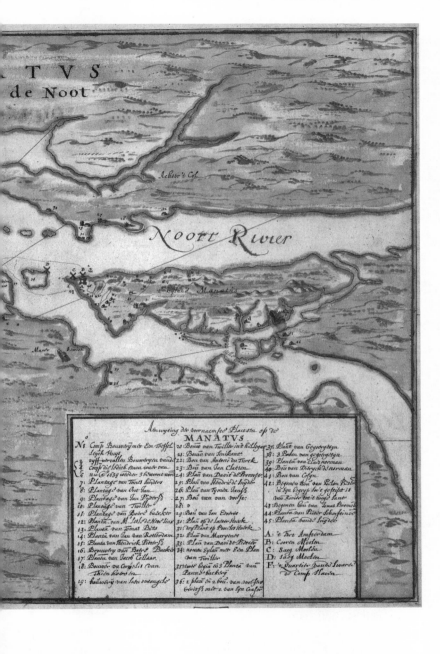

undertaking it; the only significant success was Rensselaerswyck near Beverwyck, granted to the principal figure behind the policy. Significantly, and much to van Rensselaer's displeasure, patroons were initially denied the right to participate in transatlantic commerce with the Netherlands, a trade restricted to city merchants.

The close involvement of New Netherland with the Dutch commercial world—especially within the context of a sparsely populated commercial venture—meant that the colony from an early date acquired one of the characteristic forms of labor emerging in the Atlantic economy: African slaves. In the early seventeenth century, merchants of the Dutch West India Company were major suppliers of slaves to the New World, and the African trade was an integral part of the Dutch West India project. The first Africans arrived in New Netherland as early as 1626. Unlike the plantation colonies, where many slaves early on were treated as lifetime workers, Africans imported by the West India Company had the opportunity to achieve partial freedom —"half-freedom," it was called—allowing slaves after many years of service to achieve the freedom to travel and to own limited property, paying the Company a fixed sum in return. Even some slaves of private owners were allowed to obtain a degree of freedom. The result would be an extremely diverse African community in New Amsterdam, combining slaves, free people of color, and the half-free. By the 1640s, Dutch ships arrived in New Amsterdam with large cargoes of enslaved Africans for sale, and the city had become the principal slave market for mainland North America.

Dutch merchants were especially aggressive traders. From the beginning they cruised the waters not only adjacent to New Netherland but up and down the Atlantic coast from New England to Brazil. They played important roles in the trade of nearby English colonies, including Virginia and New England, and they quickly connected New Netherlands commercially with both of those places. They also promoted the colony's trade with the Caribbean possessions of the English, French, and Spanish as well as their own.

The main deviation from the structure of a trading colony developed on eastern Long Island, where migrants from New England began to establish some of that region's characteristic forms of commerce and community. Like their New England countrymen, settlers in that region envisioned a diversified economy, incorporating agriculture, fishing and shell-fishing, whaling, and trading with their neighbors across the Sound and farther afield. After the English conquest, eastern Long Islanders requested to be placed under Connecticut's jurisdiction, a request James's government steadfastly denied. They continued to trade principally through Boston, however, and towns such as Easthampton developed very active commercial sectors.

Those New England natives established their settlements largely on the model of their former homes. They acquired their titles to land in large community grants, redistributing the land over time to the original inhabitants and their descendants, along with any newcomers they chose to permit. Some towns continued to take in new families as full members; others would separate the original holders who maintained a claim in future land distributions from later arrivals. Thus Easthampton established a separate Board of Trustees, representing those descendants of original inhabitants who were to share in the ownership and distribution of town lands. The principal exceptions on Long Island were the large manors created by men such as Lion Gardiner on Gardiner's Island and Nathaniel Sylvester on Shelter Island, whose properties lay beyond the jurisdiction of the towns and answered to no one but the manor lord.

The system that emerged in the towns was both patrilineal—with lines of descent largely following the male line of family and inheritance—and male-dominated, or patriarchal. In those respects it stood in sharp contrast to local native communities, which were matrilineal and matrilocal. In the new English communities, property was passed down from parents to children, and families placed a premium on obtaining sufficient land to provide substantial portions to all of their children, or at least all their male children. One historian has referred to those units as "linear families," in which sons succeeded their fathers on family lands for generations.[4] Women probably had fewer property rights than among other groups, owing to the emphasis on transmitting land through the generations. Eastern Long Island farmers came to value freeholding—the outright ownership of land by families—to a degree not shared by other colonists in the region. Families tended to remain together within particular townships, and over time they became quite inbred. This is easily detected by the association of large clusters of individuals and families with a single surname within the various towns. In the New Jersey town of Newark, also settled by transplanted New Englanders, those extended families would be grouped together in the church records as "tribes."[5]

CONQUEST AND CONTINUITY

The society that followed the English conquest built upon its predecessor. That was partly the result of continuity in population. New Netherland in 1664 housed as many as nine thousand inhabitants, many of them having come in the previous decade. Immigration from the Netherlands virtually ceased thereafter, but most of the population remained, with only a small group of English newcomers. While direct commerce with the Netherlands was severely diminished, trade with the Netherlands never ceased, often carried out illegally. More importantly, Dutch traders along the Atlantic coast continued to act as leading players in local commerce, linking the mid-Atlantic to such sites as the Chesapeake and the Caribbean.

Like his Dutch predecessors, James was concerned less with possessing and developing the territory than with broader commercial and imperial goals—hence his willingness to part with much of the colony. Nor did he have much interest in offering land to recruit small farmers in order to promote migration. Instead, his government further developed both hierarchical and commercial aspects of the Dutch colony.

One of those was the patroonship, a creation that appealed to James's associates and other members of England's landed class. While the Dutch had originated the grants, the English government gave away many more large properties, which they called manors, in places ranging from the Hudson Valley to Long Island's southern shore. These would be much more successful than their predecessors. By the end of the century they had distributed much of the land along the Hudson from New York to Albany and beyond in large blocks.

Among the largest of the properties was Livingston Manor, patented to the Scots migrant Robert Livingston in part for his services to the government in Indian affairs. Livingston was a shrewd operator and continually added to his claims through active politicking and even more aggressive extension of claims beyond his patents; his property eventually reached 160,000 acres. The estate was developed slowly, but over the years the Livingstons added inhabitants along with the acreage until they presided over one of the principal properties in the colony.

A similar set of large estates developed in East Jersey, where the presence of Dutch settlements and the strong involvement of James's associates among the Scots proprietors created a social order closely related to that of New York. Like their countryman Livingston, several Scots proprietors created manors that functioned continuously as working estates throughout the colony's history. Other properties lay dormant for decades until an aggressive group of owners began to develop them in the second quarter of the eighteenth century. Those manors would be important both for their lands and for their mining deposits, and several would house working iron plantations, complete with foundries and forges. And, like large properties elsewhere, the proprietary estates in East Jersey housed a combination of tenants, servants, and slaves.

With much of the better and more accessible land patented to wealthy landowners and with an initial form of government granting fewer liberties to its inhabitants than did those of its neighbors, New York's population grew sluggishly. Close to twenty thousand persons inhabited its colonial settlements by the end of the seventeenth century, and perhaps seventy thousand by the middle of the eighteenth, but that was less than half the population of Pennsylvania.

The surprising thing may be how little the conquest of New Netherland altered basic patterns of economic and community life. Up-river commerce, including the fur trade, remained substantially in Dutch hands. So also did much of the coastal trade between colonies. And rural Dutch settlers continued to live in what looked like Dutch-style communities. Dutch houses, for example, were long developed in what became characteristic Dutch building styles, with sloped roofs and Holland brick and gables facing the street.

One of the keys to maintaining the forms of community was a continuing adherence to the Dutch social system, defined by Dutch patterns of community, gender, and inheritance. Dutch settlers derived from a society that was not only highly commercial but markedly mobile as well. As Europe's principal Protestant refuge, the Netherlands experienced a constant influx and outflow of both natives and outsiders. The Netherlands funneled diverse peoples into the Dutch commercial empire; the diversity of New Netherland was very much the norm. Over the years, those who lived in the Netherlands developed significant strategies for maintaining community life in the midst of extensive commercial undertakings and movement in general.

Compared to their English neighbors, Dutch New Yorkers had only a modest stake in landed property. Property functioned more as a commodity for sale and distribution than as an essential pillar of society, and territorial acquisition was never the goal of the colony. Thus Dutch inheritance provided for the strict division of property among heirs, with women receiving equal portions, rather than privileging the inheritance of male heirs or the firstborn, as was common among the English on Long Island, for example. Dutch women had much greater rights of property-holding than did their English neighbors, and Dutch widows were frequently able to carry on family businesses and active trading. Some married Dutch women were even able to trade under their own names, and Dutch laws allowed a form of marriage in which women kept their own property intact, although those were eventually succeeded by English laws of coverture, giving husbands legal control of family property. Unlike English wives, Dutch women traditionally kept their own family names at marriage. This suggests the importance of maternal kin groups among the Dutch, which provided much of the cohesion in a Dutch commercial society that did not derive its roots from the transmission of landed property.

Among the most prominent of the Dutch trading women was Mary Spratt Alexander, granddaughter of a female merchant, widow of a Dutch trader, and wife of the prominent New York attorney James Alexander, a Scot. Alexander traded on her own account in eighteenth-century New York, although laws of coverture meant that sometimes payments owed to her went to her husband, regardless of her preferences. She imported dry goods and other items from London and dealt them across New York and New Jersey and was among the wealthiest women in the colony. Other Dutch women traded on a more modest scale, either because of lesser wealth and connections or because for some it was an occasional activity. An example of the latter was Mary Gardiner, wife of Lion Gardiner on Long Island, with trading interests in New York.

The economic legacies of Dutch New Netherland would be considerable. They included a strong commercial base for the colony, specializing in fur, flour, and other provisions, still surrounded by only a modest colony of settlement within a larger native landscape. They included strong trading links to European colonies in the Caribbean—although competition from active traders in the new colony of Pennsylvania would begin to eclipse New York's role there—and to the Five Nations. They included the presence of a substantial and diverse African population as well as significant social divisions. There were commercial rivalries between upstate Indian traders and their downstate brokers in the export trade. There were divisions as well between Dutch and English but also between those Dutch elites who benefited from the conquest and those rural families who became increasingly removed from the commercial connections that brought them there. Ironically, for rural families left behind by the removal of the Dutch commercial empire, with their links to external trading diminished, New York was becoming less a commercial colony than something that had not been intended: a colony of settlement.

QUAKERS AND THE ATLANTIC ECONOMY

To most observers, the economic landscape that best seemed to represent the Middle Colonies developed not in the previously Dutch territories of the Hudson Valley but in the new Quaker settlements along the Delaware. Pennsylvania and its surroundings were noted for efficient and prosperous family farms, connected to their markets through a network of local traders and overseas merchants. The opportunities those farms provided led observers to describe the countryside there and throughout the region as the "best poor man's country in the world."[6]

While casual observers imagined a uniformity to both the economy and the landscape of the region, even the Delaware Valley contained considerable variety. As one traveled beyond the enclosed farming country of Pennsylvania's eastern counties, other landscapes emerged. Scattered through the region one found numerous Indian village settlements, even as the constant quest for farmlands pushed the overall native landscape ever farther into retreat. At many of the trading crossroads of central Jersey and eastern Pennsylvania, one found interlocking networks of small hamlets. That was especially true where migrants from upland regions of Scotland, Ireland, or northern England had settled. These were people who derived from pastoral societies in which mobility and dispersion, as well as extended regional trading networks, had long been basic to their ways of life. One also found occasional large manors, along with tenants, servants, and slaves. And despite the evident prosperity of the region, poverty and inequality were also permanent features of the countryside.

The largest influence in Pennsylvania came from the Quakers, comprising perhaps half of the settlers between 1680 and 1700. They took up farms in Philadelphia and in eastern Pennsylvania, chiefly in Bucks, Delaware, and Chester Counties as well as in Burlington and Salem Counties across the river in New Jersey. As the first substantial group of farmers in the colony, Friends laid claim to some of the best agricultural lands as well as the most accessible to market, both of which were significant factors in the success of Quaker agriculturalists.

The prosperity of farming families among the Society of Friends cannot readily be separated from their religious practices. Just as Quakers combined spirituality and discipline in their faith, so also they attempted to balance the world and the spirit. That included the competing imperatives of religious purity and the need to preserve their vision by passing their faith on to others. One of the principal motivations of Quakers for coming to Pennsylvania was the prospect of acquiring farms large enough to settle their families and provide future homes for their children so that they would not have to move outside of their families, their communities, and the Society.

The religious practices of Friends, like the family habits of that other commercial people, the Dutch, provided an enhanced role for women in community, household, and meeting. Quaker families were unusually egalitarian, relying less on paternal command than on parental persuasion. Quaker women had substantial decision-making authority within the family and within their own women's meetings. And because Friends shunned the idea of an ordained ministry, Quaker women could preach and prose-lytize as women could in few other churches or sects.

The Quaker faith also provided for a balance between religion and enterprise. Quakers had distinct rules of trading: merchants were not to haggle over prices but were to establish fixed charges as a matter of fair dealing. They were not to ask for a higher price in a transaction than they were willing to accept. Friends were to behave honestly in their transactions or risk the censure of the meeting, which maintained an intense interest in seeing that the actions of individual Friends did not undermine the reputation of the Society. While this did not ensure their complete com-pliance, Quaker merchants were well-respected and trusted as long-distance traders, especially by other Friends. Of course, all of this assumed that they were trading within a protected British Atlantic economy.

Quakers who fulfilled their obligations to those formal rules could be among the most aggressive of traders. Early on they established some of the best-developed commercial networks in the Atlantic world. That was partly a result of the willingness to travel of early Quaker preachers, who established a presence at many key ports of call. Quakers were well established from an early date in the West Indies, for example, and played leading roles in Philadelphia's commerce with that region.

Merchant networks such as those that Friends employed, in which a group establishes its own members across the globe as commercial partners, are referred to as "trading diasporas." Friends were one of several such diasporas to locate in Middle Colony ports; Scots and Jews were other prominent examples. The latter built upon their existing connections in the Dutch world to connect families in New York and Philadelphia to Am-sterdam and commercial sites around the Caribbean.

The impact of Friends on local economic activity was wide-spread. One of Penn's first initiatives was to establish the Free Society of Traders led by Quaker merchants. Those traders had extensive contacts through much of the Atlantic world, from London, Bristol, and Cork to Rhode Island, the mid-Atlantic, and the West Indies, and the grain and flour produced by Quaker farmers quickly began to find their way into the expanding Ca-ribbean market. There it served to feed the growing slave population on the sugar plantations. There was a considerable irony in that situation: Quaker farmers found a freedom and opportunity that was underwritten by the profits of slave labor. But individual farmers would hardly have been aware of that connection. Those few who were would help lead early Quaker antislavery efforts.

The migration of Friends to the Delaware Valley affected not only the country landscape but that of Philadelphia, the Quaker city. In line with the leading planned communities of the latter part of the seventeenth century, Philadelphia was set out as a neatly ordered city—as orderly as any according to the proprietor's vision—with parallel streets and a regular series of grass-covered town squares, intended to create a "greene country town," in Penn's plan. Along the banks of the Delaware the leading merchants established wharves and stores. Penn's commercial ambitions were large enough that he planned for a second set of wharves along the Schuylkill River to the west of the city, but few merchants were willing to set up there, and settlement did not extend that far. For many years the banks of that river lay undeveloped.

If the manor-dominated landscape of New York led to a period of sparse settlement, the commercial and family-farm economy of Pennsylvania combined with religious toleration and a long period of peace to attract many new immigrants seeking liberty, prosperity, and security for themselves and their children. By 1700, the colony had close to 20,000 settlers, and it continued to grow rapidly thereafter. Moreover, Penn specifically sought to bring artisans and other skilled workers to Pennsylvania, and tradesmen thrived in Philadelphia.

In Benjamin Franklin's *Autobiography* we get a vivid picture of the life of a tradesman in early Philadelphia. Franklin was an unusual individual, to be sure, and his success in the printing trade was hardly typical of his peers. Indeed, many of his early friends and associates failed in their trades, and some landed in lives of poverty and dependence. The great majority had much less success than Franklin. Nonetheless, opportunity was there. When Franklin arrived in Philadelphia in 1723, he faced only modest competition in the printing business, and there was a shortage of skilled workers of all kinds. Those who combined a measure of wit, a modicum of skill, some useful personal connections, and some general good luck—all of which Franklin had in abundance —had reason to hope for lives of reasonable prosperity.

HOUSEHOLD AND TRADE

One of the keys to growth in the Pennsylvania region was the development of internal trading networks to diversify what was available in local markets and to provide goods to trade abroad. Here the geography of the region was a considerable advantage, since Philadelphia was closely linked to productive regions accessible to its merchants. One was the central Jersey corridor from Newark to Trenton, linking Philadelphia to New York. New Jersey ports failed at attracting overseas commerce, but as an internal trade network it connected fertile lands with easily traversed commercial paths, which were augmented by the development by regional traders of regular ferries at the major transfer points. The region would become a significant engine of growth.

Other areas of growth could be found down-river. One such area was Chester County to the south and east. There a regime of mixed agriculture by farmers and cottagers was combined with the growth of craftwork by men and women, increasing what county householders could make available to the market. Further down-river were the lower counties, or northern Delaware, where important flour mills grew up along the Brandywine Creek near Wilmington.

Much of the growth resulted from an increasing productivity in Middle Colony households, especially in the Pennsylvania region. In the preindustrial age most production occurred at the level of individual households, in which all family members participated. Thus major gains could come from the activities of women, even if their production does not necessarily show up in the records. Young women sometimes took part-time work outside of the home to contribute to family incomes, but all women were active producers. They produced such commodities as food and cloth for their own consumption and for sale, and nearly all participated in local networks of exchange. The growth of household economies was an important part of economic growth in the region.

One of the ways the economy grew was through a diversifica-

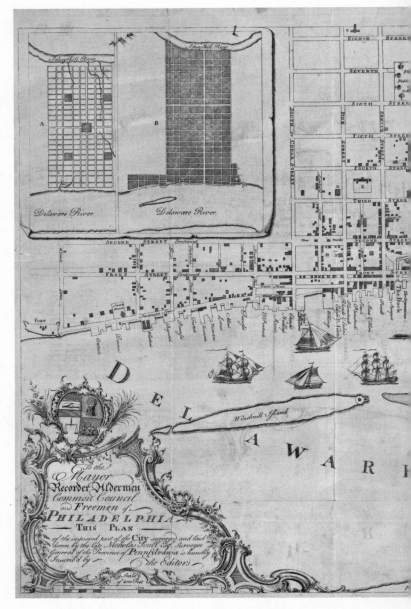

Plan of the Improved Part of the City of Philadelphia by Nicholas Scull, 1762, showing the importance of the city's waterfront as well as its regular rectangular grid. Courtesy of the Library of Congress.

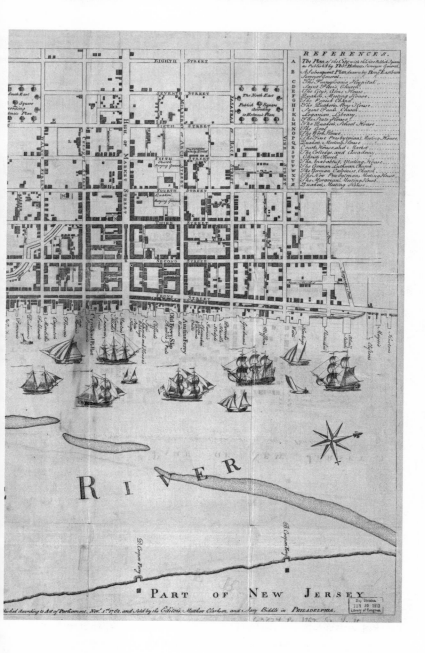

PART OF NEW JERSEY

tion of activities such as milling, mining, and craftwork. Throughout the region, farm households introduced both spinning and weaving, especially of linen cloth, into their household activities. Spinning was usually performed by women; weaving, almost exclusively by men. The milling of flour was an activity that was especially useful for selling the region's extensive grain crop to distant markets. While local mills were a necessity for every farming community, by the middle of the eighteenth century merchants were building larger mills explicitly for crop exports. Mining was another important activity in northeastern Pennsylvania, northern and northwestern New Jersey, and upper New York, usually organized on merchant estates.

An example of the way household production and internal trade networks could link local households to the Atlantic market was the cultivation and exchange of flaxseed. Flax was a valuable crop used for linseed oil and especially for the weaving of linen cloth. Middle Colony farmers had grown flax from the beginning, often for household use, but circumstances in the eighteenth century led to markedly increased production. The cause was the vast expansion of linen production in Scotland and especially Ireland, and the consequent demand from those places for a supply of seed. Farming households were thus able to expand their crops, keeping what they needed at home for their own use and selling the surplus seed to overseas merchants. Across central Jersey, that was especially true of Scottish farmers, who were linked to Scots and Irish merchants who controlled many of the internal points of transit in that region as well as the Irish trade.

NEW MIGRANTS AND FRONTIERS

In the development of the Delaware Valley, Quakers represented a "charter group," a group whose early and substantial presence in a new society creates conditions that influence the development of that society even as the numerical dominance of that group diminishes. The profitable economy of individual farm families producing wheat and flour for a larger Atlantic market spread beyond the Quakers. In particular, German migrants who began arriving in Pennsylvania in response to Penn's recruiting campaign established their own farming communities as early as 1683 among German Friends and Mennonites at

Germantown. Thereafter, the commercial opportunities the region provided created both a demand for labor and a highly commercialized means of obtaining it.

The early influx of German migrants had little lasting significance; more important was the Palatine migration to New York in 1708. Governor Hunter's promises to the group went unfulfilled, and soon thereafter a group led by the young Conrad Weiser, the future Indian negotiator, departed for the Pennsylvania's greater Susquehanna Valley. Others would follow in their wake, and over four decades perhaps eighty thousand German-speakers departed the Rhine Valley for Pennsylvania, drawn by the prospect of land and the promise of toleration. They included persons of the Lutheran, German Reformed, Mennonite, Moravian, and other groups. Religious networks as well as commercial links played important roles in directing their moves, with Dutch and English merchants tied to their religious communities organizing much of the movement to the New World.

For those who could not afford the rather hefty cost of passage from the Rhine Valley to Pennsylvania, the option of indentured servitude—selling one's labor for a period of service to pay for the cost of the passage—was always present. Among German-speakers a special kind of servant emerged, the "redemptioner." Unlike servants from Britain, who usually signed labor contracts before their departures, many German-speakers indentured themselves to merchants and ship captains, who would then auction off their labor upon arriving in the New World for periods sufficient to pay off their debts. It could be a difficult sum to raise; for many, the voyage up the Rhine to reach their point of departure—often England—cost much more than they had anticipated and left them with fewer resources and greater obligations than they had planned. Moreover, for those who traveled in families, the death of a child or a spouse after the journey had reached the halfway point—no rare thing—could leave the remaining family members with the obligation to pay for the passage of the deceased. The most unlucky redemptioners arrived in the New World in the throes of grief and saddled with debt.

The former servant Gottlieb Mittelberger left a vivid description of the redemptioner trade. Mittelberger wrote to protect his fellow Germans who might be lured by false promises, describing at length the risks that awaited such travelers. How effective it was is hard to say; it did not appear until the peak of German migration to America had passed, and the harsh picture Mittelberger painted of the voyage was at least partially balanced by a much more favorable presentation of Pennsylvania itself.[7]

Whether the migration of German speakers was motivated more by the attractiveness of Pennsylvania or by the difficult conditions they were attempting to leave behind is also a difficult question. The colony was only one of several options for the large number of persons displaced by hardships in the Rhine Valley. Pennsylvania, in fact, attracted only a fraction of those who departed from the German territories, usually those who had direct connections with fellow villagers or family members who had already departed for Pennsylvania. Most of the rest went to the east, especially to Poland, which often offered terms as good as or better than those given by Pennsylvania promoters. Migration to Pennsylvania peaked in the brief period of 1748–54 that separated imperial wars and fell off dramatically thereafter. Henceforth, most migrants went east rather than west. The achievement of a lasting peace in 1763 did not lead to any significant resumption of movement to America.

Mainstream German-speakers looked to establish farm communities much like those of the Quakers, settling in Pennsylvania as far west as the Susquehanna Valley and then southward into the backcountries of Maryland and Virginia. Ironically, German sectarian groups such as Mennonites, who were closest to Quakers in their spirituality, were more likely to diverge from the pattern they set in economic roles and community forms. Where Quakers looked to balance commerce and spirituality, those groups more often opted for purity. They often located in isolated settings, even at the expense of their ability to pass on the faith to others or to future generations. The most radical, such as the Ephrata group in Lancaster County, abandoned reproduction altogether in favor of celibacy and communal control of property.

Groups who moved farther from the original Quaker territories were less likely to follow the patterns they initiated. As early as the 1680s, East Jersey's Scots proprietors, including Quakers, established a set of estates or manors largely on the Scottish model. Few of the proprietors actually moved to the colony, especially among those who were Quakers, and many sold off their lands. Others rented lands to tenant farmers. At the same time, Scottish merchants and petty traders, long accustomed to establishing ethnic trading networks on the European Continent, began to develop intensive commercial ties across central Jersey, and at every crossroads or transit point between New York and Philadelphia, they established trading stations and small clustered hamlets, where most of the settlers located.

Scots and Irish settlers who ventured into the backcountries of Pennsylvania and New York would extend that landscape into new settlements. Irish migrants were predominantly Ulster Protestants, most of Scots birth or descent. It was a highly unsettled population, with many families who had moved back and forth across the Irish Sea during the previous century in response to persecutions, religious wars, and economic troubles in both Scotland and the north of Ireland.

Both Scots and Irish settlers, like the Dutch, derived from populations that traditionally experienced exceptionally high rates of mobility, although of a rather different sort from that of the Netherlands. The migration strategies they developed were suited to the maintaining of community ties among a mobile people. Rather than settling down in large communities, family members frequently spread themselves among the numerous small hamlets they established in the region. In the process they created extended family networks that linked widely separated settlements over a substantial territory.

With little attachment to particular family holdings, Scots and Irish families, like the Dutch, divided their inheritances quite equally among their children. Women thus received full portions for themselves and retained considerable influence in their communities. Those who married outsiders regularly brought them into their local community networks just as Dutch women did. They also retained their own family names.

Ulster migration to North America began in earnest in 1717, promoted initially by Penn's secretary, James Logan, a Quaker and native of Ulster himself, who thought that after their experience of battling with Irish natives, the people would make good frontiersmen. That growth accelerated in the following decade, prompted by declines in the linen trade—Ulster's principal manufacture—as well as continuing resentment by Presbyterians at their second-class status as dissenters from the established Episcopal Church of Ireland. By 1729, so many Ulster settlers were arriving in Pennsylvania that Logan lamented, "It looks as though Ireland is to send all its inhabitants hither. . . . It is strange that they crowd where they are not wanted."[8]

Over the first three-quarters of the eighteenth century, perhaps forty thousand left the North of Ireland for America, with the great majority landing either at Philadelphia or at Newcastle in Delaware; from the latter port they usually made their way into lower Pennsylvania. That far exceeded the movement from Scotland directly, where the migrant stream was greatly reduced by substantial depopulation at the end of the previous century. Many Irish went as indentured servants, that is, as individuals who signed indentures to work for someone in the New World for a period that ranged from four to seven years. Children served until they reached maturity.

The attraction of new migrant populations to the region was influenced by two rather separate sets of market forces. One was the need for labor, which was reflected in the many thousands of indentured servants who left Europe for the region. Most servants were young, usually single, and predominantly male, although female servants also played a substantial role in households. The demand for laborers in the region was fairly consistent, and though the rate of servant migration certainly had its peaks and valleys, new servants were a rather consistent presence in the Middle Colonies.

The migration of families, usually as aspiring farmers rather than servants, was more variable. It depended as much on "push factors"—the willingness of families to leave their homes—as on the particular opportunities offered. It also depended on the interest of families at any particular juncture in moving to Pennsylvania or to the Middle Colonies rather than to another site, such as eastern Europe. Family migration came largely in waves, coinciding with peak periods of emigration: the late 1720s from Germany and Ireland; Germany again between the two wars at mid-century (1748–54); Ireland and Scotland after the conclusion of the Seven Years' War in 1763.

The end of the Seven Years' War had another effect on immigration: the center of movement to the Middle Colonies shifted from Pennsylvania to New York as the back parts of the latter colony began to fill up with Scots and Irish settlers. That was partly the result of the beginnings of overcrowding: long years of far greater migration to Pennsylvania left accessible land there scarce and expensive. New York prices were lower, and more land was now available in desirable locales. Moreover, for the first time the end of the war provided real security for New Yorkers beyond the immediate vicinity of New York City, who had lived under the threat of attack from the French or their Indian allies. The Treaty of Paris ended France's presence on the mainland and left New York secure. By contrast, during the Seven Years' War Pennsylvania became the principal point of frontier warfare for the first time, and peace left tenuous relations between the colony and its Indian neighbors.

As more migrants moved to the frontier, that movement accelerated the development of one of the most unusual community forms in the Middle Colonies, the mixed settlements of Indians and Europeans. Those settlements were sites of exchange—commercial, diplomatic, cultural, and spiritual. Many of the inhabitants were persons capable of navigating across cultural boundaries, who were sometimes referred to as "go-betweens." They included European traders such as George Croghan, an Irish-born settler who established a Pennsylvania trading enterprise west of the Appalachian line in the Ohio Country and dealt extensively in furs and other commodities. They included native women who cohabited with frontier traders. There were also persons of mixed parentage, European and Indian, who sometimes inhabited the spaces between cultures. Cross-frontier trading at such places formed a regular and significant part of the commerce of Pennsylvania merchants.

An example of such a mixed settlement was Shamokin, in the Susquehanna Valley of Pennsylvania. The settlement was hardly controlled by the colony, however. It was inhabited by a mixed and variable group of Delawares, Iroquois, and other native peoples; German Moravians; Presbyterian missionaries; British-American soldiers; and Scots-Irish traders, nearly all of whom came and went without establishing permanent residence. Most influential of all was the Oneida Indian Shikellamy, the principal Iroquois representative in the town, which served as the diplomatic center of the region. Shikellamy was visited regularly by traders and negotiators of all groups.

In mixed settlements such as Shamokin, women could play unusually large roles. There were women of European descent, most of whom were married or attached to soldiers or traders, or served in the missions. Some achieved considerable influence. Near Shamokin lived one Madame Montour, a French-Iroquois *métis,* herself a power to be dealt with in the region by all sides. But perhaps the greatest influence belonged to Indian women, who probably did more than anyone else to cross the cultural boundaries as traders, translators, hostesses, and either occasional or long-term sexual partners. Indian women regularly established relationships with European traders who moved into border areas, creating sites for multiple forms of exchange while at the same time helping their nations in the competition for trade goods.

Another mixed settlement of a rather different sort was the Mohawk Valley estate of the Indian trader William Johnson, an Irish native, military officer, and leading figure of New York's political and diplomatic life. His manor house, Johnson Hall, bridged the boundaries between Europeans and natives, inhabited by both, and became the center of economic and diplomatic exchange between the New York colony and its Mohawk neighbors. Johnson played the role of broker to the hilt. He cohabited for many years with Molly Brandt, sister of the powerful Mohawk chieftain Joseph Brandt, and they raised a family of nine children together. In all of his diplomatic activities Johnson made sure that Britain delivered a full bounty of goods to the Mohawk, who insisted in return that they would carry on diplomacy in the region with no one other than Johnson.

Still another new form of settlement in which native peoples participated were religious missions such as those the Moravians established in the Susquehanna Valley. Other important missions could be found at the Forks of the Delaware in Pennsylvania and in Cranbury, New Jersey, a Lenape town where the famous Presbyterian missionaries David and John Brainerd preached. While the Indians at Cranbury moved into a relatively compact settlement, giving up the wider swath of territory on which they had previously existed and living within the confines of European control, they managed to maintain much of their lifestyle, with the ability to move from place to place as their activities and the seasons required, at least for a time. In addition to planting corn, they hunted on open lands, gathered cranberries, fished, and continued to trade in brooms, baskets, fish, and other commodities. Still, wherever native communities were fully surrounded by European settlement, as they were at Cranbury and the Forks, they were almost invariably sites of considerable poverty.

PROSPERITY AND POVERTY

Those sites of poverty developed within a rapidly growing economy. Economic growth in the region was impressive, especially in the Delaware Valley. Pennsylvania's population grew from about 20,000 at the beginning of the eighteenth century to about 180,000 by 1760, and Philadelphia grew into the largest city in North America, with nearly 30,000 inhabitants. New York, with more than 20,000, passed Boston for second place. At the same time the commerce of the region grew even more rapidly, with a marked increase in the grain and flour trade to West Indies and southern Europe, especially from Pennsylvania, and a large surge in imported goods. And the gains were widely distributed. It was the countryside of prospering farms that led observers to call Pennsylvania and its surroundings the "best poor man's country." And in the city, where few could match the meteoric rise from lowly artisan to independent gentleman that Benjamin Franklin would describe in his famous *Autobiography,* many skilled tradesmen still managed to make their way to a decent living.

Accompanying the increase in wealth and trade was a rise in the overall living standard. As the eighteenth century progressed, more and more consumer goods made their way into Middle Colony markets, both from Britain and from the production of local tradesmen. Again, Benjamin Franklin offered a good illustration of those developments. For his early working years, as Franklin tells it, he and his wife ate off of nothing but earthenware. Then one morning at breakfast, he found in front of him a china bowl, his wife informing him that her husband deserved them as well as any of her neighbors. Franklin went on to concede that over the years, as the family's finances improved, they eventually accumulated china and plate worth several hundred pounds.[9]

The increase of imports was dramatic. By the middle of the

eighteenth century all kinds of consumer goods were finding their way into the mid-Atlantic market, from fine china, to tableware, to all kinds of fancy cloth, to furniture, to books, to imported beverages such as coffee and tea. So dramatic was the growth in the import of manufactured goods that historians have come to speak of a consumer revolution in the mid-eighteenth century, with the Middle Colonies at the very forefront of that movement. In Pennsylvania, for example, between the 1740s and 1760s, the value of imported goods from Britain nearly quadrupled, and New York was not far behind. Merchants advertised their wares in New York and Philadelphia papers, including a continually increasing variety of consumables. Families who previously had few possessions began to furnish their homes and their lives with more and more things. Not only genteel households but also middling farmers and tradesmen participated.

The advent of commercial prosperity did not bring an end to poverty, however. On the contrary, the ranks of the impoverished also seemed to grow both in absolute numbers and in relative terms over the course of the eighteenth century. That was a direct result of the region's close involvement in the world of Atlantic commerce, which increasingly required participants to involve themselves in a world of markets and a world of risk. Where some made fortunes in land and trade and others achieved a modest prosperity through the benign influence of the market, still others suffered from its iron hand. Commerce required the use of credit, which made advancement possible for some but consigned others to failure and indebtedness. Even tradesmen found that in order to survive in the competitive market they had to enter the world of trading and risk. In times of economic contraction, often connected to wars and the disruption of trade, many who had prospered were led into ruin. And while living standards improved overall for the majority of inhabitants, those at the bottom accumulated little or no property and lived in ways that were decidedly substandard. For those groups, the distance between their possessions and those of their betters only widened.

Poverty in the region took a variety of forms. In the countryside, even as the wealthy built themselves ever finer estates, with genteel houses, fine orchards, and profitable mines, the number of rural families unable to acquire land of their own grew. Some of those families rented farms, others became squatters on hold-ings claimed by the great landlords, while still others were mere workers on the agricultural and iron plantations. Even poorer, of course, were servants or slaves. By 1750, tenancy was becoming increasingly common in a number of areas, including the Hud-son Valley, East Jersey, and Pennsylvania's Chester County.

Not all tenants were impoverished. Some rented properties out of choice, either because tenancy allowed them access to better lands than were available for sale as good farmland be-came scarce or because landlords, who often could not easily obtain tenants to work their properties, simply offered better deals to renters. That was especially likely after the resumption of imperial warfare in the 1740s began to make the Pennsylvania frontier appear far less secure. Yet for most, tenancy was not an enviable position. Most tenancies remained insecure, and the disparities in wealth increased. In Chester County, for example, the number of adult white males without property of their own grew from no more than a fifth of the population near the end of the seventeenth century to roughly double that by 1760, even as the distribution of wealth grew increasingly stratified.[10]

Poverty was no stranger to the city either. New York and Philadelphia housed a great many laboring people who lived on the margins of subsistence: day laborers, the working poor, wid-ows, seamen, and servants all lived under the most precarious conditions, and their numbers were increasing. In prosperous times, able-bodied workmen could usually get by. But few had the resources to put away savings, and an economic downturn, illness or injury, or simple bad luck left those who relied on their muscles little margin on which to maintain themselves. Among the unskilled, few could even dream about emulating the mete-oric rise Benjamin Franklin achieved in a skilled trade. For nearly all workers, the prospects for substantially advancing one's po-sition declined toward mid-century as competition increased. Moreover, proximity to the world of commerce provided little protection: seaman, as well as dockworkers who depended on their strength and the continuity of trade, were among the most susceptible in difficult times. In urban spaces nearly everyone was involved in trading, with the result that when economic troubles hit, almost everyone except the well-to-do was at risk.

The situation of the women of working families was especially precarious. Many were in domestic service. Women's wages were considerably lower than men's, especially in rapidly growing urban economies where manual labor was the most likely to be in demand. A woman with an able-bodied husband or a daughter in a family remained secure so long as her circumstances held. And while widows in well-off families might continue to run their husband's businesses, sometimes with great success, a widow with children in a family without property had little place to turn. That was recognized by the authorities, who were more likely to grant poor relief to women than to men, whatever hardships the man might encounter.

An even more visible manifestation of poverty was the slave population of the mid-Atlantic. By definition, slaves owned no property at all, not even their own labor. The growth in trade and the increase in wealth amassed by the more prosperous citizens enhanced both the availability of slaves and the demand for their services. In the cities one found especially large numbers of enslaved persons: slaves would form up to a third of the labor force in New York City, where they pursued nearly every kind of available work.

In spite of that colony's relatively northern situation, the highest proportion of slaves in the mid-Atlantic lived in New York. That was partly a legacy of active Dutch slave trading; it also resulted from the modest pace of free settlement and a relative shortage of labor in a colony so dominated by large landowners and wealthy merchants. After the end of Dutch rule, few Africans in the colony were permitted to obtain their freedom or even half-freedom. Close to 15 percent of the New York population was enslaved by mid-century, whereas in New Jersey it was only about 10 percent, and even less in Pennsylvania.

The concentration of slaves in New York, along with the harsh conditions they confronted, subjected that city to the two principal slave rebellions that occurred, or were thought to have occurred, in the region. In 1712, a group of slaves set fire to a home in the city and then lay in wait to attack those who rushed to the scene. Eight whites were killed and another dozen injured. Authorities responded with a wave of repression, convicting twenty-one conspirators and executing eighteen in brutal fashion. The bodies of those executed were displayed in public places long after as a deterrent. The crackdown would have been worse, except that Governor Robert Hunter recommended pardons for several—to the chagrin of city officials—believing that to be the best way to discourage future rebelliousness.

There is less agreement about what happened in 1741. It all began with a fire in Fort George in New York City, followed by further fires in the city and its surroundings in the days thereafter. Authorities soon decided that more than mere arson was afoot, and suspicion turned to several slaves and their associates, including a young white servant named Mary Burton, who worked at John Hughson's tavern, where slaves and other inhabitants would often meet. Once she was accused, Burton began to accuse others in exchange for her freedom. Accused slaves, threatened with execution, began to do the same, leading to an ever-widening circle of alleged conspirators. Over the next year more than 150 slaves were accused, and 30 were subjected to grisly executions. More than 20 whites were accused of being ringleaders, and several were put to death.

Historians have not always been convinced that such a conspiracy in fact took place. That some of the Africans were hostile and rebellious in temper is hardly surprising and was characteristic of slave populations almost everywhere. Certainly, when they met over drink, both Africans and some less-privileged white persons likely expressed their anger at their lot in New York society. Until recently, most historians have doubted that it went much farther than that.

It is clear that New York authorities were more than ready to panic at the threat of slave rebellion. Slaves were a conspicuous and important part of New York society. Moreover, as the demand for slave labor increased, New Yorkers took into their workforce several new groups of slaves with few ties to the community. Some of those were slaves imported directly from Africa rather than the West Indies, a group less accustomed to the slave system as practiced in the New World. There was also a group of "Spanish Negroes" in New York—slaves who had been captured illegally from Spanish ships. Many of those were Catholic, which added to the suspicions of New York's overwhelmingly Protestant population.

Recent historians have been more willing to credit the stories of rebellious intent on the part of the slaves. For one thing, there is considerable evidence of frequent meetings and the formation of secret societies among the slaves. There is also evidence, previously unrecognized, that among African slaves in particular, many identified by group with particular African nationalities. That suggests close connections among some slaves and a belief that by organizing their countrymen they could assemble a large group of potential rebels. Moreover, what we have learned about communications in the Atlantic world suggests that New York slaves knew about other slave conspiracies elsewhere. The Spanish Negroes in particular brought tales of rebellions in the West Indies and of the willingness of Spanish colonies to take in escaped rebels.

The case does illuminate the extent to which New York slaves, as well as free Africans and whites of the lower classes, were involved in an underground economy, one that went well beyond sanctioned activities. Those included the sale of stolen property and otherwise restricted goods. Such activities formed a safety-valve in economic hard times and were readily carried out in a port city, where goods were constantly being brought in and out. In taverns such as that of John Hughson, those transactions apparently crossed racial lines. White servants, wage workers, seamen, prostitutes, and working-class women with goods to sell all engaged in extralegal transactions in the underground economy to keep themselves solvent in the risky urban economy.

Even after the end of the conspiracy trials, slaves in the city continued to manifest their displeasure with the system. There was apparently another arson conspiracy soon after in the city, and various other threats from slaves. Even more, city officials and slave owners worried about reports of slave resistance in other colonies. For a few years New Yorkers cut back on the number of slaves they imported into the city, whether because of fear of slave uprising or the advent of war. By 1750, however, slave imports rose again. Whereas previously most Africans arriving in New York came from a prior stint in the West Indies, New York merchants now involved themselves directly in the African trade.

The close involvement of the Middle Colonies with the commercial world of the Atlantic eventually led to a narrowing of some of the diversity of social and economic life. Of prime importance would be a diminishing variety in the physical forms of the countryside, as everywhere the native landscape gave way to the farming settlements the Europeans brought with them. As it did, the options for Native Americans in the region narrowed. They could move to remote regions, where they settled among and either assimilated or conflicted with other native peoples, while at the same time trying to secure for themselves new economic roles in intercultural trade. In the best cases they ended up in settlements such as Shamokin, where diverse natives carried on varied tasks in mixed cultural environments. If they remained within the region of colonial settlement, they had to adopt an increasingly settled and usually impoverished existence, with territories such as that which the Delaware held at Cranbury or the native settlements on eastern Long Island providing only a modest respite. In most of New York colony the situation was often better, since the Six Nations continued to dominate a wide swath of territory.

After the middle of the eighteenth century the differences between New York and Pennsylvania also began to narrow, with the diminishing of the native landscapes of the former colony. That process accelerated with the end of the Seven Years' War in 1763, with the wave of new immigration from England and especially Scotland and Ireland that followed. The newcomers came principally in search of farmland, and they extended settlements into the upper Hudson and Mohawk Valleys into territory previously the exclusive preserve of the Six Nations. Those lands provided a whole new set of opportunities for Middle Colony migrants. With diminished security in Pennsylvania and the high price of lands, upper New York increasingly became the best poor man's country for new immigrants.

Toward the end of the colonial era, economic activity also increasingly transcended its regional bounds. Growing international demand in the Atlantic market meant that the trade in wheat, for example, extended beyond the mid-Atlantic into the plantation regions of southern Delaware, Maryland, and Virginia, as wheat began to replace tobacco as a Chesapeake crop, even on some slave plantations. Middle Colony merchants more and more involved themselves in the trade of their neighbors north and south, bringing places such as Fairfield County in western Connecticut increasingly into their trading zone. Households from Maryland to Connecticut acquired imported goods from the mid-Atlantic consumer market. Pennsylvania merchants extended their trade onto the frontier lands of Ohio and the southern backcountry; New York landlords and merchants extended their sway into the Vermont lands and, after 1763, Quebec. As an economic unit, the mid-Atlantic was coming to extend well beyond the Middle Colonies, calling into question the extent to which they composed a distinct economic region at all; the mid-Atlantic economy was integrating an ever-larger region.

The presence of slaves and slave rebellions in the Middle Colonies points out one of the anomalies of life in the region and its effects on those left behind. For many, the impetus to move to the mid-Atlantic was the opportunity the region afforded to common farm families from Europe who could move there and function independently, with no lords and few landlords and with a ready-made market for their produce. Few stopped to consider that favorable market conditions for their produce owed as much as it did to the ability of mid-Atlantic merchants to sell their produce to the plantation colonies, where it fed and supported the unfree laborers who produced the staple crops of sugar, rice, and tobacco. The presence of slaves in colonies that had little real necessity for them is itself an indication of the penetration of the commercial system of the Atlantic into the heart of mid-Atlantic life.

The second trade upon which the region had been founded—the fur trade—illuminates another anomaly of the mid-Atlantic economy. That trade placed Middle Colony merchants at the center of imperial rivalries among European and Indian nations. The more furs that traders acquired, the farther their Indian contacts had to range toward the edges of the region. Yet still the supply of furs receded. The farther native hunters pushed into the interior, the closer contact and the more conflict they experienced with one another, and the more competition for lands and for trade. As traders and their native suppliers brought both war and disease to those peripheries, the ranks of the hunters and their people dwindled along with the supply of the animals they hunted. The new roles they adopted—on the farther frontiers or in confined settlements—often left them in poverty and conflict.

FIVE

The Crossroads of Cultures

DIVERSITY, TOLERATION, AND PLURALISM

ONE OF THE MOST often-cited descriptions of mid-Atlantic society ever published appeared in 1782 in *Letters from an American Farmer,* written some years before by a French-born writer living in the colony of New York, J. Hector St. John de Crève-coeur. In the third letter of that volume, the author, posing as a farmer in Pennsylvania, asked the famous question: "What is the American?" He provided the following answer: "He is either an European, or the descendant of an European; hence the strange mixture of blood, which you will find in no other country. . . . Here individuals of all nations are melted into a new race of men."[1]

There are many questions one could ask about the American Farmer's description—about the nature of groups and nations in the mid-Atlantic, about families and lineage, and even, in our gender-conscious age, about the particular connotations of a new race of *men*. But the aspect that has always attracted the most attention has been his depiction of the mixing of peoples, which has become one of the classic statements of American pluralism. It is fitting that such a passage was penned in the mid-Atlantic, for there more than anywhere else in British America one found early and extensive intermingling of diverse groups of settlers—English, Dutch, French, Scots, Irish, Swedes, Finns, Jews, and German-speakers from diverse jurisdictions—

along with similarly varied African and Native American peoples, whom Crèvecoeur failed to mention. There one found as well the most often-noted system of religious toleration found in British America, if not the whole of the western world. The Middle Colony region surely was, in Michael Zuckerman's apt phrase, "America's First Plural Society."[2]

The presence of toleration and pluralism by no means describes all there is to know about diversity in the Middle Colonies. Implicit in Crèvecoeur's description is not only the fact of an extensive intermingling of peoples, but two quite distinct portrayals of how they mixed. In the passage cited above, the Farmer wrote of people of many nationalities "melted into a new race," a phrase that seems to anticipate the depiction of America as a melting pot in which diverse peoples were molded into a common American culture. Yet at other times the Farmer described people of varying beliefs and habits living side by side, suggesting that those peoples were not really melted together at all. Those passages emphasized instead the toleration of difference, where religious and cultural variety flourished and where people lived together without bothering themselves about what others were doing or thinking. Moreover, there were clear limits to the author's general sense of inclusion. If the Farmer viewed Americans as assembled from "all nations," the nations he listed were exclusively those of northern and western Europe.

The ambiguities that appear in Crèvecoeur's presentation were characteristic of the region almost from its beginning. For while toleration and diversity were among the distinguishing characteristics of the Middle Colonies, the ways in which people mixed, including the degree of integration and the extent of tolerance, were quite varied. The practice of pluralism included a large degree of intermixing in some areas, which often appeared to reduce distinctions among peoples; in other areas, diverse communities lived side by side while maintaining markedly distinct identities. Religious accommodation within the region ranged from the limited and often grudging acceptance of denominational differences one found under the policy known as toleration, to something much closer to true tolerance and full religious liberty. If Middle Colony societies were in fact the principal precursors of American pluralism that is because nearly all of those varied forms of interaction would have echoes later in American history.

For all of the attention it has received, the nature of early American pluralism has not been well understood. Too often we view it as simple and straightforward: the more pluralism the better. In fact it was complex, and its varying forms were each designed to serve distinct interests and purposes. In the Middle Colonies, those included a settler pluralism intended to increase the population and prosperity of European migrants while bypassing native claims to the land; a proprietary pluralism aimed at enhancing civil authority by reducing religious conflict; a Protestant pluralism designed to diminish denominational disharmony to counter the Catholic imperial challenge; and a spiritual pluralism that opposed the creation of religious establishments or formal creeds that might dampen the inward experience of faith.

Nor were the ethnic and national groups involved in the American settlement as clearly defined as is often supposed. While we tend to think of ethnicity in early America as the simple carry-over of Old World identities—of Dutch or English or German nationalities—in fact, those identities were historical creations that often did not fully develop until after arrival in the New World. Thus Reformed Protestants from the German Palatinate did not necessarily envision themselves as sharing an identity with German-speaking Lutherans or sectarians from elsewhere in the valley of the Rhine; in Pennsylvania, they would all come to be identified as Pennsylvania Germans. That kind of group pluralism created large groups out of small, a process that affected not only Europeans but African American and Native American populations in the region as well. The Middle Colonies, more than any other region, displayed the varied models of group formation and ethnic interaction that would come to constitute American pluralism and that would form a large part of American identity.

PROTESTANT PLURALISM

The colony that the Dutch established in New Netherland was among the most diverse of societies. As we have seen, the settler population of that colony comprised a complex combination that included natives of the Netherlands, German-speakers from various locales in central Europe, French-speakers from France and the Low Countries, English and Scots, Finns and Swedes, Africans from Angola and Senegambia, Jews from Portugal by way of Brazil, and more. Although the early-arriving French-speaking Walloons established themselves in a distinct settlement north of New Amsterdam, on the whole the small population lived substantially intermixed. Many worshipped together in the Dutch Reformed Church, in large part because there were rarely other ministers available to preach.

The diversity of New Netherland derived from several sources. Common to most of the early non-English settlements in eastern North America was a shortage of settlers and the desire to attract them from wherever they could. Just as important, the Netherlands itself was among the most diverse societies in Europe, serving as the principal center for Protestant refugees in an age of religious wars. Moreover, the extensive commercial ventures of the merchants of the United Provinces brought a constant stream of peoples into and out of Dutch cities. The Netherlands housed a population in motion—inward, of foreign Protestants seeking secure places to live and trade, and outward to the vast reaches of the Dutch commercial empire extending as far as the East Indies.

The openness of the society of the Netherlands was not unlimited. The Dutch Revolt against Catholic Spain (1572–88) had created a Protestant haven in the northern regions that became the United Provinces, leaving the southern or Spanish Netherlands under Catholic control. Refugees flocked to the United Provinces less for its tolerance than for its Protestantism. It was a center of "Protestant pluralism," one that accepted Protestants of diverse backgrounds and beliefs, tolerated Catholic populations where they already lived, but offered little encouragement to others to come.[3]

Even for Protestants in the Netherlands, toleration was not universal. For much of the seventeenth century the Dutch Reformed Church was engulfed in a series of struggles between competing religious factions that were linked to other fissures in the society: Amsterdam and the trading community were more likely to support theological flexibility, if for no other reason than an aversion to driving out productive workers on the basis of small religious distinctions; their strict Calvinist or Reformed opponents were stronger in rural regions and among the populace at large. Thus, while in Amsterdam one often found tacit acceptance of non-Calvinists such as Lutherans, Quakers, and even Jews, elsewhere those groups were far less free to worship. The question of toleration in the Netherlands, then, was never whether or not to accommodate diversity, but rather about the kinds of diversity that would be accepted. Even where strict Reformed principles prevailed, certain variations were readily allowed. National distinctions, at least those of northern European nations, were never a problem in the United Provinces. As England and Scotland fought their civil wars in the middle of the seventeenth century, Puritans and Presbyterians from those nations often flocked to the Low Countries, where they were fully tolerated because of their Calvinist principles in spite of modest variations in religious practice. Thus in the Netherlands, one often found not just Protestant pluralism but a Reformed Protestant pluralism.

New Netherland was affected by some of the same forces that influenced the United Provinces. As an offshoot of the larger Dutch commercial empire, the North American colony attracted migrants not only from the already diverse population of the Netherlands but also from Dutch colonies in the Caribbean and South America, especially after the loss of Brazil in 1654. Thus in addition to the varied European settlers arriving from the Netherlands, the colony on the Hudson drew upon several additional populations. Among them were Portuguese Jews, many of them "Conversos," who had abandoned Judaism for the Catholic Church under severe pressure; some reverted to Judaism in the Netherlands and its empire. They arrived in New Netherland principally from Brazil or the Caribbean. Another group consisted of African slaves, most brought from other Dutch colonies by that nation's wide-ranging merchants. That population included adherents of various African religions and very probably Catholics and Muslims also. Apparently, no one thought it necessary to avoid purchasing slaves who did not share their religious principles.

Like the United Provinces, New Netherland experienced a continual contest over the tenor of religious life, as commercial interests seeking to attract settlers to the under-populated colony competed with political leaders wanting to maintain Calvinist orthodoxy. The West India Company itself was formed largely at the behest of Calvinist merchants, many from the outer provinces, who were jealous of the privileges that Amsterdam merchants had garnered in the East Indian trade. But the New Netherland colony was long directed by the Amsterdam chamber of the Company, which served as a moderating influence on the strict Calvinism of other Company members. During the tenure of the orthodox governor, Peter Stuyvesant, the colony repeatedly worked to suppress the worship of Lutherans, Quakers, and Jews; but the Amsterdam chamber resisted his efforts. At the very least, New Netherland consistently provided a home to diverse groups of Reformed Protestants, while other groups often managed to make places for themselves in spite of official disapproval.

The situation in the Dutch world suggests the need to distinguish between toleration and tolerance. Toleration is a matter of policy: it is in the interests of the state or society to allow for a degree of variation in religious belief or practice to foster commerce, diplomacy, or the public peace. Toleration does not require either ecclesiastical equality or full religious liberty. It is less about the rights of individuals than about the needs of society. The Dutch Reformed Church remained the established, state-supported communion in both places, while other churches were allowed to maintain worship only at the discretion of state authorities, who granted it or not for their own reasons.

Nor does toleration necessarily imply the willing acceptance of diversity of the sort that could be called true tolerance. In Protestant Europe, toleration was a means to forge a measure of harmony among churches tending too often toward schism, while at the same time firming up support against a common Catholic adversary. It did not require the abandoning of doctrinal confessions or the notion of religious certainty. In the Netherlands, advocates of toleration endorsed a limited freedom to disagree over what were deemed minor questions—what the English philosopher John Locke would describe as "things indifferent"—but did not license individuals or churches to pronounce an unlimited public dissent. In New Netherland, one found considerable tolerance of most Reformed Protestant groups; for others, the degree of toleration depended greatly on the interests of those in power at the time.

The English conquest of New Netherland marked a new era in group relations. A colony of settlers and traders established to extend the reach of the Dutch commercial empire now found itself governed by its English commercial rivals. The varied Protestant peoples who came together voluntarily under the protection of the Dutch Republic now found themselves conquered subjects of a Catholic proprietor. A new form of toleration emerged in the colony, one designed to provide Catholics with full civil and religious liberties, diminish the powers of the aggressive Protestant churches in New Netherland and on Long Island, and promote obedience to proprietary and royal authority over all. Thus efforts to suppress Lutheran and Quaker worship were ended. The rights of Catholics and Jews were expanded. Protestant pluralism gave way to a toleration that was broader in form but just as committed to furthering particular political and ecclesiastical interests.

For the inhabitants of New Netherland, the most immediate change was not the appearance of newcomers, who were relatively few, but the severing of the settlers' outside connections. The terms of the surrender guaranteed the property of the inhabitants of the Dutch colony and their right to continue their mode of worship, but they were only permitted to continue trading legally with the Netherlands for six months. Migration to the colony from that country and the Dutch empire was essentially cut off. Those who remained thus had to adjust their relationships both within and beyond their local communities.

New conditions affected different groups in varying ways. In the port of New York, wealthy merchants at the top of the social ladder found substantial new opportunities. While they sacrificed direct legal commerce with the Netherlands, they could still trade with the numerous Dutch merchants active along the North American coast. Moreover, they would develop new alliances with British traders. Elsewhere, new commercial regulations forced up-river merchants to conduct their overseas trade through New York City but also gave them a monopoly position in the fur trade. That provided unusual opportunities for those able to work between the English and Dutch trading communities, such as the Scottish emigrant Robert Livingston, fluent in

Dutch and raised in the Dutch commercial city of Rotterdam. The Albany merchant community remained strongly Dutch for many years as well as staunchly independent.

Farther down the social scale there was often less reason for close contact with the newcomers. Especially for those living outside of New York City, a sense of distance from the conquerors and the lack of new migrants from the Dutch world led to the development of more uniform and insular communities than had existed in New Netherland. The most dissatisfied inhabitants of New Amsterdam moved out of the city altogether, settling in the towns of the rural Hudson Valley or northern New Jersey—away from both the English authorities and those Dutch merchants and clergy who were allied with them. There they developed identifiable Dutch communities with Dutch national churches and a widespread use of the Dutch language. They often maintained a degree of isolation that has led one historian to speak of the "thinness" of Dutch public culture, owing to the very modest Dutch participation in public life.[4]

One of the ironies of the situation was that a large portion of those increasingly insular Dutch inhabitants had not originally come from the Netherlands at all, but had come from all over western Europe. The experience of the English takeover led Dutch settlers, not to Anglicization, but to their "Batavianization"—their assimilation into the culture of the previous proprietors of the land.[5] The intensity of the "Dutchness" that developed there came not from close contact with the Netherlands but from the lack thereof.

In important respects, it was the later experience of conquest and isolation that established the cultural legacy of Dutch New York. It was very "Dutch" in its identification with Dutch traditions—in religion, in language, in architecture, and in community. But it was a very different Dutchness from that which had existed before. With little direct contact with the Netherlands, the Dutch population developed a greater attachment to their communities than they previously had. The Dutch Reformed Church they now supported was becoming less a pillar of Protestant orthodoxy than a marker of their new ethnic and linguistic identity.

Paradoxically, the ability of rural towns to retain their Dutch character within a growing colony depended in large part upon their ability to absorb outsiders. It is often assumed that strongly ethnic settlements maintained their identities in part by limiting out-marriage, but that is often not correct. With New York cut off from further Dutch immigration, the establishment and retention of a national community required the continuing integration of outsiders. One historian has maintained that rural Dutch communities maintained an intense "tribalism" at the upper levels of society—where the top positions within the community were largely limited to members of the lineage or "tribe"—while continually absorbing new people into the larger community.[6]

Much of that was accomplished through the influence of Dutch wives; the unusual authority that Dutch women maintained in the economic realm extended their influence into the community at large. In the early years of English rule, English men far outnumbered English women in the colony; thus, Dutch women were considerably more likely than Dutch men to marry outside of their nationality. Yet women in Dutch communities also retained considerable control of family property and were the central figures in preserving an ethnic identity. They usually formed the bulwark of the Dutch Reformed Church. Even those who married outsiders rarely left the communion; when Dutch women married men from non-Dutch households, the husbands were far more likely to join the Dutch Reformed Church than to lure their wives into other communions. The children of those marriages were raised in the Dutch Church, especially the girls, who usually remained within close Dutch female networks within the New York colony.

At one level, Leisler's Rebellion involved the playing out of the various roles that the Dutch inhabitants could adopt. Leisler himself, of German and Huguenot origin, was deeply involved in the trading world of the Dutch Atlantic, a rigorous Protestant with an acute interest in the fate of Protestants everywhere. The community his followers formed was Calvinist and international. Leisler's son-in-law and second in command, Jacob Milborne, came from staunchly Protestant New England. Part of the anger in Leisler's actions was sparked by the recent persecutions of French Protestants following the revocation of the Edict of Nantes. The targets of Leisler's wrath included not only James and his Catholic appointees but also those English, and especially Dutch, elites who worked with James's government and against the Reformed Protestant interest. An example was Nicholas Bayard, a longtime member of the Dutch Reformed Church who now sometimes worshipped in the Anglican communion and increasingly identified himself as English. In the wake of Leisler's execution, his followers arrested Bayard for treason and sentenced him to death, although the sentence was not carried out.[7]

Outside of New York City, even Reformed Protestants were wary of Leisler, preferring to keep as much of their governance as possible under local control. Thus Dutch Albany refused Leisler's demand to surrender the city to his control. The same was true of eastern Long Island, whose Puritan townsmen felt much greater affinity for those who shared their New England backgrounds than for their fellow Calvinists among the Leislerians and the Dutch Reformed Church. The defeat of the Leislerians spurred further withdrawals among the Dutch of New York, both from the direct control of the English government and from their Anglo-Dutch allies in New York City and its Dutch Reformed Church.

With only modest movement of new settlers into the conquered colony, groups other than the rural Dutch developed inward-looking communities. One of those consisted of New Englanders who had settled the eastern Long Island communities of Southold, Southampton, and Easthampton. For much of their early history, those communities participated in a thriving trade with New England across Long Island Sound; Easthampton in particular was an active port from which settlers conveyed the products of their lucrative whaling trade. But gradually, in the wake of the English conquest and the absorption of eastern Long Island into New York, their ties beyond their local world began to diminish along with the supply of whales. There was very little influx of population to those towns, which instead took on a more insular character with their own "tribal" characteristics. Many of the leading families remained descendants of early settlers, and they controlled an increasing portion of town property and important aspects of church life.

The relatively slow growth of New York and the dispersal of the population allowed still other groups to maintain a considerable degree of insularity in the New York countryside. They included German-speakers, drawn largely from the region of the

Palatinate along the Rhine, who had settled in New York in 1709 with a promise of land and support in the Mohawk Valley. While some left in a group for Pennsylvania, those who stayed remained largely in the vicinity of their original settlement, where, living in relative isolation, they would long maintain a distinct identity as "Palatines"—a name that was rarely applied to their countrymen who settled in larger numbers in other colonies.[8]

The principal exception to ethnic insularity was New York City, where the upper levels of Dutch society Anglicized much more quickly. So also did French Huguenot settlers who had attained a similar social level. Even so, a fair portion of the Dutch population of the city retained strong community attachments into the eighteenth century. There also, Dutch women who married non-Dutch men usually retained their affiliations with the Dutch Reformed Church; the few Dutch men who married other than Dutch women were likely to choose brides of at least partial "Dutch" ancestry. And even as they learned and spoke English in public, Dutch was still often used as the language of home and church.

If the subordination of Dutch settlers intensified their community consciousness, that was probably even more true of the city's African population. Included among them was a free black population composed largely of former company slaves to the Dutch West India Company who were of diverse African origins. At least two dozen former slaves inhabited a cluster of farms of their own in the Bowery shortly after the English conquest, and nearly as many lived northward toward Harlem. Still others moved to the outskirts of the city, to New Jersey or to Long Island. The community remained small, with few slaves freed after the Dutch period, but over the years free blacks met together in taverns and markets and established their own physical and cultural spaces. They participated in community festivals such as Pinkster, the Pentecostal holiday of the Dutch Reformed Church, which became an important ritual for New Yorkers of African descent, identified both with Dutch and African traditions.

The African community in New York was long a diverse group. Its members originated in several different parts of west Africa, although most who came in the seventeenth century first experienced a period of "seasoning" in the West Indies. Some who were raised in African trading ports had accumulated language and craft skills. They came from varied cultural and linguistic backgrounds, and that diversity would be amplified in the eighteenth century as the growing involvement of New York merchants in the slave trade meant that more slaves than previously were imported directly from Africa rather than from other colonies. Advertisements for runaway slaves demonstrated their linguistic diversity. Slaves spoke Dutch, English, Spanish, French, and a variety of African languages; many spoke more than one. They established a variety of linkages among themselves, some based on common African backgrounds, some on ties of community first established on shipboard, and some simply as sharers in the common position as slaves or members of an urban underclass. Their religious heritages were equally varied among diverse African religions, the Catholic or Islamic traditions some brought with them, or membership in Dutch or eventually other Protestant churches. A recently discovered African burying ground in lower New York has revealed burial patterns suggesting the continuing influence of both African and Islamic religious practices.

As New York society devolved into a composite of separated national communities, James's government imposed a new system of toleration upon them. The terms of the conquest allowed the inhabitants the freedom to continue to worship in the Dutch Church—a freedom extended to Lutherans and Quakers as well. The Duke's Laws went further, providing an ordained Protestant minister for each parish, supported by all of the inhabitants. The result was a system of local ecclesiastical establishments, with each community having its own form, supported by all. So long as they remained local establishments, none was sufficiently powerful to challenge proprietary authority.

On the surface, the duke's government provided New Yorkers greater religious liberty than they had before. Groups whose worship was previously challenged, such as Lutherans and Jews, now had practically full liberty to practice their religions as they wished. Public support, previously restricted to the Dutch Reformed Church, could now go toward whatever Protestant communion the inhabitants desired. In some respects, this was toleration on the French model as it was practiced during the years James lived in that country. For nearly a century following the Edict of Nantes (1589), Protestant worship was permitted in Catholic France but was restricted to designated Protestant towns. Toleration of that sort worked against the development of an aggressive Protestant challenge either to Catholic privileges or to civil authority.

Following the Glorious Revolution, James's successors altered the workings of toleration but not toleration itself. Whereas the duke had been determined to prevent a Protestant establishment, the governors who followed were by law committed to support the Anglican Church. In 1693 the New York Assembly passed the Ministry Act, which borrowed from the Duke's Laws, providing that, in the lower four counties around New York City, all congregations were to be supplied with "good sufficient Protestant" ministers at the people's expense. While the act referred only to Protestant clergy, a series of aggressive Anglican governors used it to impose ministers of the Church of England, in spite of the relatively small membership of that communion.

The most aggressive of those governors was Edward Hyde, Lord Cornbury. In the town of Jamaica, where the Presbyterian population had erected and paid for a church and manse, the governor evicted the local Presbyterian preacher and handed the property to an Anglican clergyman. Cornbury believed in toleration, but of a rather grudging sort. In his view, toleration should be extended to local populations in out-of-the-way locales, distant from the centers of power, and only where dissenters composed an irresistible majority. Elsewhere, the position of the Church of England was to be advanced at every opportunity.

The system of toleration that developed in New York after the Revolution largely followed the English model. The Toleration Act of 1689 under William and Mary was an act only for exempting their Majesties' Protestant subjects from penal laws. Toleration was granted only to Trinitarian Protestants: Catholics, non-Christians, and Protestants who questioned the doctrine of the Trinity were excluded. Toleration in England also implied much less than ecclesiastical equality; dissenters were denied civil office or even the right to attend Oxford and Cambridge. They were simply allowed to worship without fear of arrest. In both England and New York, toleration was intended to diffuse overt opposition. In pluralist New York, that principle was extended further to allow whole communities of dissenters beyond the lower counties to maintain de facto local establishments where they posed little challenge, even as the authorities worked toward Anglican hegemony in the New York City region.

What one found in the early history of both New Netherland and New York was toleration without a great deal of tolerance. From the beginning, successive authorities in the colony, while allowing for a measure of diversity, continually worked to promote the interests of a religious establishment. New Netherland governors established the Dutch Reformed Church, tolerated local branches of the Reformed Churches of other nations, and struggled with the more tolerant Amsterdam authorities to suppress Lutherans, Quakers, and Jews. James appointed Catholics to positions of leadership, did his best to reign in the strict Protestant establishments on Long Island and in Dutch New York, and tolerated diverse local churches that would accede to his authority. Leislerians promoted Reformed Churches while suppressing Catholics and their enablers. The New York government thereafter worked to establish the Anglican Church in lower New York, tolerating only those dissenters who fully acknowledged their status as dissenters while surrendering their claims to property and tithes.

In 1692 Charles Lodwick described the social order of New York City as having "too great a mixture of nations," a revealing representation of official attitudes toward pluralism in early New York.[9] The population was heavily mixed, and to most authorities, that was not a good thing. As Richard Nicoll recognized at the time of the English conquest, there was little alternative to toleration, and the old inhabitants were guaranteed their property and their freedom of worship. But successive governments set out to structure pluralism to serve their own ends. In New York City, that would mean promoting conformity to English and Anglican ways. Those who objected were free to remove themselves to rural places, where their viewpoints posed little challenge.

SPIRITUAL LIBERTY

The grant of Pennsylvania to a Quaker proprietor opened a vast new territory to English settlement. As a Quaker, Penn held beliefs markedly different from those of the Catholic James, yet in important respects their ecclesiastical goals were complementary. If James's principal worry was the emergence of a powerful Protestant establishment on his colony's western border, he had nothing to fear from Friends, whose spiritualist leanings made them equally wary of such establishments. The grant to Penn extended the range of territory open to Catholics while drawing some of James's Protestant adversaries away from his kingdom and his colony.

Whereas in New York the emergence of diverse and largely separate national groups led to a tactical toleration of local religious establishments, in Pennsylvania one found a situation much closer to true religious liberty. That was largely the work of Penn and the Society of Friends. In the late seventeenth century, Quakers emerged as the most vocal advocates of spiritual liberty in the British world. That was partly a result of their own experiences of persecution, for Penn and many of his co-religionists had suffered fines and imprisonment for their Quaker beliefs.

As important as their prison experiences was the nature of Quaker beliefs themselves. Unlike most orthodox Protestants, who believed that God had delivered his full revelation to humankind in the Bible, Quakers believed in a continual unfolding of divine truth through the inner light—the voice of the spirit in everyone. If revelation was ongoing, then no one group could set down a single creed that all were obliged to follow. And if God's word was communicated to all, then knowledge of the truth could not be the preserve of any one church. Believers were obliged to listen to the voice within them, something that could not be enforced by law or by arms. Quakers were a "Society" rather than a Church; a formal Quaker establishment would have been an oxymoron. Penn's goal was to make the world safe for spiritualist beliefs.

In the first Quaker effort to establish those beliefs in a New World colony, the West Jersey Concessions of 1677, Quaker proprietors went farther than any other group in the granting of religious liberty, guaranteeing that "every person might freely enjoy his own judgment and the exercise of conscience in matters of worship." Penn's promise in Pennsylvania was not quite so universal; indeed, he had previously written against tolerating Catholics. And while the draft version of the "Fundamentall Constitutions of Pennsylvania"—one of the early plans for the colony—had provided "that every Person that does or shall reside therein shall have and enjoy the Free Possession of his or her faith and exercise of worship towards God," the *Frame of Government* he published to the world stipulated that such liberties would be granted only to those "who confess and acknowledge the One Almighty and Eternal God to be the Creator, Upholder and Ruler of the World," which was, of course, still a very liberal set of privileges for the day.[10]

Religious liberty in Pennsylvania had its political and practical side. In encouraging the migration of Friends and their close spiritual allies in particular, Penn was both promoting the success of his enterprise and (he thought) creating the conditions for the maintenance of Quaker government, while lessening the risk of a powerful Protestant establishment that would threaten the spiritual liberty he promoted. Penn's idea of religious freedom did not include the liberty to foster such establishments, which threatened the liberty of others. That was part of the reason for the proprietor's ambivalence toward Roman Catholics. When James ruled, Penn usually endorsed a broad view of religious freedom, but in other writings on toleration, he suggested it should not be extended to Roman Catholics, who, he feared, could not be trusted to live peaceably under Protestant rule and would seek to promote their own church in its place.

If the presence of diverse national groups was an important factor in promoting religious toleration in early New York, in Pennsylvania it was the other way around: religious liberty led to national diversity. The mixing of peoples went a good deal further than Penn had planned. From the beginning, Penn used his religious contacts to attract diverse populations of Quakers, Baptists, and other voluntarist sects from across Britain and central Europe, promising a religious liberty far exceeding that which existed in their homelands. As they came, their countrymen from orthodox Protestant churches began to follow them—sometimes with the direct assistance of those Penn had recruited. Moreover, where conquest and a slowing of migration to New York led to the gradual consolidation of groups in that colony, continuing movement into the lightly regulated Pennsylvania environment produced an almost bewildering religious and ethnic diversity, and several distinct new community forms.

An important target of recruitment for Penn was the cluster of German-speaking principalities in the Rhine Valley in central

Europe. Working through the agency of the Rotterdam Quaker Benjamin Furly, Penn set out to recruit Friends on the Continent as well as German Baptist groups such as the Mennonites. As early as 1683 a group of Friends from the Rhine Valley established a German-speaking settlement at Germantown outside of Philadelphia.

German settlement was sporadic in the early years, and Robert Hunter's attempt to settle Palatine migrants in New York might well have directed most of it to the northern colony. But the poor conditions in New York led a group among them to establish a foothold for German speakers in Pennsylvania. Their numbers began to increase in the second quarter of the century, promoted by an active group of merchant entrepreneurs in Amsterdam, Rotterdam, London, and Philadelphia, who were linked to one another by religious networks as well as the profit motive. Together they organized the lucrative trade in redemptioners, in which German settlers were granted free passage in exchange for their promise to work for an owner to whom they were auctioned upon their arrival in Philadelphia.

In their homelands, German-speakers, like their Dutch neighbors, were accustomed to regular and frequent migrations, but the migration experiences of the peoples of those places differed substantially. Where the Netherlands was a magnet for Protestant refugees during the seventeenth century, the German lands—wracked by wars and economic difficulties—were primarily exporters of migrants, who were generally looking for land. Before they began embarking for America in significant numbers, many German-speaking Protestants had migrated east to Poland and other parts of eastern Europe; those places would far surpass Pennsylvania as destinations for German migrants in the eighteenth century. Given the cheaper and safer travel involved in migrating to the east, and the often more favorable terms those migrants received, it is doubtful that there would ever have been significant German migration to Pennsylvania had it not been for the presence of those early settlements.

In their movements to the east and west, German migrants followed a pattern of chain migration that would become frequent in mass movements. The initial move to a particular place was usually begun by a small group of migrants whose paths were then followed by others from the same villages or regions.

Not all German-speakers who ended up in a community necessarily came from the same region, but they almost always settled in clusters, with enough local links to ensure that those who went would find significant connections and a ready acceptance wherever their journeys took them.

Where immigration to the mid-Atlantic from the Netherlands largely ceased after 1664, German migration would be almost continuous through the first half of the eighteenth century. The migrants came from varied backgrounds, including members not only of the Lutheran and Reformed Churches but also smaller groups such as Mennonites, Moravians, and Schwenkfelders. Unlike the Dutch of New Netherland, whose eventual isolation from migration streams led them to withdraw from much of public culture and coalesce within a single church, the continual influx of varied groups from the lands along the Rhine kept the German-speaking population diverse and publicly active. While there were distinct clusters of German-speakers of varying backgrounds, especially among the sectarian groups, most came to inhabit mixed regions of Pennsylvania, albeit each with a substantial German-speaking presence. Thus no group in Pennsylvania took on the distinct "Palatine" identity that so marked the much smaller German community in New York. Instead, they became part of a larger language community of German-speakers.

By the middle of the eighteenth century, migrants from German-speaking lands were playing a much larger role in the public culture of Pennsylvania. Led by the Pietist printer Christopher Sauer in Germantown, the German press began publishing everything from political writings, to works explaining the workings of English law, to Pietist religious tracts. German migrants also began injecting themselves into colonial politics, and thousands of German speakers had themselves naturalized so that they could vote in the elections.

German involvement in public culture was promoted by several key issues. One of those was property. German-speakers who emigrated retained claims to family property in the villages from which they came, and one of the most important publishing activities instructed emigrants in navigating the legal system, both for the properties they were to receive from abroad and that which was to be passed on in Pennsylvania. German-language almanacs gave explicit directions for preparing wills that would conform to German traditions of partible inheritance rather than English property law. Similarly, the protection of land claims in Pennsylvania was one of the first issues that drove German-speakers to apply for naturalization.

Another issue that encouraged public expression among German speakers was migration itself. Those who traveled as redemptioners faced an arduous and expensive voyage from the Rhineland to the Netherlands to England to Pennsylvania, often suffering hardships along the way. German letter writers set out to warn prospective settlers of the dangers, some addressed to Sauer, and it became a subject of discussion in print. The most famous publication appeared in Europe: the account of Gottlieb Mittelberger, whose *Journey to Pennsylvania* was published in Frankfort in 1756 after the author's return from Pennsylvania.

Settling alongside German-speakers in the Pennsylvania backcountry were the Irish, principally Presbyterians from Ulster in the north, where English and especially Scots Protestants had begun establishing a presence at the beginning of the seventeenth century. Their arrival in Pennsylvania also was prompted by Quaker invitations, in this case that of Penn's secretary James Logan, himself an Ulster native born to Scottish parents, who helped establish Ulster migrants in the Lancaster County town that would be named Donegal. Like migrants from the Rhine, Irish settlers were drawn to Pennsylvania both by economic opportunities and by the greater religious freedom they encountered there. In Ireland most had been dissenters from the Episcopal Church of Ireland, and they had suffered substantial civil penalties for their allegiance. In Pennsylvania they found both religious liberty and the opportunity to build an expansive church of their own.

The culture of those Ulster emigrants, known variously as "Scotch-Irish," "Scots-Irish," and "Ulster Scots," has never been well understood. The name did not signify a mixing of Scottish Protestants with the native Irish, who were largely Catholic and Gaelic-speaking. Nor were all Ulster Protestants descended from Scots; there was substantial English Protestant settlement in Ulster also, although the two groups concentrated their settlements in different parts of northern Ireland.

One of the most important points about the culture of the Ulster Scots was that they were not descended from a single wave of settlers, as is often imagined. The original Scots plantation of Ulster dates from the first quarter of the seventeenth century, but settlement during the plantation years was modest. By far the largest influx of Scots to Ulster came during the 1690s, when widespread famine struck parts of Scotland just two decades before the beginning of sustained Scots-Irish migration to America.

Scots-Irish culture, then, was still quite fluid when emigration to North America began in earnest early in the eighteenth century. Contact between Scotland and Ulster had been continuous, as was return travel to Scotland on the part of Ulster Scots. Glasgow University was the principal college attended by Irish Presbyterians, and Glasgow city was in many ways Ulster's cultural capital. Thus at the beginning of the eighteenth century, Ulster Scots had not established a wholly distinct identity. That is evident in the difficulty people then and now have had in naming them. Contemporary documents referred to them variously as Scots, or Irish, or "Scottish and Irish Presbyterians." A recent historian has called them "the people with no name."[11]

The largest element of Scots-Irish identity was an attachment to Presbyterianism, but even that affiliation was quite fractured. The population included some of the staunchest advocates of orthodox Scottish Presbyterian tradition, emphasizing strict conformity to the Westminster Confession of Faith. Others, called "New Lights," advocated a much greater degree of theological latitude, inspired by the ideas of the Enlightenment.[12] Still others adopted the new evangelical mode of preaching for conversion. And some among the Irish joined breakaway or "seceder" churches that claimed adherence to Presbyterian principles even stricter than those of the orthodox Presbyterian Church.

Ulster Scots developed a reputation as a violent people and aggressive Indian fighters, and both labels were well earned. In Pennsylvania, Scots-Irish Presbyterians formed the principal element among the Paxton rioters, a group of men from the town of Paxtang and surrounding villages who in 1763 went on a rampage, slaughtering a group of peaceful Conestoga Indians who lived in their vicinity. They proceeded to threaten the government, which they believed was not doing enough to protect the colony's frontiers, marching on Philadelphia in search of other Indians under the colony's protection until Benjamin

Franklin met them and promised to attend to their grievances. That was not the only time Irish Presbyterians were involved in frontier violence.

The violent actions of Ulster emigrants were partly the products of their persistent presence in the backcountry, where they served as a buffer between Native Americans and eastern farmers. Even German migrants on the frontiers, who had a far more peaceful reputation, played a role in the violence of the Paxton years. The settlement of Ulster migrants in the backcountry was no mere coincidence. It was partly the result of their relatively late arrival in the colony; it was also a product of their propensity to migrate, as they had with considerable frequency between Ireland and Scotland also. Like their German neighbors, Ulster migrants moved in clusters, maintaining ties of kinship and friendship in older townships even as they moved on into new ones. Unlike the Germans, Irish migrants often did not end their motions with their arrival in Pennsylvania but continued to move around. For those settlers, the constancy of migration among an interlocking group of settlements, rather than isolating individuals and families, served as a principal bond of community across the region.

The Presbyterianism of the migrants was well suited to mobile communities. In form, Presbyterianism constituted something of a middle way in eighteenth-century American religion. Lacking the formal hierarchy of the Anglican Church, Presbyterians did not require metropolitan involvement to ordain ministers or create their organization. Yet unlike New England Congregationalists or other voluntarist groups, whose congregations were essentially independent of one another, Presbyterian churches were joined together under regional presbyteries. Moreover, the meetings of the presbytery, composed of ministers and elders from each congregation, linked dispersed congregations across the region.

The participation of Ulster men and women in frontier violence was also a product of their strict Calvinist heritage. Like many religious groups, orthodox Scottish and Irish Presbyterians were firmly wedded to the notion of an unvarying religious truth, but the manner in which they defended it often gave it an unusual rigidity. The Presbyterians of Scotland and Ulster traditionally upheld their faith through acts of public testimony, such as the signing of covenants that affirmed the status of Presbyterianism as a providentially ordained religion, or subscribing to articles of faith. During the Restoration years, Presbyterians were fined, imprisoned, or banished from their homelands for refusing to subscribe to a test oath renouncing the obligations of Scotland's national covenants.

In a published pamphlet supporting the Paxton men, a spokesman referred to them as the "distressed and bleeding frontier inhabitants" of Pennsylvania, and the language suggests a lot about the culture of Scots and Ulster Scots. The imagery derived from the persecutions of the seventeenth century that united the experiences of Presbyterians in Ulster and the west of Scotland, who had circulated between those places while avoiding or resisting the Stuart regime. One Paxton pamphlet called them "descendants of the Noble Enisknillers," a reference to the inhabitants of an Ulster town that had held out bravely against James's army in 1688 in defense of the Protestant succession.[13]

Those words were also part of a language of martyrdom and resistance, a nearly ubiquitous popular tradition in Ulster and western Scotland, which consistently invoked displays of divine favor in the cause of religious truth. It was a language that brought an especially marked sense of moral certainty. These were godly people who believed that they were suffering grievous trials on behalf of divine truth. Their enemies included the native Irish during the Civil War years of the seventeenth century and, of course, the Indians on the Pennsylvania frontiers. Behind those "un-Christian" agents were persecuting authorities, a Stuart dynasty or a Quaker government that denied fair representation to the back settlements, ignored their requests for security and assistance, and protected native inhabitants more vigorously than Christian subjects.

Beyond their commitment to Presbyterian traditions, the culture of Ulster migrants was less uniform than most portrayals suggest. Successive waves of migration from Ulster brought a variety of styles to the backcountry. If Irish emigrants in those areas did indeed display much violent and intemperate behavior, they also brought a contrasting culture of civility. Thus Ulster Presbyterians were among the greatest promoters of education in the mid-Atlantic, and especially in the backcountry, creating an unparalleled network of colleges and academies that one writer has called an "evangelical educational empire."[14] Through those institutions, they may have done more than any group to bring the ideas and perspectives of the Enlightenment to America—including the new moral philosophy, with its emphasis on sympathy and sensibility, which contrasted sharply with their often violent behavior. Moreover, even the violence toward Indians exhibited by many was partially balanced by the considerable involvement of Ulster migrants both as Protestant missionaries and as frontier negotiators.

The continual influx of Irish and German migrants into Pennsylvania during the eighteenth century contributed both to the diversity of their populations and to considerable intermingling. While Irish and German newcomers concentrated their settlements within particular Pennsylvania counties, those often bordered on the communities of other inhabitants. Thus even as they maintained regular connections with those of similar religious, cultural, or linguistic heritage, they rubbed shoulders with other settlers far more often than did the Puritan townspeople of eastern Long Island or many of the Dutch of rural northern New Jersey and the Hudson Valley.

Diversity in Pennsylvania extended to church life, and here migration and diversity went hand in hand. Whereas in New York the number of different denominations remained relatively stable during the first half of the eighteenth century—incoming French Protestants, for example, often simply attached themselves to extant Protestant churches—in Pennsylvania denominations proliferated, a result of the freedoms the colony provided and the continuing influx of newcomers of varied faiths. German migrants included members of the Reformed Church, Lutherans, Moravians, Mennonites, Swiss Brethren, Amish, Schwenkfelders, and Dunkers, among others; Scots and Irish settlements housed not only Presbyterian churches but various denominations of breakaway Presbyterians, including both burgher and anti-burgher seceders, and Cameronian and Reformed Presbyterians. There were also Anglicans, Quakers, Keithian Quakers, and, by the end of the colonial period, Methodists, Catholics, and Jews.

Intermingling would not always be peaceful. Mobile Irish and German populations continued to expand and to involve themselves in the public affairs of Pennsylvania, creating rivalries and hostility that would manifest themselves in skirmishes, attacks, and massacres after mid-century. Those conflicts were both ethnic and racial, pitting Irish and Germans against both the colonial authorities, especially Quakers, and their Native American neighbors. In the process, they would begin to define Native Americans, collectively, as enemies, neglecting the distinctions they had often formerly made between allied Indians, sometimes Christian, and hostile nations allied with the French.

For Native Americans also, the frontiers were a site of much mixing. Indeed, for those groups nearly everywhere was a frontier, and from the seventeenth century onward Indian peoples of the mid-Atlantic were involved in an intense struggle to add population. Along the way, many smaller groups died out, with their populations absorbed into larger nations, including most prominently the Six Nations. From mourning wars they added captives, especially women and children. In the early eighteenth century they adopted a whole nation, the Tuscarora, who moved northward from the southern backcountry to form the sixth nation of the Iroquois League. They added others as well, such as the Susquehannocks, who accepted their offer of absorption at the founding of the Covenant Chain.

Not all of the Susquehannocks joined the Iroquois. Another group was absorbed into the Delaware Indians of Pennsylvania. The Delaware, themselves a composite of several smaller Indian nations, also divided. Some, who remained in eastern Pennsylvania, largely lived in positions subordinate to their European neighbors. Others moved westward in the wake of the Walking Purchase, into western Pennsylvania and the Ohio Country, where they joined with Shawnees and groups who split away from the Six Nations and maintained an acute hostility to Pennsylvania settlers that led to frequent outbreaks of violence.

PROTESTANT LIBERTY

While the pattern of pluralism was not wholly uniform in either Pennsylvania or New York, the most diverse cluster of cultural practices was probably found in New Jersey. In that colony one found aspects of group life present among both of its neighbors with additional features not present elsewhere. In the north were communities possessing many of the traits of their rural New York neighbors, including distinctly "Dutch" communities in and around Bergen, a group of relatively insular towns founded by former New Englanders in the vicinity of Newark and Elizabethtown, and the town of Perth Amboy, dominated by Anglican proprietors. In south Jersey one encountered a landscape of diverse settlements of Quakers; Presbyterians from Scotland, Ireland, and New England; Anglicans; Baptists; and Swedish Lutherans. Yet the influx of migrants was slower in southern Jersey than in its Pennsylvania neighbor, and some groups there still maintained a rather isolated existence. Others, even in the most rural areas, established surprisingly cosmopolitan communities connected to cultural circles in Philadelphia and in Princeton, where the new College of New Jersey was situated.

As the place where different forms of pluralism met, New Jersey was for a time the center of religious contestation in the Middle Colonies. As in New York, leading members of the Church of England worked aggressively to promote Anglican ascendancy, especially in the eastern section. In New Jersey, as elsewhere, they confronted vocal and aggressive proponents of religious dissent, who were in a much stronger position there than they were in their northern neighbor. The contest that developed extended throughout the mid-Atlantic and helped to create still other meanings of toleration and religious liberty.

An important reason for the intensity of conflict in New Jersey was its central position between the two larger colonies. Leading citizens of New Jersey played significant roles in the affairs of its neighbors, especially New York; there was, in fact, considerable overlap between the elites of northern New Jersey and the New York City region. There were two additional reasons. One of those was the assertive character of the dissenting population in New Jersey, which was much more willing than its New York counterpart to engage in public debate over political and religious matters. The other was the substantial presence in the Jerseys of migrants from Scotland. Their involvement in the region began with the Scottish proprietary colony in East New Jersey in 1683. While the size of the Scots migration never rivaled the numbers of Germans or Irish who came to the Middle Colonies, it would be continuous throughout the period. More importantly, the unusually high profile of the Scots migrants gave them an influence in colonial life well out of proportion to their numbers.

In several respects, the experience of the Scots was much like that of the Dutch of New York. Both came from societies with strong migratory traditions. Both were Protestant nations with staunchly Calvinist churches. Both were highly commercial peoples who devoted considerable effort to venturing abroad in the pursuit of foreign trade. Both had legal systems derived from Roman law, including systems of partible inheritance that funneled property into both the male and female lines of descent and significantly greater protection for women's property rights than was found in English Common Law. Moreover, the religious wars of the seventeenth century had sent many Scots to seek refuge in the Netherlands, some of whom would subsequently involve themselves in the mid-Atlantic.

There were crucial differences between the two nations, however. Whereas the Netherlands in the seventeenth century became among the wealthiest countries in western Europe, Scotland remained among the poorest. While the Netherlands, as a trading center as well as religious refuge, experienced substantial inflows and outflows of population, Scotland, which had few products or resources that others valued, had only outflows. It was probably the most consistent provider of net out-migration in Europe.

A second distinctive aspect of Scots migration was how far up the social ladder it extended. Not only the poor went abroad with regularity; so also did merchants, officers, ministers, medical men, and professional persons of other sorts. For Scots to participate in almost any aspect of commercial, cultural, or professional life, they had to be willing to travel abroad. Scots developed an image and an identity in early modern Europe as a nation of arms, commerce, and letters. None of those would have been possible had Scots of substance not been willing to venture abroad to pursue them. And while their continuing involvements in Europe meant that Scots in general were relatively slow to involve themselves in transatlantic migration, the number of skilled and educated persons among the migrants was disproportionately high.

With the exception of a few distinct groups of migrants such as the Highlanders, who settled in Argyle, New York, in the 1730s, Scots did not form a separate and easily identifiable group in the region. Most were Lowlanders, and they tended to settle at commercial and cultural crossroads: in the cities, along the principal trade routes, and in what became the cultural centers. Outside of New York and Philadelphia, their primary presence in the mid-Atlantic was in the busy central Jersey corridor that connected those cities. Rather than inhabiting insular enclaves of the sort the rural Dutch developed, Scots became an integral presence in many aspects of public life.

Their avoidance of ethnic insularity did not signify the absence of national community. Although Scots in the mid-Atlantic spread out across considerable distances, they maintained substantial ties with one another across the region. Like their counterparts in Europe, Scots developed extensive trading primarily with their own countrymen. That originated as a way of overcoming the disadvantages they faced competing against the better-supplied merchants from larger and wealthier nations. In the mid-Atlantic, Scots merchants in the leading cities participated in trading networks that spanned the Atlantic from the British Isles to the Caribbean to Africa. Just as importantly, they extended those networks within the region, linking Scots farmers, artisans, and petty traders across the central Jersey corridor and eventually through an extended backcountry of what would become upstate New York and western Pennsylvania.

Scottish migrants were pioneers in the formation of national clubs, including the Saint Andrews societies of New York and Philadelphia, open to natives of Scotland and their descendants. In keeping with the character of their community, those clubs combined the pursuit of sociability with commercial motives, linking Scots merchants across a wide swath of territory. The New York club, for example, in a vivid display of the extensiveness of their trading networks, included members who resided as far from that city as Albany, Philadelphia, Quebec, and Glasgow. Like the trading networks the merchants established, the society incorporated less-wealthy persons into its network; a principal purpose of the society was to provide financial relief to any natives of Scotland in distress.

The relative prominence of many of the Scots who came to the region, combined with the intensity of their connections, accounts for some of the contentiousness of the pluralism that developed where they settled. Although Scots proprietors governed East Jersey for only twenty years, members of that group retained considerable wealth, power, and prominence for many decades thereafter. The hard stance taken by Scots on the proprietary board against the land claims of the inhabitants of the townships of Newark and Elizabethtown—both settled by former New Englanders—led to one of the most sustained outbreaks of land rioting in the American colonies during the middle decades of the eighteenth century (see chapter 7 below). They regularly constituted a contentious force in the politics of New York as well as New Jersey. And the Episcopalians among them—both government officials and members of the clergy— were among the leading proponents of foisting an Anglican bishop upon the unwilling colonists of the region.

Paradoxically, Scots were just as important among leaders of their principal adversaries within the region: the Presbyterians. Central New Jersey was long the institutional home of that resistance, led first by the aggressive presbyteries of New York and New Brunswick and, after 1746, by the College of New Jersey. From that base, Presbyterians would forge alliances with neighboring dissenters among the Congregationalist and the Dutch Reformed Churches that extended far beyond the bounds of the colony.

The religious situation in colonial New Jersey varied considerably from that of its neighbors. Whereas in New York the Anglican elite allied itself with leading members of the Dutch and Huguenot communities, in New Jersey Presbyterians forged the most important alliances both with Dutch Reformed congregations and with the descendants of New Englanders. Most of the congregations of the latter group placed themselves under the protection of the Presbyterian Church. Moreover, whereas in Pennsylvania Presbyterian opposition was directed at a tolerant ecclesiastical environment, Presbyterian interests in New Jersey and New York were able to voice their dissent through the aggressive use of a rhetoric of religious liberty.

The creation of the Presbyterian college is itself a good illustration of the fact that the balance of power in the region was shifting. When Presbyterians first pushed through a charter, the measure met with predictable objections from Anglican leaders. Those were quickly waived aside by the governor, Jonathan Belcher, a native New Englander. By contrast, when, several years later, Anglicans sought their own college in New York, the request provoked a bitter public debate led by the Presbyterian William Livingston.[15] Anglicans were reduced to arguing that in fact they would hold only the most limited power in the college and that what they were seeking was nothing more than what Presbyterians already had in New Jersey. Anglicans would get their college in New York, but Presbyterian opposition managed both to delay the charter and to put the church on the defensive.

The Church of England would remain on the defensive thereafter. In the 1760s, Anglicans in the mid-Atlantic, led by the New Jersey minister Thomas Bradbury Chandler, embarked on a campaign to obtain an Anglican bishop for the region. Chandler's proposal was put forward in very muted terms. It disavowed any secular authority for bishops through ecclesiastical courts. It denied them any authority over non-Anglicans. It limited their work to those colonies where Anglicans already had a substantial presence. Chandler in fact contended that he was asking only that Anglicans be granted the same liberty as other denominations to maintain their full ecclesiastical structure. Nonetheless, the proposal brought about a flurry of publications from dissenters and a new effort among Presbyterians to unite behind the New Jersey college in opposition.[16]

Perhaps the most interesting aspect of those debates is that Presbyterians were able to counter those Anglican efforts on the basis of religious liberty. It was a very particular kind of liberty that they endorsed. It was not opposition to state-supported religions: William Livingston and his allies stoutly defended the state-chartered Presbyterian College of New Jersey. Nor was ecclesiastical establishment the problem: Presbyterians bolstered their position by forging active alliances with the established Presbyterian Church of Scotland and New England's Congregational establishment.

By the middle of the eighteenth century, the idea of religious liberty had attained broad appeal throughout the British world. Liberty did not possess a single meaning. It was widely proclaimed by Protestants, who viewed their religion as granting people the freedom to think for themselves—a view that provided a ready rationale for denying liberty to Roman Catholics who were, in such a view, liberty's inherent enemies. To the Church of England, the liberty of the nation required a strong Protestant establishment intertwined with the state. To those outside of the Anglican Church, it required an additional limitation, signifying the freedom of the church *from* the state, and of the community from a church—such as the Church of England —with a state-supported hierarchy. Nor were church officials to be part of the state. The government might well provide support for the church, which Presbyterians would eagerly seek in New Jersey; it was not to control it.

By defining religious liberty as the independence of the church from the state, dissenters were able to muster a substantial coalition of Reformed denominations to campaign actively against Anglican initiatives. Where dissent in New York was diffused through separate and often isolated communities, in New Jersey those denominations would consolidate in opposition. There the rhetoric of liberty served as a partisan tool, supporting a New Jersey college as promoting liberty, piety, and prosperity, while opposing an Anglican institution as one that would lead to backwardness and lethargy. In a pluralist mid-Atlantic, Reformed groups endorsed state support of any religious institutions not subordinate to the state; within the British empire that disqualified none but Anglicans and Catholics. The emerging consensus on the meaning of religious liberty led not to the separation of church and state, but rather to the emergence of an aggressive Reformed counter-establishment.

While diversity of religion and nationality were indeed distinguishing characteristics of the Middle Colonies, the region exhibited several markedly different kinds of pluralism. In New York, an aggressive English authority structured and directed a Protestant pluralism that encouraged much of the local population to retreat into consolidated religious and ethnic enclaves under a toleration designed to bolster high-church authority. The spiritual liberty for which Pennsylvania was famous, by contrast, supported a far greater degree of religious and ethnic intermingling and interaction among more fluid populations. And in New Jersey, the combination of a New York–style Anglican elite and a more assertive Reformed population led to a contentious colony and an aggressive coalition of dissenters in reaction.

Those varying systems of pluralism were not simply the results of preformed conceptions; they emerged in conjunction with the development of the colonies in which they were located.

The limited toleration that prevailed in New York both fostered and was in turn furthered by the relatively slow influx of population, encouraging the promotion of group cohesion and precluding challenges to authority. Spiritual liberty in Pennsylvania supported the dynamic growth of the colony; the resulting diversity in that colony, in turn, rendered any reconsideration of tolerance and diversity inconceivable. And the quest for Anglican ascendancy in a deeply divided but expansive Jersey colony fostered active opposition to Anglican supremacy and a de facto counter-establishment.

By the middle of the eighteenth century, increasing diversity was causing anxiety among observers and participants. No less a figure than Benjamin Franklin, in a 1751 essay on population, noted the rapidly increasing presence of German-speakers in his home colony of Pennsylvania, and he famously asked why "Palatine boors" should be "suffered to swarm into our Settlements, and by herding together establish their Language and Manners to the Exclusion of ours?" He went on to question why colonials should continue to "increase the Sons of Africa, by Planting them in America."[17] During the Paxton uprising of the following decade, Franklin expressed similar misgivings about the Irish, characterizing them and not the natives as the true savages in the affair. The Paxton pamphlets published during those years were full of religious and ethnic aspersions cast upon the Irish by opponents of the uprising, and on their principal adversaries, the Quakers, by its supporters. And the drive for an Anglican bishop prompted a similar range of sentiments—and a similar reactive trend toward an exclusionary group pluralism—among both Anglicans and dissenters.

Crèvecoeur was among the keenest observers of diversity in the mid-Atlantic and one of its leading interpreters. One of the ways to understand the passage with which we began the chapter is as an attempt to impose an order on the diversity of group life that surrounded him. In affirming the value of pluralism, he was at the same time attempting both to define and confine it. While the Farmer repeatedly referred to the variety of groups that coexisted in Pennsylvania, his goal was to consolidate many of them into a single figure, *the* American.

One of the ways Crèvecoeur achieved this was to project a unity upon Americans that was greater than what actually existed.

Even as he celebrated the general diversity of the region, he restricted those he considered Americans to Europeans, or the descendants of Europeans. He then declared that what those Europeans in America shared, which was the common experience of diversity, gave Americans a "strange mixture of blood, which you will find in no other country." In fact, that assertion was highly misleading. It overlooked the actual experience of such nations as the Dutch, whose homeland was a veritable meeting ground of nationalities. More dramatically, it silently excluded those other inhabitants, Africans and Indians, for whom slavery and displacement had led to levels of intermixing that those Crèvecoeur referred to as Americans could hardly approach.

The particular beliefs and traditions that European peoples held mattered less to the Farmer than their shared values. That is well illustrated in the author's description of a tour through the Pennsylvania countryside. On one side, he wrote, "lives a Catholic, who prays to God as he has been taught and believes in transubstantiation; he works and raises wheat, he has a large family of children, all hale and robust; his belief, his prayers, offend nobody." Nearby lived a Scots seceder, "the most enthusiastic of all sectaries; his zeal is hot and fiery. . . . He likewise raises good crops, his house is handsomely painted, his orchard is one of the fairest in the neighbourhood." The Farmer then asks, "How does it concern the welfare of the country, or of the province at large, what this man's religious sentiments are, or really whether he has any at all? He is a good farmer, he is a sober, peaceable good citizen."[18]

The implication, of course, is that the fact that the seceder was a good farmer and citizen, unlike his strict religious principles, *did* concern the welfare of the country. The values the population expressed were settler values; the greatest good was in the settling and improving of the land. The toleration of even the most enthusiastic of believers was justified by their labors. The Farmer praised national groups repeatedly for their industriousness, "which to me who am but a farmer is the criterion of everything." All the rest were minor matters, fading into religious "indifference."[19]

Crèvecoeur's writings would help to enshrine pluralism as an American virtue. Yet the model of pluralism that the Farmer depicted was considerably less varied and less contentious than the group pluralism that was emerging in the Middle Colonies, where peoples differed not only in the nationalities they acknowledged and the faiths they followed, but in their very composition as peoples. As incidents from Leisler's Rebellion, to the Paxton march, to the debate over the Anglican episcopate suggest, there would be continual struggles over identities and power in the region. Yet whatever the issues, they were increasingly voiced through a language of pluralism, toleration, and liberty.

SIX

The Crossroads of Philosophy and Faith

In matters of religion and philosophy—in the organization of spiritual life and the understanding of the human place
within the divine cosmos—Middle Colony inhabitants stood at a
significant crossroads. During the eighteenth century, the colonies were whipsawed by two of the major intellectual crosscurrents of the eighteenth-century Western world: the movement for a rational, experimental, and progressive foundation
for knowledge that came to be known as the Enlightenment, and
the evangelical and pietistic efforts at spiritual renewal represented in North America as the "Great Awakening." That both
of those often opposing movements attained prominence within
the mid-Atlantic suggests the location of the region as a cultural
crossroads.

Neither the Great Awakening nor the Enlightenment originated in the Middle Colonies; both were brought to the region
through its extensive external connections. Yet there were distinctive features to the way both manifested themselves within
the region. The unusual diversity of the Middle Colony population led to uncommonly diverse responses to evangelicalism and
the Enlightenment, including the appearance of some of the
more extreme expressions of both. At the same time, the wide
range of manifestations that developed encouraged the creation
within the region of a broad middle position about matters of
spirituality and enlightenment that was organized around some
often-unrecognized commonalities between the two. The result

was a powerful synthesis that stood at the very center of mid-Atlantic culture and that placed the region at the cultural center of British North America.

THE MID-ATLANTIC ENLIGHTENMENT

To the larger world beyond the Middle Colonies, the face of the Enlightenment within the region, and of the American Enlightenment in general, was Benjamin Franklin. Renowned as a printer turned inventor, a man of science and of public spirit, he was the very model of what Pennsylvanians and British Americans could become—even if outsiders often portrayed him, somewhat incongruously, in Quaker garb. His prominence was no accident. As he recounted in his famous *Autobiography,* Franklin worked hard throughout his life to attain the reputation of a respectable and enlightened citizen with a passion for science and an ethic of public service. The *Autobiography* itself was in part an effort to publicize his efforts and the ethic that underlay them, first to his son and then to a larger audience, to spread and secure his and (after 1776) the new country's rank among the enlightened peoples of the world. And the Quaker attire, although not authentic to Franklin, was indicative of the role that the Friends' legacy, rooted in radical spiritualism, Protestant traditions, and a commercial and tradesmen's culture, played in shaping the mid-Atlantic Enlightenment. Like Franklin, advocates of Enlightenment in the region often blended the progressive outlook of the new science with a firmly Protestant basis for morality deriving from the civic cultures of merchants and artisans.[1]

The movement that has come to be known as the Enlightenment represented an effort by the literary classes in Western society to reorganize their approach to knowledge in order to place it on a more secure footing. In that sense it was partly a response to an age of exploration and discovery—of unknown continents, new cultures, and diverse peoples. The Enlightenment was also an extension of that other set of discoveries known as the "scientific revolution," which, through Copernican arguments for planetary motion, Francis Bacon's advocacy of an experimental or scientific method, and Newton's establishment of a system of universal laws of the physical world, seemed to provide a general model for the advancement of knowledge by questioning received assumptions, the accumulation of facts, and the search for underlying order. For Christian thinkers, the Enlightenment provided as well the opportunity to demonstrate through philosophical and scientific argument that the universe followed a regular design. Such a design, in the view of proponents of an enlightened or "natural religion," could only have been created by an omnipotent divine being.

The Enlightenment as a movement had several main characteristics. The first was a belief in the principle of doubt: the questioning of inherited knowledge of all sorts, whether handed down from scripture or antiquity, and a belief in experience or experiment as the only means of acquiring certain knowledge. A second principle was that knowledge was progressive: through the application of reason, experience, and experiment, humankind could come to understand an ever-larger portion of the world around them, continually building upon the discoveries of their predecessors. A third aspect was an antipathy both to bigotry in religion and to religious "enthusiasm"—the belief that one could be directly possessed by the divine spirit, thus placing one's faith and one's actions beyond the principle of doubt. The Enlightenment promoted instead a toleration of at least those variations in belief that could be termed mere "opinion" or "things indifferent," in the philosopher John Locke's words, rather than the essentials of religion or those aspects that had public consequences.

Historians have come to recognize that the Enlightenment was a diverse movement; indeed, its leading figures articulated positions that often sat uneasily with one another. They included staunch advocates of reason such as the French *philosophe* Baron d'Holbach or skeptics such as the philosopher David Hume, who applied his analytical skills to the project of demonstrating the limits of human reason. Some, such as the French philosopher Voltaire, were outspoken critics of the church; others, such as Frances Hutcheson and Joseph Priestley, were ministers themselves. Some were prominent opponents of government and the standing order, like the international revolutionary Thomas Paine, who took his campaign to England, France, and America; others owed their livelihoods to the patronage of kings and the court.

Part of the reason for the diversity of the Enlightenment was its geographic reach. Manifestations varied from place to place among the different national, religious, and social groups and between the metropolis and the provinces. The Enlightenment in the Middle Colonies was distinguished both by the unusually large number of enlightened styles that were brought together within the region and by the variety of social groups that responded to its ethos. The mid-Atlantic Enlightenment also extended unusually deeply into the region's social order.

There were several important sources of Enlightenment in the region. One set of influences came through the Society of Friends. Quakers such as the botanist John Bartram and especially the statesmen James Logan played leading roles in advancing Enlightenment in Philadelphia and beyond. Moreover, the extensive mercantile networks that Friends maintained throughout the Atlantic world kept Quaker merchants abreast of intellectual developments far away. Friends of a scientific bent were closely linked to a London circle of Quaker naturalists led by the merchant and scientific entrepreneur Peter Collinson, whose correspondence spanned the British Atlantic. The influence of the Society of Friends helped turned Penn's capital into the leading city of Enlightenment in North America; it was thus not surprising that Europeans depicted Franklin as the enlightened American in Quaker attire.

The connection of Quakers to the Enlightenment was not an obvious one. The first Friends had been radical spiritualists who looked to the inward voice of the spirit for understanding and guidance. Early Quakers were allied to other radical groups of enthusiasts such as the Ranters and Fifth-Monarchy Men, who would long be remembered for challenging the most basic tenets of government and society. The consolidation of the Quaker movement under George Fox, which had rationalized the *structure* of the Society, had done so partly through the invocation of visions, prophecies, and the voice of the spirit—hardly conducive to the appeal to reason, experiment, or the search for universal laws that would characterize the Enlightenment. Even in its most conservative formulations, the Quaker belief in the inner light signified ongoing revelation through the voice of the spirit, a view seemingly at odds with the rational Protestant trend toward envisioning a God who laid down immutable laws of nature and humanity, the uncovering of which became the principal work of enlightenment natural and moral philosophers.

There was another side to Quaker piety, however. A good illustration can be found in the life of John Bartram (1699–1777), whose Philadelphia garden was famous for its collection of botanical specimens. Bartram was no ordinary Friend, and in 1758 he was "disowned" by the Darby Monthly Meeting for allegedly refusing to affirm in public his belief in the divinity of Christ. Yet his religious dedication remained firm; Bartram continued to attend meeting, and he maintained his commitment to Quaker practices of worship and self-examination. He expressed his devotion through his garden and the temple of nature, and within his personal library, which he termed his "chapel." To Bartram, nature was alive with God's work, but he never followed the deists in reducing God to nature. Bartram's God remained an active force, constantly energizing the natural world and infusing it with mysteries that always remained beyond man's full comprehension. The result would be humility and reverence, or the Quaker form of piety referred to as "Quietism," a movement away from the loudly confrontational stance of the early Quakers toward contemplation and silent devotion.[2]

Quaker spiritualism was compatible with other enlightened ideals as well. Quakers believed in tolerance and in spiritual equality, including equality for women. Their tolerance derived from their antipathy to man-made creeds, which could not stand up to the voice of the spirit, in their view. Quakers allowed women to play unusually active roles, both in Society meetings and within their own families. Whereas most religious bodies refused to allow female preachers, among Friends women represented nearly half of the traveling missionaries. Moreover, since the days of George Fox, Quakers had been masters of organization, and the quest to organize would play an important role in the many civic organizations that Friends, like Franklin, would work assiduously to create. From the beginning, Quaker emphases on spiritual equality and antipathy to violence led a few Friends to become just about the only voices in the English-speaking world to question the morality of slavery, although it would be many decades before Quakers as a whole would come to accept that position.

Quaker belief in the inner light also led to a substantial affinity for another important aspect of the British Enlightenment, known as the new moral philosophy. Deriving from the work of earlier moral writers such as Anthony Ashley Cooper, the third Earl of Shaftesbury (1671–1713), the British school of moralists established a branch of ethical philosophy that pervaded the English-speaking world. Led by the Irish Presbyterian preacher Francis Hutcheson, later professor of moral philosophy at Glasgow University, and carried forward principally by a group of Scottish philosophers, those writers would attribute human moral action to an innate moral sense common to humankind, which Hutcheson and his closest followers described as a sensibility analogous to that of aesthetics or taste. There were innumerable varieties of moral sense philosophy, some of which gave morality a much more rational foundation than Hutcheson had proposed. What they shared was the idea that moral sensibility, presumably God-given, existed in everyone—alongside the often even more powerful urges toward selfishness or the gratification of the selfish passions. The job of the moralist was to encourage its development.

That philosophy was strongly rooted in Protestant theology, another important source for the mid-Atlantic Enlightenment. One of the key contentions of the Protestant Reformation was that the mere performance of benevolent actions was not in itself moral. Sanctification came through God's grace, not the doing of good deeds. What mattered to Protestant philosophers, then, was not the character of an action, but rather the spirit in which it was carried out. An act of benevolence undertaken for mere selfish purposes was no more moral than was the sinner whose vanity caused him or her to carry it out. It was thus the duty of Protestants to search their souls to uncover the inner motives for their actions and to struggle against their sinful and selfish natures.

Quakers, rooted in a spiritualist version of radical Protestantism, took the injunction to search their souls a good bit farther. Whereas orthodox Protestants believed that a renovated moral principle could only be found through faith, Quakers found it within themselves, in the indwelling voice of the spirit. As to the character of that voice, Friends differed widely among themselves. Some maintained the radical Protestant sense of the voice as markedly spiritualist, conveyed through active voices and visions, leading to conflicts with organized spiritual and worldly authorities. For others, the inner voice was more regular, something much closer to an indwelling moral sense, approximating what many would call natural conscience, although Friends themselves were always careful to maintain that distinction.

A good example of the latter kind of Friend was Penn's secretary and longtime Pennsylvania statesman James Logan. Born and raised in the north of Ireland to Scottish Quaker parents, Logan, like most Scottish Friends, was strongly concerned with questions of theology and philosophy. Another Scottish Quaker, Robert Barclay, composed the most significant codification of Quaker doctrine of the period, the *Apology for the True Christian Divinity of the People Called Quakers* (1676). A concern for Christian doctrine led yet another Scots Quaker, George Keith, to initiate his break with Pennsylvania's Friends. Logan himself shared the bookishness of the Scots Friends as well as Bartram's interests in nature and devotion. He composed a treatise on moral philosophy supporting the notion of the moral sense, studied mathematics, conducted scientific experiments on his estate, and collected an extensive library, the largest in North America. He loaned his books to artisans, apprentices, and other promising young men. At his death, he possessed a library in excess of two thousand volumes.

THE SCOTTISH ENLIGHTENMENT

Logan's Scottish roots and his interest in moral philosophy lead us to a second set of influences on the Enlightenment in the Middle Colonies: its close connections to what we call the Scottish Enlightenment. From the late seventeenth century, Scotland was both an unusually active center of enlightenment activities and a place that was highly influential in North America in general and the Middle Colonies in particular. The Scottish Enlightenment derived largely from two sets of circumstances. One was that Scotland was a relatively remote and unproductive land that historically had a highly mobile population, even among the elite and the educated classes. With scarce opportunities at home, they traveled abroad with considerable regularity in search of connections and employment. In the process, Scots came to identify themselves as a nation of letters with a cosmopolitan outlook.

A second circumstance that led to the proliferation of enlightenment activities in Scotland was the Union of Parliaments of

1707, which joined England and Scotland into Great Britain. Not all Scots were enthusiastic about the union, since it left them as the smaller, weaker, and poorer partner within the new British state, located at a considerable distance from the new capital at Westminster. One of the results was to lead Scottish thinkers to devote considerable attention to the situation of the province within the state, and in particular to explore the dynamics of wealth and power. That led to the new science of political economy that Scottish authors such as Adam Smith, David Hume, and others made famous, and to the analysis of the moral authority of communities of citizens reflected in the new moral philosophy.

Several things tied the Middle Colonies to the Scottish Enlightenment. One was the presence of prominent Scots in the region from an early date. The original East Jersey proprietary group was followed by other Scotsmen willing to look abroad for opportunities. These included Logan and a circle of Scots attracted to the region by the Scottish governors Robert Hunter and William Burnet of New York and William Keith of Pennsylvania, such as the lawyer James Alexander and the scientist-politician Cadwallader Colden.

Another factor that linked the Middle Colonies to the Scottish Enlightenment was the growing presence of Presbyterians in the region. Presbyterianism was the national church of Scotland, and while the English universities of Oxford and Cambridge were restricted to those who took communion in the Church of England, Scotland's universities, under Presbyterian control, were not so limited. With a substantial Presbyterian population and only a minority of adherents to the Church of England, the Middle Colonies would send many students to Scotland's universities, and most of the region's educational institutions would be modeled on the Scottish universities and academies, widely considered the most progressive and enlightened of the day.

Scottish influences came early to the Middle Colonies. An important source was the intellectual circle associated with the Aberdonian bishop, Gilbert Burnet, who have come to be known as Latitudinarians.[3] Burnet, an Episcopalian, had been a leader in the promotion of learning at Aberdeen's two colleges before moving on to London. A firm Whig in politics, the bishop fled Aberdeen for the Netherlands during the later years of the Stuarts, returning to Britain with William of Orange in the Glorious Revolution of 1688. Among his protégés were several who would play prominent roles in North America, including the Quaker controversialist George Keith as well as Burnet's son William, who became governor of New York.

Among those who absorbed Burnet's legacy at Aberdeen was the Reverend William Smith. In 1751, at a time when Anglicans in that colony were attempting to create a local college, Smith traveled to New York in search of prospects. While there he published two proposals for educational innovation based on recent reforms in pedagogy implemented in the colleges at Aberdeen, which had recently modernized their curricula, emphasizing moral and natural philosophy and what was termed "practical education." Smith's writings attracted the attention of Benjamin Franklin, who invited him to Philadelphia to join the academy he was working to establish there and then to head the new College and Academy of Philadelphia.

Ambitious, quarrelsome, and intemperate, Smith managed to alienate almost everyone he worked with during his years at the college. Yet during his tenure the institution flourished, helping to create a literary culture of polite letters in Philadelphia second to none in North America. Part of the reason was the non-denominational character of the institution: Smith as provost shared the leadership with his deputy, Francis Alison, an Irish Presbyterian clergyman who had studied at Glasgow under the renowned moral philosophy professor Frances Hutcheson. Alison had previously run an academy of his own at Newark, Delaware. Inevitably, Smith and Alison fell out over political matters as well as Smith's attempts to increase the Anglican identity of the college, but it continued to inspire enlightenment ideas among students of all faiths.

One manifestation of Smith's efforts was the literary magazine he edited, the *American Magazine*, compiled principally from the writings of Smith's circle at the college and devoted to the cultivation of polite letters in Philadelphia society. The contributors were a distinguished group: Thomas Godfrey, glazier, poet, and accomplished mathematician; Francis Hopkinson, the young poet and future political leader; Ebenezer Kinnersley, Baptist preacher turned public lecturer on the subject of electricity; and many others, including James Logan and Francis Alison.

Penn's Treaty with the Indians, 1771–1772, by Benjamin West.
Commissioned by William Penn's son, the proprietor Thomas Penn.
Courtesy of the Pennsylvania Academy of the Fine Arts, Philadelphia.
Gift of Mrs. Sarah Harrison (The Joseph Harrison Jr. Collection).

Smith and most of his colleagues shared an interest in science, or natural philosophy as it was called in the curriculum, and in the promotion of scientific meetings. In 1743 Benjamin Franklin and John Bartram, intending to attract members from across the North American provinces, helped organize the American Philosophical Society, a colonial counterpart to the famous Royal Philosophical Society across the ocean. It proved to be short lived. Not until 1767 would Philadelphians attempt to resurrect the society, along with a rival American Society for Promoting and Propagating Useful Knowledge, founded the year earlier. The two would merge in 1769 to form the American Philosophical Society, held at Philadelphia, for Promoting Useful Knowledge. In all of those activities, the literary leaders of the city worked to make Philadelphia into the cultural capital of the American Enlightenment.

The interests of Smith's circle extended beyond natural and moral philosophy to poetry and the visual arts, especially paint-

THE

GENERAL MAGAZINE,

AND

Historical Chronicle,

For all the *British* Plantations in *America.*

[To be Continued Monthly.]

JANUARY, 1741.

ICH DIEN

VOL. I.

PHILADELPHIA:

Printed and Sold by B. FRANKLIN.

Title Page of Benjamin Franklin's *General Magazine and Historical Chronicle,* 1741, a Middle Colony publication addressed to *all* of the British plantations in America. Courtesy of the Rare Book and Special Collections Division, Library of Congress.

ing. The young men with whom Smith surrounded himself often took an interest in a broad range of the arts. Among those, the most renowned would be Benjamin West, whom Smith had tutored at the Philadelphia Academy and encouraged to pursue his art. West traveled to Rome to study painting, and he would later settle in London, where he would head the Royal Academy.

As they expanded their aspirations in the literary fields, members of the Philadelphia elite began to envision a broad role for their city not only as a center of culture but as a focal point for the whole of the British colonies on the western shore of the Atlantic. In 1741 Benjamin Franklin would begin the publication of a magazine that he called "The General Magazine and *Historical Chronicle* for all the *British* Plantations in *America*." William Smith's publication was *The American Magazine, or Monthly Chronicle for the British Colonies*.[4] And the philosophical society they began was not the Philadelphia society, but the American society *held* at Philadelphia.

WOMEN'S AND TRADESMEN'S CIRCLES

The kind of literary culture Smith encouraged extended not only to men but also to women. A good example was the literary circle that grew up in and around Philadelphia, at the center of which sat Elizabeth Graeme Fergusson of Graeme Park. Born into a family of a prominent landowning family, Elizabeth became one of the most active writers in the mid-Atlantic. She would later be dubbed "the most learned woman in America."[5] Eventually her poems would be widely published, but before that time she circulated her manuscript writings among a network of neighbors and friends. Her family home at Graeme Park in some ways resembled the famed literary salons of Paris and other enlightenment cities, where prominent hostesses entertained leading literary figures. The principal difference was that Graeme Fergusson was herself an accomplished writer, as were the women in the circle of its most frequent attendants. Still, men as well as women participated in her gatherings, and Graeme Fergusson provided a bridge between her own circle of women writers and the larger group of predominantly male authors in the Philadelphia vicinity.

For women of the day, the circulation of manuscripts was an important means of sharing them with a reading public. While

Portrait of Elizabeth Graeme Fergusson, a literary woman of
distinction. Copy of a miniature in the Historical Society of
Pennsylvania. Courtesy of the Library of the State University
of New York at Stony Brook.

British and British-American women did occasionally publish on
certain topics in the eighteenth century, chiefly about spiritual
experience or in the emerging literary form of the novel, such
publications were still uncommon, and much of the male public
disparaged and distrusted female writers. Women wrote nonetheless, perhaps in the eighteenth century more than in any previous era, and their writing was for more than personal consumption. They relied instead upon passing around works
written out in longhand, a method that allowed the writers to
direct their productions toward carefully selected audiences.

Like the men associated with the College of Philadelphia,
the women who visited Graeme Park came from varied back-

grounds: Graeme Fergusson remained firmly loyal to her Anglican upbringing, but others in her circle were Quaker or Presbyterian. The topics on which they wrote varied greatly, from letters and poems on friendship, love, and marriage to religion to literary parody. Yet the women of the group seem to have considered the production and discussion of manuscripts as something of a community project. They not only read each other's work, but they commented on them and often copied them in their own works. Thus the only copy still extant of portions of Elizabeth Graeme Fergusson's journal of her travels to Britain in the 1760s is in part transcribed in Milcah Moore's commonplace book, in which she also transcribed writings by several important female Friends as well as a few letters of such renowned public figures as Benjamin Franklin and Patrick Henry.[6] Elizabeth Graeme Fergusson and her friend Annis Boudinot Stockton exchanged manuscript books of their own poetry.

The use of commonplace books, in which women copied things they had read and wanted to save, whether published or in manuscript, was itself a common feature of women's literary circles. It suggests that the women maintained a notion of authorship different from that of the more familiar single male writer who published his works to the world. Women wrote for a more select group, and their writings were perused, copied, shared, and even read aloud.

The Enlightenment thus affected groups other than the most prominent literati. Especially in Philadelphia, it reached well down into the artisan community, where young tradesmen participated in reading and discussion groups, scientific experiments, and the dissemination of new ideas. There is an excellent description of such activities in Franklin's memoirs, which have come to be known as the *Autobiography,* and which surely ranks as the best book ever written about the American Enlightenment. When the young printer first arrived in Philadelphia, he was quickly drawn into a network of young artisans, especially several connected to the printing trade, and all "lovers of reading." While none of the others achieved the level of success that Franklin did, they were similarly committed to reading and learning about the latest advances in the world of knowledge. At about that time, Franklin and a group of acquaintances among the youthful tradesmen of Philadelphia formed a club for mutual improvement that they called the Junto. Their purpose was to hold discussions and compose occasional essays on topics in morals, politics, or natural philosophy. The rules Franklin drew up for the club included beginning each meeting with a question to the members about whether anything had transpired among them that could be described for their mutual edification and improvement. That was followed by an affirmation of tolerance, that the members "love mankind, of what profession or religion soever."[7] For tradesmen, mostly men of relatively low status, they were an impressive group: Thomas Godfrey, a glazier, who was also a poet and a self-taught mathematician would be noted for his role in the invention of Hadleys' Quadrant, an instrument of maritime navigation; Nicholas Scull, a surveyor would later be attorney general of Pennsylvania.

Their emphasis on advances in knowledge reflected one of the leading characteristics of the Enlightenment. Knowledge was viewed as progressive, or cumulative. The creation of the scientific method, combined with the willingness to challenge inherited knowledge, they believed, had newly provided society with a path for regular, incremental increases in human knowledge in countless areas. Thus young Franklin and his friends were always eager to obtain the very latest writings on every subject—in science, religion, philosophy, literature, or whatever was new. The principles of acquiring and increasing knowledge were assumed to be the same in all of those areas, and individuals believed they could both learn about and contribute to all.

Science, or that part of it that was referred to in the eighteenth century as "natural philosophy," the study of the natural and inanimate world, were particular subjects of interest in the tradesmen's community. In part that reflected the aspects of life with which they were familiar: artisans worked with tools and the products of nature, and they were accustomed to examining and measuring them and designing new ways to achieve older ends. There was less in their lives to direct them to study literary subjects or general principles of philosophy and morals, which were considered more often by gentlemen or members of the clergy. In the tradesmen's community, invention and improvement were closely linked.

The most renowned of the scientists was Franklin. It is clear from his *Autobiography* that his interest in science was part of his larger interest in projects for the betterment of humankind, whether they be hospitals, libraries, associations, rules of conduct, or inventions for increasing comfort and efficiency, such as the lightning rod and the Franklin stove. Yet he was always aware that his scientific speculations placed him in other circles as well, associating not only with those who devised practical inventions but with those who conducted polite conversations about philosophical matters and who circulated their ideas through circles of correspondents and through print.

Franklin was best known for his achievements in the field of electricity. In that, his polite contacts played an important role, since he first became interested in the subject after viewing the electricity lecture and demonstration of a traveling Scottish lecturer, Archibald Spence, given to paying audiences in leading cities. Franklin obtained his own electrical apparatus and began a series of experiments, the most famous of which proved that lighting and electricity were one and the same. However, Franklin's interests always extended beyond displaying his knowledge in polite circles. He was uncommon among learned scientists in his ability to adapt his experiments to practical use; the lightning rod stands as an example.

For Franklin and his colleagues, the distance that separated religious and philosophical speculations was narrow. For some, this meant that enlightened thinking led away from formal religious worship, or at least toward a less doctrinal, more rational religion. Franklin was a case in point. As a young man he became a deist—one who believed in a deity who created the world and then left it alone to follow the divine plan that was embedded in nature. To Franklin, the best way to honor God was moral: by doing good to his creatures. For others, philosophical musings led instead to original speculations about God and religion and about good and evil that maintained a far closer relationship to religious worship. For example, Franklin's first employer, the printer Samuel Keimer, was a mystic and former member of the enthusiastic sect known as the "French Prophets."

For all of their skepticism, the young tradesmen shared a distinctly Protestant ethic of self-improvement and self-worth. Franklin himself was raised in a pious Presbyterian household in New England, and some of the most important influences on his ideas and behavior came from dissenting writings. Those included Boston minister Cotton Mather's *Essays to Do Good* and Daniel Defoe's essay on "projectors." Franklin himself was the ultimate projector, constantly at work devising projects to improve the lot of his community, his province, his nation, or humankind, in almost every walk of life, from politics to morals to material comforts to charitable enterprises. Early in his life he wrote out a strict set of rules intended to serve as guideposts for his morality. They were, in important respects, a secularized version of Christian morality: temperance, silence, order, resolution, frugality, industry, sincerity, justice, moderation, cleanliness, tranquility, chastity, and humility. But what linked them in particular to Protestant and even evangelical morality was his approach. Franklin tells us that his goal was not so much the accomplishment of a finite set of moral actions, but rather "to acquire the *habitude* of all of these virtues"—in other words, a virtuous temper and frame of mind.[8]

Tradesmen's philosophizing could lead to political radicalism as well. In Britain, such trends were common, and artisanal societies played important roles in radical politics. But with greater opportunities in the Middle Colonies for skilled workers, artisanal engagement in politics was less evident until the 1760s, when, in the aftermath of the Stamp Act, artisans would play major roles in defense of political liberty. In New York, artisans would support the political radical Alexander McDougall against the actions of a hostile legislature, and across the region Sons of Liberty with roots among the tradesmen would be vocal supporters of political resistance.

ENLIGHTENMENT IN NEW YORK

Whatever the political awareness of artisans and workers, literary culture in New York seems to have been less developed than in Pennsylvania. In some respects that is surprising, since the Netherlands itself was among the first and most prominent centers of the Enlightenment in Europe. But as the Dutch community withdrew from cultural leadership in New York, its connections with the homeland also declined. There are occasional glimpses in the records of enlightenment activity; for example, Isaac Dubois left New York during the 1730s to attend the world-renowned medical school at Leyden. When he returned, he brought with him with the writings of the famous

Swedish naturalist Carl Linnaeus.[9] In general, however, the records are silent on the participation of Dutch New Yorkers in the Enlightenment.

Other New Yorkers played more conspicuous roles. Among those were several associated with East Jersey's Scottish proprietors, who often had close connections to the world of early Enlightenment Scotland. Among those were the surveyor John Reid, author of the first book published on Scottish gardening and a correspondent of prominent members of scientific circles. They were soon joined by Scots newcomers, the most prominent of whom arrived in New York during the governorships of Robert Hunter (1710–1720), who was a Scotsman, an author, and associate of prominent British literary figures, and his successor, William Burnet (1720–1728), the bishop's son.

Among those we can connect to Hunter were James Alexander and Cadwallader Colden. Alexander, one of the leading lawyers in New York and a prominent politician, was noted for his numerous political essays as well as his interests in mathematics and science. Colden migrated first to Philadelphia, where he befriended James Logan before Hunter lured him to New York with the offer of political preferment. Colden had a long career as a (mostly unpopular) politician in New York. His greater interests lay in natural philosophy and what was called natural history—the study of the plant and animal kingdoms—as well as in the history of people. His *History of the Five Indian Nations Depending on the Province of New-York* (1727–1747) became a leading source on the Iroquois Confederacy. It was read on both sides of the Atlantic and was used by political leaders to promote diplomatic alliance with the Five Nations as well as by writers on history and natural history.

Some members of the New York elite would delve into the realm of polite essays. A key figure here was William Livingston, a lawyer and cousin of the lord of Livingston Manor. Livingston studied law with James Alexander's law partner, William Smith Sr., but he found the law a dull profession. He much preferred essay writing, and in 1754 he and William Smith Jr. began the publication of a literary journal, *The Independent Reflector,* modeled on very popular and polite English journals such as *The Spectator* and *The Gentleman's Magazine.* Their original plan was to write on manners and civic affairs, but they soon found themselves in the midst of political controversy over the founding of King's College as an Anglican institution, which the paper vociferously opposed. Thereafter, more of Livingston's and Smith's writings concerned political topics, but they continued to address issues of civic culture, religious liberty, and the connection of liberty to progress and prosperity.

While New York lacked a circle of literary women like that which surrounded Elizabeth Graeme Fergusson in Philadelphia, individual women could still play an active role in Enlightenment projects. One who did was Cadwallader Colden's daughter Jane. Raised on the rural Colden estate in the Hudson Valley, Jane Colden developed an interest in botany from her father. In fact, she became the foremost naturalist in New York colony, collecting plants, some of which had never been cataloged before. She sketched them, described their attributes, and classified them according to the new scientific system of the Swedish naturalist Carl Linnaeus. Introduced by her father to a circle of natural history scholars in Britain and North America, Jane Colden corresponded with all of the leading (male) naturalists of the day, a number of whom visited her while traveling through the colonies. Her descriptions and drawings appeared also in European publications.

A GREAT AND GENERAL AWAKENING

A different kind of women's literary circle from that surrounding Elizabeth Graeme Fergusson developed in the region among a group of pious Protestant women, at the center of which stood Esther Edwards Burr and Annis Boudinot Stockton. Burr was the wife of Aaron Burr Sr., Presbyterian minister in Newark, New Jersey, and president of the College of New Jersey, which moved to Princeton in 1756. She was the daughter of the famed New England theologian Jonathan Edwards, who succeeded Aaron Burr at the Princeton college two years later. Annis Boudinot was the daughter of the prominent Huguenot commercial figure Elias Boudinot and sister of a prominent political leader of the same name. She would later marry Richard Stockton, another important member of the Princeton community.

The involvement of orthodox women such as Esther Burr and Annis Stockton in women's writing circles suggests that there was another side to enlightenment culture in the Middle

Colonies that was different from the Anglican and polite culture that William Smith promoted at the College of Philadelphia—even if a woman such as Anna Stockton was able to move easily between them. For the devout men and women affiliated with the College of New Jersey, Enlightenment stood, not in opposition to piety and orthodoxy, but rather as an enhancement. Learning and experiment led not only to knowledge but to awe and wonder at the perfection of the divine creation. Thus it was that Esther Burr could write to her friend, upon looking for the first time through the new telescope at Princeton and viewing Jupiter's moons, "I want you here prodigiously to see and wonder with us."[10] Annis Stockton would express similar sentiments when she sent a packet of garden seeds to her daughter, Julia Stockton Rush, wife of the renowned Philadelphia physician Benjamin Rush, writing, "May it bloom like eden and when you are meditating in it on all the vanity of this changing scene—may your thoughts be led to admire the glorious architect of universal nature and by what he is pleased to discover of him in his works be impelled to love and adore."[11]

The sentiments expressed by Stockton and Burr were products of the flourishing evangelical movement that had taken hold in the region in the eighteenth century, at the center of which was the religious movement proponents referred to as a "Great and General Awakening." Associated most often with the spectacular evangelizing tour through British America of the English itinerant preacher George Whitefield in 1739 and 1740, the Awakening was in fact part of a larger and longer transatlantic evangelical movement, one dedicated to reviving religion through the preaching of spiritual conversion.

That movement had been conspicuous within the region for more than a decade when Whitefield arrived. The first evidence of a new evangelical preaching style occurred among the Dutch settlers of eastern New Jersey, some of whom came from families who had left New York in the aftermath of Leisler's Rebellion. They did so in part out of distaste for the Anglicized politics and the haughty clerical style of that city's Dutch religious establishment. During the 1720s, a young minister of the Dutch Reformed Church named Theodorus Frelinghuysen appeared in New Brunswick and soon began to preach sermons that were highly affecting to his hearers. Frelinghuysen had been strongly influenced by the European religious movement known as Pietism, which placed a strong emphasis on personal faith and a life of devotion, and he instigated a local revival of religion within Dutch communities in the vicinity.

Frelinghuysen's immediate influence among the Dutch community in the vicinity appears to have been short-lived, but he had a larger effect upon their English-speaking neighbors. His New Brunswick counterpart among the Presbyterians was a young minister named Gilbert Tennent, and Tennent seems to have learned much by watching his Dutch colleague. Within a few years, the Presbyterian had begun preaching what were described as "searching" sermons, designed to awaken sinners from their slumbers and convince them to convert at once. Tennent challenged his hearers to examine their inner selves, exhorting them not to rely on outward religious behavior for their security in the afterlife when the possibility of eternal damnation awaited; only inward piety assured salvation. For his expressive and emotive style he earned the nickname "Son of Thunder." His sermon titles tell the story: *A Solemn Warning to the Secure World, from the God of Terrible Majesty* (1735) and *The Necessity of Religious Violence in Order to Obtain a Durable Happiness* (1735).

Gilbert Tennent would become the leading evangelical preacher of the American Presbyterian Church and of the Middle Colonies in general. His father, William Tennent Sr., was a native of Ulster who had originally taken orders in the Irish Episcopal Church. Upon arriving in the mid-Atlantic, the elder Tennent joined the Presbyterian Synod and eventually settled in Neshaminy, Pennsylvania, where he established a school for ministers that critics dubbed the "Log College." There he trained about a dozen ministers, almost all Ulster natives, including Gilbert and his three younger brothers. The Log College ministers became the foremost evangelical party in the region.

In developing an evangelical style, the Tennents drew upon their origins among Scottish and Ulster Presbyterians. William Sr. was raised in Ulster, but like most Ulster Protestants he was educated in Scotland's Presbyterian universities. Since the middle of the seventeenth century, Presbyterian ministers who crossed the sea between the west of Scotland and the north of Ireland had often employed a popular, revivalistic preaching style. That style was developed at large annual communion celebrations and in the many religious "conventicles" that had grown up as opposition religious meetings during the civil war years of the 1640s and again after the Restoration, when the Stuarts were attempting to impose an Episcopal religious order and Anglican ritual on Scotland and Ulster.

Glasgow and Edinburgh were also important early homes of the Enlightenment. Indeed, while William Tennent was studying there, the controversial divinity professor at Glasgow University, John Simson, was training a group of Ulster clergymen who would become important members of what came to be known as the "New Light" party in Ireland. Several became members of the "Belfast Society," which came to oppose the Presbyterian practice of requiring ministers to formally subscribe to the Westminster Confession of Faith in favor of the Protestant right to private judgment. That position would divide the unity of the Ulster Synod, and a similar dispute would envelop American Presbyterians thereafter.

Glasgow University was also radically restructuring its curriculum at around that time to incorporate influences from the "new learning" of the Enlightenment, even as it remained a center of Presbyterian orthodoxy. At Glasgow, more than elsewhere in Britain, the literary classes exhibited an unusual merging of orthodox and enlightened styles, and leading clergymen and commercial men in the city managed to combine fervent piety with the progressive framework of the new learning. None of this was lost on the elder Tennent, who retained his commitment to doctrinal orthodoxy but merged that with an emphasis on secular learning and a belief in the necessity of inward faith that would profoundly affect the careers of his students.

The first evidence that the evangelical style was taking hold among Presbyterians in the Middle Colonies emerged around 1730 in the congregation in Freehold, New Jersey, about twenty miles from New Brunswick, whose population largely descended from Scots settlers of the East Jersey proprietary. The minister there was Gilbert Tennent's younger brother, John, a man with a history of mysticism and bodily illness, both of which he used to good effect. Shortly after his arrival there, Tennent, who was already ill, sparked a dramatic religious revival in the community. John Tennent died in 1732, in the midst of the revival, and was succeeded by his brother, William Jr., who had had an even more noted mystical past than his brother. On one occasion, William had fallen into a deep trance for more than three days and was laid out for burial before he suddenly awoke, to everyone's surprise. William combined his mystical reputation with the evangelical preaching style of his two brothers, creating an almost continuous revival movement in the vicinity over the next dozen years.

The preaching of the Log College men soon spread the revival to nearby communities in central Jersey and eastern Pennsylvania. More broadly, it prepared local Presbyterians to receive George Whitefield's visits in 1738 and 1739. Whitefield, an ordained minister of the Church of England and colleague of the Methodist founders Charles and John Wesley, developed a whole new style of ministry based on itineracy—constant traveling from pulpit to pulpit—for the purpose of winning converts. In the traditions of most established communions, ministers sought to be installed within particular parishes. Whitefield did not. Instead, he spent his time traveling about, on both sides of the Atlantic, preaching conversion to all who would hear. His audiences were huge, the largest yet seen in North America. In Philadelphia, Whitefield claimed to have attracted tens of thousands of hearers, and thousands more in surrounding places. Gilbert Tennent in particular aligned himself with the Englishman, even taking up itinerant preaching himself, following Whitefield to New England in 1740, where he traveled about preaching conversion for several months before collapsing in a fit of exhaustion.

Whitefield's success derived from several sources. One was his booming and melodic voice. Benjamin Franklin maintained that in Philadelphia the preacher could be heard distinctly at a distance of several city blocks, sufficient to reach thirty thousand hearers at a time. Another was his dramatic style. Before attaining faith and studying divinity, Whitefield had trained as an actor, and he was not reluctant to employ his dramatic skills on his new stage. Whereas traditional Protestant sermons were written as learned expositions of scriptural text, Whitefield embellished his with performance. He would act out parts for his audience like an actor in a biblical play. He would use dramatic inflection. He would appeal to the emotions of the audience, playing on their sympathy, their affections, and their fears.

Another part of Whitefield's success came from careful preparation. Rather than arriving unannounced in the places he was to preach, Whitefield had his associate, William Seward, visit beforehand. The purpose was not only to arrange for the event but to publicize his coming. By the time Whitefield arrived in the mid-Atlantic, the public well knew who he was. As early as 1739, printers in Philadelphia began publishing Whitefield's journals in individual volumes, and they also appeared in newspaper accounts serving the places he was to visit. Those journals reported on the crowds he had drawn, the excitement he had inspired, and—most importantly—the large number of converts he claimed to have made. That same year Benjamin Franklin announced his intention to publish Whitefield's bound journals by advance subscription, which turned out to be a popular and profitable enterprise for the young printer. Franklin subsequently developed a longstanding business and professional relationship with the evangelist, which proved extremely beneficial to both of them.[12]

ALLIANCES AND DIVISIONS

Whitefield and the Tennents drew many allies. They included the other Log College men among the Scots and Scots-Irish Presbyterians, as well as Presbyterians in New York and Long Island. Most of those were New Englanders by heritage; they had joined the Presbyterian Synod after moving outside the bounds of that region's Congregational establishments. Frelinghuysen and some among the Dutch community supported the revival, as did some of the German Reformed and sectarian groups in Pennsylvania, although others, as we shall see, did not.

From the time of Whitefield's visit, Philadelphia and surrounding communities in eastern Pennsylvania and central New Jersey became in effect the evangelical headquarters of the region. In 1743 Gilbert Tennent left New Brunswick for a new Presbyterian congregation in Philadelphia. By contrast, New York was much less involved in the revivals, even though New York City would house the evangelical Presbyterian Synod. The Dutch population there remained largely aloof within their own local religious communities, while the leading Dutch Reformed pastors in the city became increasingly connected to their Anglican neighbors, who were almost uniformly hostile to the revival. The principal exception in New York colony was eastern Long Island, where evangelical preachers of New England background drew fervent responses from the region's Presbyterian congregations. Not everyone was pleased with the preaching of Whitefield or the Log College men. Some considered them creators of disorder, provoking disharmony within communities, preachers who stirred the emotions to produce "counterfeit" exhibitions of faith. The opponents were called "Old Lights" for their opposition to the supposed "new light" of spiritual faith spread by the Awakening. The terminology here can be confusing, as many of the Irish Presbyterian "Old Lights" owed their opposition to their adherence to enlightenment influences learned from those who in Ulster were called "New Lights," a term that in North America signified supporters of the Awakening. And despite Whitefield's Anglican ordination, most Anglicans opposed him as a danger to a national church and a settled ministry, one who undermined the refined faith that elite Anglican preachers tried to spread.

Few Friends supported the Awakening either. Although Quakers in their early days had been strongly moved by spiritual experience, by the middle of the eighteenth century they were more likely to be Quietists, proponents of inward devotion and, in the domain of the Philadelphia meeting in particular, good order. To them, Whitefield was noisy, disruptive, and emotive. Away from Philadelphia the revival was less antithetical to Quaker practice, but only on Long Island did the descendants of early Friends who had never been under the authority of the Philadelphia meeting retain their active spiritualism. In Oyster Bay, former Quakers joined with local Baptists in a movement of spiritual renewal influenced by the Awakening, as did others in the East Jersey settlements.

Even Presbyterians were far from unified; the Awakening in fact led to a schism within the church, which divided into "New Side" and "Old Side" factions. At least two groups of Old Siders opposed the Awakening. One, led largely by Scots and Irish Presbyterians, valued doctrinal orthodoxy and disciplinary order above all else and feared that the practices of the Tennents and their associates were threatening both. An example was John Thomson of Lewes, Delaware, and later of Pennsylvania. Educated at Glasgow in traditional Reformed doctrines and influenced by those orthodox Irish Presbyterians who battled with Ulster's New Lights, Thomson, in 1727, proposed making subscription to the Westminster Confession a requirement for all ministers. This was a position firmly opposed by most of those raised in New England and Congregational traditions, who placed much greater emphasis on individual liberties and congregational independence. The "Subscription Controversy" was compromised in the Adopting Act of 1732, which required ministers to subscribe to the Westminster Confession but allowed them latitude to express their understandings of its doctrines in their own words

Opposition came also from the opposite end of the Presbyterian spectrum. Some among the Irish immigrants in Pennsylvania had associations with the Irish New Lights and were looking toward a religion with a more rational and enlightened message than the emotional preaching of the evangelicals. They were also wary of the imposition of subscription to any man-made creeds. Their leader was Francis Alison of Newark, Delaware, formerly a student at Glasgow, where he had studied with the Enlightenment moral philosopher Frances Hutcheson. Alison was noted as an educator and a teacher of science and moral philosophy, first at the academy he ran in Newark and later as vice provost and second in command to his Anglican colleague William Smith at the College of Philadelphia.

Alison inspired his students not only with the learning he had imbibed at Glasgow but also with his ability to combine that learning with personal piety and, later, with the politics of liberty as well. To Alison, the benefits of such learning came not only from the specific knowledge it provided but also from the limits on the powers of human reason that it demonstrated. In the tradition of Scottish skeptics such as the philosopher David Hume, who had attacked the assumption of "natural religion" that religious faith could be proved by reasoning from experience, Alison criticized those he believed to be "too sanguine" about their beliefs and who drew "too universal conclusions from their experiments that are too few to sustain their Fabricks."[13] Reason, he argued, "cannot teach the wonders of redemption." Rather, its effects were inspirational, influencing the "will and affections of men," and their "internal frame and temper." The demonstration of the limits of human reason in comparison to God's infinite power would lead believers to piety and devotion.[14]

Disagreements over evangelical preaching split the Presbyterian Church. In 1739, the Philadelphia Synod, alarmed by the progress of the Log College men, voted that henceforth ministerial candidates who lacked certification from European or New England universities would have to be examined by the whole synod. The New Side resisted, and in 1741 the synod divided, with the New Side withdrawing to form its own synod in New York. A number of churches also split into Old Side and New Side congregations.

Other churches were also divided by the Awakening. Among the Germans of Pennsylvania, reactions to the revival were extremely diverse. The largest denomination was Lutheran, most with Pietist backgrounds, but the evangelical movement split German Pietism into two factions that spanned the Atlantic. One, of long standing and centered in Westphalia, emphasized a personal faith continually lived through faith and devotion. It opposed demonstrative displays of divine possession resembling those found in evangelical conversions. Its leader in Pennsylvania was Henry Melchior Muhlenberg. In opposition stood Count Nicholas Zinzendorf of Moravia, who had been influenced by John and Charles Wesley as well as by Whitefield, and who defended instantaneous conversions. Zinzendorf also settled in Pennsylvania, where his "Moravian" followers adopted a spiritual life incorporating such extraordinary rites as the use of the lot—rooted in chance—in the making of all major decisions. Moravian support for such practices alienated many "Church Germans"—those in the Lutheran and German Reformed communions—as well as non-Germans, including even the Presbyterian evangelical Gilbert Tennent. Tennent feared that association with a group many considered "enthusiasts"—trusting in direct and personal revelations of the spirit—would undermine the overall appeal of the revival.

One communion that expanded during the Awakening was the Baptist Church. Members of the Baptist communion were quite diverse in their beliefs, sharing an aversion to the practice of infant baptism but otherwise strongly divided in their theological opinions. The emphasis on inward personal conversion that came out of the Awakening fit well with the Baptist argument that none but true believers were entitled to the rite of baptism. Baptists drew new adherents from former Quakers who grew dissatisfied with that communion's increasing emphasis on order and organization, and from New Lights of other denominations seeking a communion that was wholly voluntary and evangelical.

Part of the appeal of the Baptists, like other communions that strongly privileged individual faith, was that leadership was often open to persons of low social status. Whereas orthodox denominations generally insisted that ministers be men of substantial education and training, some Baptist ministers had little of either. A learned background hardly rivaled the authority of the voice of the spirit, in their view, and that voice could reach the lowly and unlearned as well as any others. Occasionally, women preached to Baptist congregations, as at Oyster Bay on Long Island, where during the 1770s a "Madam Sarah Townsend" was the leading exhorter in a congregation that, in the manner of Quaker meetings, allowed multiple voices, including those of female believers.[15] And in several New Light and Baptist congregations, African Americans were admitted as full members. A few Africans began to preach in their own communities, although they were never recognized by Christian denominations.

Outreach to Indians was even greater. Connecticut evangelist David Brainerd established Presbyterian missions near Cranbury in New Jersey and the Forks of the Delaware in Pennsylvania with the goal of ministering to and converting local natives. On his death, he was succeeded by his brother John. On Long Island, ministers such as Azariah Horton also took on missionary efforts during the Awakening, and there an Indian convert named Samson Occum was ordained a minister in 1759. In Pennsylvania, the Moravians who located in and around Bethlehem in 1740 made a special effort to convert native peoples, and a town of Christian Indians emerged nearby.

Other native peoples had their own form of religious revival. In western Pennsylvania and the Ohio Country, Indian communities feeling pressured by the encroachment of settlers on their land responded in part with a religious awakening that combined elements of traditional native religions with occasional Christian themes and an evangelical style into a message of cultural renewal. A major figure was the Lenape Indian Neolin, the "Delaware Prophet," who at the end of the Seven Years' War began to preach to his people about the necessity of rejecting European goods and European ways in favor of a return to traditional ways. His preaching influenced many Indians in the region, resulting in what has been called an "Indian Great Awakening" in the region.

ENLIGHTENED EVANGELICALS

For all of the passion the Awakening caused, the actual differences between Old Lights and New Lights were often less than the rhetoric implied. That was certainly the case among Presbyterians. Old Side Presbyterians trained by Irish New Lights came to accept a measure of subscription as necessary to define their faith in a plural society—hence their willingness to accept the Adopting Act. And whereas Congregationalist ministers in England and New England who opposed Whitefield began moving toward a theology that was explicitly anti-Calvinist, mid-Atlantic Presbyterians in general did not follow them. Nor did they defend in principle the concept of church schism, the idea that permanently breaking away from an impure church was an acceptable course of action, as some outside the region would. Even as the synod divided; nearly all members on both sides still upheld the principle that the church ought to remain a single body.

With Old Side preachers such as Francis Alison emphasizing personal piety rather than rational religion, the differences between the sides were less about goals than tactics: how best to promote piety in congregations. As their larger aims converged, the crux of the argument between Old Side and New came to be very much about history: whether the events that had occurred during the early 1740s as part of the Great Awakening were in fact real works of God or the work of overly passionate preachers persuading the gullible to respond to their emotions. The dispute had been severely aggravated by Gilbert Tennent, who in 1740 had preached and then published a sermon on *The Danger of an Unconverted Ministry,* in which he had attacked opponents of the revival as Pharisees interested only in maintaining their own power within the churches. He had also defended worshippers who abandoned their ministers in favor of more inspiring evangelical preaching. Tennent would later disavow those positions.

The disagreement remained an emotional sore point for both groups, but there was little in their core beliefs that prevented ultimate agreement.

As the New Side, or evangelical party of the Tennents expanded, they also began to moderate their positions. Gilbert Tennent himself went from preaching on the taking of heaven by storm in *The Necessity of Religious Violence* (1735) to *The Necessity of Holding Fast the Truth* (1743)—an attempt to put a brake on evangelical enthusiasm—to *The Necessity of Studying to Be Quiet, and Doing Our Own Business* (1744) to *The Necessity of Keeping the Soul* (1745). He followed the disputatious *Danger of an Unconverted Ministry* (1740) with the more reflective *Danger of Spiritual Pride* (1745). By 1748 Tennent was formally attempting to heal the breach within the Presbyterian Church, preaching on *Brotherly Love Recommended*. It took another decade to accomplish the reunion, but long before that it seemed a foregone conclusion, with two sides so firmly committed in principle to the idea of unity.

The New Side began to moderate its doctrine as well. Partly, that was the result of the extreme actions of some supporters of the Awakening: James Davenport, a New Englander installed as Presbyterian minister of Southold on Long Island, led a notorious book-burning of "heretical" works, including some written by orthodox clergy, while preaching in New London, Connecticut. In Pennsylvania the Moravian leader Count Nicholas von Zinzendorf scandalized many orthodox evangelicals in Pennsylvania with his reliance on sensory perceptions and what they regarded as superstitious rites, such as the use of the lot. The growing moderation of the New Side was also a result of the enlightened education many received at the Log College and elsewhere, where they were taught that the best preaching involved not just terrorizing hearers but persuading them with rational argument and an appeal to the affections and the moral sense.

A good exposition of the newer style of New Side preaching was offered by John Blair, Log College graduate, minister in New York, and (later) professor of divinity at the College of New Jersey. Blair wrote extensively about regeneration and the new birth. The surest sign of conversion, to Blair, was in the moral life, but in orthodox terms, he argued that it was not moral behavior per se that signified a true conversion. Rather, it was found in one's inner temper, "a settled activity of the mind to right activity toward spiritual objects." It became evident over time, through the constant and habitual avoidance of sin. In terms reminiscent of moral sense philosophy, Blair described sin as gratifying to the passions. Thus the commission of one sin only encouraged subjects to commit more, "by giving loose reins to your lusts and sinful practices." Moral behavior and the avoidance of sin—the cultivation of inners sensibilities—were thus necessary steps towards true repentance.[16]

That moderating trend among orthodox evangelicals made possible the emerging literary culture reflected in the writings of Annis Stockton and Esther Burr, using the tools of Enlightenment—literature, friendship, conversation, scientific discovery, and an abiding faith in progress—to promote the goals of piety. Burr, in fact, began her literary correspondence by exchanging journals with her childhood friend, Sarah Prince, in Boston. In so doing, they were imitating the style that appeared in Samuel Richardson's extraordinarily popular epistolary novel, *Clarissa,* in which two friends kept journals of their inner thoughts and feelings, which they sent to one another for comment and reflection. Prince even attached the nickname "Burrissa" to her friend. Burr extended the reach of that correspondence by sharing Prince's journals with a number of friends in the neighborhood.

That the women modeled their writings on a novel might be surprising, since novels had long been considered scandalous or even subversive in religious circles. But in fact, the reading of literature was a prime subject of their discussions. Thus when Esther Burr read *Pamela*—another of Richardson's epistolary novels—she did so for the purpose of drawing moral lessons. At first she was somewhat disheartened by the novel, suggesting that the lesson it seemed to be conveying "did not well agree with so much virtue and piety." She later rather grudgingly conceded that the book contained "some excellent observations on the duties of the Married state," which made it worth her while after all.[17]

While the goal of Burr and Stockton and their friends was to encourage piety and virtue, the means they employed were very much those of the Enlightenment. For reading to do its work, it could not be a solitary activity; improvement was best brought about through sociability and conversation. The purpose of the journals the women kept was for them to converse with one another with the goal of mutual edification. Thus Burr wrote that she was fully willing to defer to her friend's judgment if her friend would set her straight about *Pamela*'s virtues. True friendship was about improving one another, and Burr distinguished what she termed "true conversation" from mere "chit-chat," meaning idle or frivolous discussion. And in a poem written to Esther Burr, Annis Stockton described how being taught, befriended, and even criticized or "reproved" by Burr would only further the basis for friendship:

> O let thy Virtue be my guide
> Thy presepts I'll improve
> Do thou ore all my ways preside
> Reprove me & I'll love—[18]

Another way the writings of Burr and Stockton assimilated the perspectives of the Enlightenment was in their progressive understanding of knowledge. Properly sought, knowledge was cumulative, and each generation could improve upon its predecessors. Thus Burr and her circle always sought the latest writings in literature, divinity, or moral philosophy because the best recent works could only be expected to improve upon their predecessors. Burr remarked to Sarah Prince that she found more "just thoughts" about friendship among "late authors" than she had ever seen before.[19]

Burr and Stockton were aware of the relative novelty of what they were doing and knew that not everyone—especially not all men—approved of women's writing circles. One of the reasons women circulated much of their writing in manuscript was to avoid provoking their opponents by appearing forward and immodest. Thus Burr declined to bring her friend, a Mrs. Browne, wife of Parson Browne, into her correspondence, for fear that "she will tell her MAN of it, and *he* knows so much better about matters than *she* that he would certainly make some Ill-natured remarks." Another, John Ewing, then a tutor at the New Jersey College, criticized Burr and Stockton and suggested that women did not know what friendship was, being "hardly capable of anything so cool and rational."[20] Her own husband was much more enlightened. Not only was Aaron Burr allowed to read the journals, but he followed his wife's example and kept his own when he was away from home.

Despite the adverse sentiments of some, Burr expressed the firm belief that the course of progress would enlighten more men in the future, as her own husband already was. Until then they would keep their writings under wraps. As she declared to Sarah Prince, "These *Hes* shall know nothing about our affairs *untill they are grown as wise as you and I are*."[21]

To maintain the privacy of what they were doing, Burr and Prince relied on manuscript journals, which they sent to one another only in the hands of carefully selected friends; only the most impersonal things were sent by the post. Stockton belonged to a diverse women's literary circle centered in the Pennsylvania home of Elisabeth Graeme Fergusson of Graeme Park. The women there might read their writings aloud, but only within their own circle. Fergusson and Stockton exchanged manuscript books of their own poetry, Stockton inscribing hers "Only for the Eye of a Friend."

As the region matured, literary circles expanded well beyond the orbit of the leading cities. Burr and Stockton extended the female literary sphere to rural Princeton; others brought enlightenment concerns into the towns of south Jersey. There a Presbyterian academy led by minister Enoch Green served as a focal point for an avid literary circle, among whom the leader would be the future minister and College of New Jersey graduate Philip Fithian. An avid diarist, Fithian is best known for his stay as tutor to the children of the Virginia planter Robert Carter, but his diaries tell us much about activities in the rural town of Cohansey. There literary friends formed a reading circle, an "admonishing society" for "the regulation of each other's conduct," and, as colonial resistance to British authority emerged, political organizations as well.

The unusual friendship that grew up between Benjamin Franklin and George Whitefield is a good illustration of the cultural crossovers that emerged in the Middle Colonies. On the surface, they were opposites: Franklin was a skeptic about religion, and at least in his early years an outright deist, who cared little for religious doctrine as such; Whitefield was a Calvinist who devoted his life to the saving of souls. Their association at the outset was a practical one: Whitefield relied upon the printer to publicize his journeys and publish his journals; Franklin's business relied heavily on the profits of publishing the works of his friends and their allies.

There was more to the friendship than mere mercenary motives, however. They shared a belief in human progress and the betterment of humankind as well. Their beliefs differed, of course, as Whitefield's progress depended much more closely upon the divine will than did his friend's. Yet whatever their goals, they both believed that the reformation of society would come about through the reformation of the individual, that progress was achievable in this world, and that it would follow from organized human effort. They were also both passionately devoted to the goal of improvement. Thus Whitefield dedicated his life to charitable efforts and to bringing religion to all possible hearers; and Franklin, upon his retirement from active business, devoted himself to the pursuit of science and projects for human improvement.

MORAL AND SPIRITUAL REFORM

The ethos of piety and enlightenment led to the development of several efforts at moral and spiritual reform within the region. Foremost in those movements were Quakers, whose Quietist piety led some to undertake active efforts to extend their spiritual impulses into the moral world. That would become especially important as issues of war and peace led many Friends to distance themselves from the world of politics and government and to turn their energies into other areas.

One such area was antislavery. That was a cause that individual Friends had taken up almost from the beginnings of settlement, but it was by no means universal within the Society. Instead, leading Quaker merchants were also active participants in the Atlantic slave trade, and the few radical antislavery Friends who vocally attacked slavery and slaveholders in the early years were disowned by the Philadelphia Meeting, which was still dominated by owners and traders of human chattel.

Some Friends persisted, and the less contentious and more methodical campaigns of men such as the West Jersey tailor John Woolman and the Philadelphia schoolmaster Anthony Benezet eventually paid off. Their victory was in part a moral revolution, for the first time convincing members of a slaveholding society that the holding of slaves was a moral wrong. It was also in part the result of a shift in power within the Society in favor of the numerous rural meetings, where slaveholding and especially slave-trading Friends were fewer than in the city. By 1758 Quakers would prohibit slave trading, though slaveholding was not prohibited for more than a decade thereafter. Eventually, such sentiments would extend beyond the Society. In Philadelphia, leading men such as Benjamin Franklin and Benjamin Rush, former owners of slaves, came to decide by the end of the colonial period that slavery was as incompatible with liberty as the words themselves suggested.

Quakers moved beyond antislavery to other forms of benevolence. With the cooperation of the London Yearly Meeting, they would form the core of a growing transatlantic humanitarian network of reformers pursuing the causes of antislavery, benevolence, and moral reform. At the local level, Quaker Women's Meetings played especially important roles in the work of charity and benevolence, another way in which Quaker spirituality and the belief in equality combined with organization to heighten the influence of the Society.

Quaker moralism did not necessarily lead to openness on the part of the sect. As Friends came to emphasize their separateness from the world, the distinctive, or tribal, aspects of their faith came to the fore. Thus Quakers could pioneer the movement against slavery and support efforts to educate and improve the lives of Africans and former slaves. They were less committed to including them in their Society, and Quaker efforts to convert slaves and former slaves lagged behind those of the more hierarchical Anglican Church.

EDUCATIONAL INSTITUTIONS

The evangelical enlightenment accelerated an already-developing movement for institution building begun some years before by William Tennent Sr. and his Log College as well as the comparable Old Side academy of Francis Alison at Newark, Delaware. The Awakening led to many new institutions, from the College of New Jersey and the Dutch College at New Brunswick to the Anglican King's College in New York led by the Puritan convert Samuel Johnson of Connecticut, and the Anglican-Presbyterian venture under William Smith and Francis

The early buildings of the College of New Jersey, 1764, showing its importance to people of status and refinement. Courtesy of the Rare Book Division, the New York Public Library, Astor, Lenox and Tilden Foundations.

Alison at Philadelphia. New academies sprang up as well at New Londonderry, Nottingham, Pequea, Carlisle, and Philadelphia in Pennsylvania before 1760, and others in New Jersey and Delaware.

The curricula at those colleges and academies were progressive, whether led by evangelicals or their Anglican and Old Side opponents. Nearly everywhere they modeled their courses of study on those of Enlightenment Scotland, with which educated Middle Colony residents developed close connections. There was a tendency toward what were viewed as "practical" subjects —history, natural and moral philosophy, the art of rhetoric, politics, and political economy—over the traditional courses in logic, metaphysics, and the classics. They purchased scientific apparatus for natural philosophy demonstrations. Moreover, everywhere at the center of the curriculum stood the moral philosophy course, borrowing from the new philosophy of the British moralists in which Scottish Enlightenment writers loomed large.

The ability of mid-Atlantic Presbyterians to fuse an evangelical spirit with the progressive intellectual framework of enlightenment made the College of New Jersey into the most vibrant educational institution in the region—and in fact, in all of North America. During the twenty years after its founding in 1746, the college employed as its presidents a succession of the most respected ministers in the region: Jonathan Dickinson, Aaron Burr, Samuel Davies, and Samuel Finley, along with Esther Burr's renowned father, the New Englander Jonathan Edwards. Fortune seemed to be against the college at the outset, and none of them survived very long in the position. Thereafter, the college decided to look abroad to Scotland for a new president. Here their luck was better. The Reverend John Witherspoon, who arrived from Paisley in 1768, headed the college for more than a quarter of a century. Witherspoon was a product of the evangelical party in the Scottish Church, but at Princeton he taught literature and moral philosophy as well as divinity, in the process establishing its reputation for piety and enlightenment and as a center of political, intellectual, and educational innovation.

Witherspoon was an excellent representative of the College of New Jersey. In Scotland he was known for his commitment to orthodoxy and his satirical representations of those who placed a polite enlightenment style above sincerity and faith. But Witherspoon was no enthusiast, and he brought to the college an intense interest in secular learning, including history, natural philosophy, the new field of political economy, and moral philosophy. He would also become a political leader in the years before and during the Revolutionary War, and many former Princeton students became active in the war and the new government, including James Madison, William Paterson, Benjamin Rush, and a host of others.

The New Jersey college stood at the intellectual crossroads of the Middle Colonies and of early America. It attracted New Yorkers and Philadelphians as well as residents of New Jersey. Moreover, leading spokesmen among Presbyterians in Scotland and Dissenters in England began to believe that the college at Princeton might in fact become the new center of religious culture for the whole of the British world. As its reputation rose, it drew New Englanders and southerners as well, including future president James Madison of Virginia. Its faculty included Old Side and New Side, evangelicals and advocates of enlightenment, and—after the coming of Witherspoon—products of a Scottish university system that was becoming the most respected in Britain. It trained ministers and laymen, physicians and politicians. Its teachings combined an evangelical sense of virtue and mission with the progressive assumptions of the Enlightenment.

One of the ironies of the Great Awakening in the Middle Colonies is that a movement begun in part in reaction against the seemingly cold and rationalizing religion associated with the Enlightenment in the end turned out to be one of that movement's principal disseminators. Evangelicals built colleges and academies across the region, from Princeton and the nearby Dutch college in New Brunswick to their many academies, substantially outnumbering the Old Light institutions—the Anglican King's College in New York, the College and Academy of Philadelphia, and Francis Alison's Newark academy in Delaware. The curricula at those institutions included not only divinity but all the modern subjects: literature, history, political economy, and natural and moral philosophy. They would train a generation of American leaders of the Revolutionary era who would be noted not just for piety but also for politics, principles, and a broad participation in public life.

SEVEN

Politics at the Crossroads

LIBERTY AND FACTION, EMPIRE AND WAR

> For the love of God, me and the poor country, be not so governmentish, so
> noisy and open in your dissatisfactions.
> — *William Penn to the Pennsylvania Council, 19 August 1685*

THE SOCIETIES ESTABLISHED in the turbulence of the Middle
Colonies anticipated several other features that would become
characteristic of American society: a consistently competitive
politics with persistent partisan divides, ever-increasing popular
participation in the political process, widespread claims of political liberty, and some of the earliest assertions of aggressively
populist or even democratic political values. From its beginnings, the region possessed an almost dizzying array of often-
overlapping factional divides: merchants versus landowners,
eastern versus western interests, up-river versus down-river interests, city versus country, proprietors versus settlers, Whig
versus Tory, a "country" party versus the "court," and many
more. Most of those groups regularly appealed to the public for
popular support. It is little wonder that, in the attempt to create a
new government for the United States in the aftermath of the
American Revolution, James Madison would argue, in an essay in
the *Federalist* addressed to the people of New York, that the
greatest benefit of a new American government would be its
tendency to "break and control the violence of faction."[1]

Factions or parties, as Madison recognized, were natural products of divisions in society, and the Middle Colonies certainly had an abundance of divisions: ethnic, religious, racial, economic, and ideological, among others. At various times individual colonies were divided between a Quaker party and a Presbyterian party (Pennsylvania); commercial and landowning interests (New York); proprietary and anti-proprietary factions (Pennsylvania and New Jersey); Scottish and English proprietary groups (New Jersey); and others. Yet the mere existence of difference did not guarantee either the persistence of parties or their influence. Thus the Quaker Party would dominate Pennsylvania politics long after Friends lost their majority in the colony, while the proprietary faction in New Jersey would win public elections even while representing only a rather small minority of the people. Moreover, periods of intense factional rivalry were sometimes broken by intervals of something closer to consensual authority, for division itself created periods of marked stability in which one party or another attained a persisting working majority.

The growth of a factious and popular politics in the New World is often treated as a natural development, as what people inevitably did when they were removed from the longstanding constraints of Old World societies. Yet the emergence of contentious factions and aggressive politics in fact resulted from the particular circumstances of the Middle Colonies, some of which were quite the opposite of what such a view envisions. One of those circumstances was proprietary rule and its aftermath. Indeed, the presence of outsized political figures making unusually large claims for their own personal authority led not to public acquiescence to their leadership—what we call "deference"—but often to its opposite. Their aspiration for authority created an uncommonly large space for the expression of political opposition in those colonies, compared to that found in colonies under direct royal governance. Even when proprietary rule ended, as it did everywhere but Pennsylvania, it left behind a hierarchical political structure that formed a convenient target for its opponents to attack, usually in the form of claims of political liberty.

The impact of those divisions was accentuated by the region's location at the center of imperial diplomacy and, by mid-century, war. The effects of empire were complex. War and the threat of war placed a lid on the intensity of political rivalries out of a belief on the part of most provincials that their security rested ultimately on British liberty and imperial power and that nothing should be allowed to endanger them. Thus politics was conducted within certain bounds. Still, the constant contest for power among prominent political leaders in the region led them to lodge ever-stronger appeals for public support. The result was that opposition to the excesses of power became a winning political strategy in the quest for votes within the region at a time when the language of liberty was paramount in the British political world. That created a foundation for enhanced popular power and something approaching a democratic politics, albeit a politics that was strongly tinged with issues of patriotism, nationality, religion, and race.

THE ORIGINS OF POPULAR POLITICS

Factious politics came early to the Middle Colonies, a result of the region's intimate connections to the troubled politics of Restoration Britain. The very existence of proprietary government reflected the hierarchical ambitions of Stuart administration; that, in turn, provoked significant opposition both in Britain and in its colonies. It was during the Restoration that "Whig" and "Tory" factions first emerged as political groupings in Britain, reflecting differing views of the king's prerogative powers. The overthrow of the Stuarts in the "Glorious Revolution" brought challenges to the authority of the proprietary circles in each of the colonies and left a legacy of political divide.

In the aftermath of the revolution of 1688, the fates of the proprietaries in the several provinces diverged. While James was deprived of his colony along with his throne in 1688, William Penn, who lost his charter in 1692 as a result of his Stuart associations, had it restored to him two years later. The Jersey proprietors surrendered the government of their colonies in 1702 but retained their ownership of proprietary lands; paradoxically, that probably left them with more influence in their colony than the Penn family retained in Pennsylvania. Thus, while New York experienced much the greatest turmoil over the fate of its government during and after the Glorious Revolution, proprietary power would remain at issue in New Jersey and especially in Pennsylvania for far longer.

The difficulties the proprietors encountered thus led to divisions in each of the colonies. What happened thereafter varied from province to province. Over time, the nature of the factional divide shifted frequently—more often in New York, which lost its proprietors, than in the neighboring colonies, where they remained. Yet the existence of partisan divisions did not necessarily signify instability. On the contrary, widespread opposition to proprietary rule in Pennsylvania led to the most stable government in the region in the eighteenth century. Toward midcentury, every colony experienced a period of relative political stability, based on the rise of a dominant faction within each province supported by an aggressive popular politics.

If political division was a regular feature of life in the Middle Colonies, in New York those divisions were more intense than elsewhere from the outset. Only in New York did politics lead to judicial murder, in the case of the executions of Jacob Leisler and his lieutenant, Jacob Milborne. Only in that colony did political opponents gain power and threaten lethal revenge. That was in large part because of the prominent role that the Duke of York—the Restoration's most polarizing figure—played in the colony. James's succession to the throne turned New York into a royal colony. It also meant that the ruling authority in New York changed with every alteration in politics at home, beginning with James's removal. The anti-Leislerian regime ruled until the ascendancy of the Whig faction in England brought Richard Coote, Lord Bellomont, to the governor's chair in 1697 and temporarily empowered Whigs and former Leislerians. The Tory Henry Hyde, Lord Cornbury, became governor in 1703; his successors Robert Hunter and William Burnet worked most comfortably with a new group with Whiggish leanings.

By that time, the continuation of factional division in the colony had less to do with the specific issues of the Leislerian divide than with the social legacy of James's rule. New York, more than its neighbors, had a collection of prominent and powerful families at the head of society; only East Jersey had a similar group. The result in New York would be continual contests for leadership among those families, who continually sought to win the favor of royal governors. Those who lost out, in turn, appealed instead to the voters, seeking to rally popular support in assembly elections by denouncing the abuse of power by their opponents. Thus, ironically, the hierarchical structure of the colony provided its own incitement to popular participation.

As frequent changes in government led to regular reversals of the families aligned with the governor or with popular opposition, factions in and out of power would vie for the reputation as spokesmen for the people against the excesses of those in authority. A colony where factions depended on leading men conducted its politics through expressions of popular power.

The event that solidified what had been a rather loose factional divide in New York politics was the 1732 appointment of William Cosby to the governorship. Cosby did not arrive until two years later, during which time council member Rip Van Dam served as acting governor. When Cosby appeared, he demanded the return of half of Van Dam's salary for the period, which the latter refused. Cosby filed suit in court, but the case was thrown out by Chief Justice Lewis Morris, who was both an ally of Van Dam and interim governor of New Jersey and therefore vulnerable to a similar demand for his salary. Cosby then removed Morris from the court. The governor also aligned himself with Morris's political rivals led by the new chief justice, James DeLancey. In so doing, he created an enmity on the part of Morris and his allies, who had been friends of the previous governors, Hunter and Burnet, but now found themselves out of office and out of power.

The Cosby years produced one of the most famous incidents in the political history of early America: the trial of the printer John Peter Zenger on a charge of seditious libel. With Cosby and his allies in control of New York's government and its lucrative political offices, James Alexander, an associate of Morris, began writing a political newspaper, the *New-York Weekly Journal,* attacking Cosby's rule. The paper was printed by Zenger, a recent German immigrant. Although there was little doubt as to the author of the attacks, Cosby and his allies were unable to prove Alexander's role. Instead, they arrested Zenger and charged him with the printing of seditious libel against the government. When Alexander and his law partner William Smith Sr. sought to defend the jailed printer, the judge, James DeLancey, had Alexander and Smith disbarred. They, in turn, recruited a respected Philadelphia lawyer, Andrew Hamilton, to defend Zenger.[2]

The case ought to have been a simple one. No one denied that Zenger had printed the paper, and attacking the administration in the public prints was in fact illegal under eighteenth-century libel laws, regardless of whether the charges were true or false.

Moreover, the decision as to whether what was printed was libelous or not was supposed to belong to the magistrates and not to the jury. Seditious libel meant defaming the government; criticism rooted in the truth was in fact all the more dangerous for being more credible.

Hamilton took a different tack. He insisted that the people had a basic right to criticize their governors and that the prospect of such criticism was necessary to guard society against corruption from above. In addition, Hamilton argued that judgments about such important matters of the public welfare should not be left to the judiciary, and that it was the right of jurors to assume authority and decide the case on whatever grounds they chose. Hamilton was persuasive, and Zenger was acquitted by the jury.

The Zenger verdict has long been cited as a milestone in the history of the press, and indeed it was, although not quite in the way that has often been assumed. It did not put an end to prosecutions for seditious libel, which continued throughout the eighteenth century, nor did it establish as a principle that the truth of an allegation was necessarily a secure defense. What it did establish, in line with growing popular sentiment against unbridled authority, was that the people had the right to criticize *magistrates,* owing to the dangers such persons posed to the public welfare. They did not necessarily possess an equivalent right to demean the legislature, since legislators were considered representatives of the people and the spokesmen for popular resistance against government corruption. The New York legislature would continue to prosecute libels against persons who attacked its members.

The line of attack evident in the Zenger case would continue to inform New York politics. Much of it was adapted from British political writing of the first half of the eighteenth century, especially from a series of essays written by two critics of the Whig government in Britain, John Trenchard and Thomas Gordon, which were collected under the title of *Cato's Letters.* They produced another set of essays under the title *The Independent Whig,* concerned largely with religious liberty. Trenchard and Gordon objected to what they considered a degradation of the political system that had developed under the leadership of the "Prime Minister" Sir Robert Walpole, who led Parliament by the use of patronage, influence, and deal-making, all of which they and other opponents of the government considered corrupt. Cato attacked the lust for power, the influence of money in politics, and the persecution of Protestant religious dissenters. He defended liberty in religion and politics, freedom of the press, and the political independence of the citizenry.

Trenchard and Gordon were popular reading throughout the British political world, but they had a particular resonance in provincial regions such as the mid-Atlantic, where it was easy for readers to relate to Cato's suspicion of concentrations of power at the center. It was therefore well suited to conveying criticism of a governing administration appointed from afar. The letters were regularly invoked by whatever local elite was currently out of power—and occasionally by those in high office as well. Their critiques worked especially well in New York, where political participation was mobilized by attacks on executive corruption, just as Cato's had been. Politics in New York was voiced in the language of liberty and power.[3]

The factional divide evident in the Zenger case appeared in other matters as well. One example was the alleged slave conspiracy in New York City in 1741. How extensive the conspiracy may have been, or indeed whether one existed at all, has long been a matter of dispute. Whatever may have been the case, there can be little doubt that panicky prosecutors were overly zealous in inducing the accused to confess and to save themselves by naming coconspirators, making whatever conspiracy there may have been into something much larger than anyone envisioned.

The incident was played out in the 1740s against a troubled New York environment with a generally uneasy class of slaveholders, renewed imperial warfare, and a divisive politics. The investigation was led by a staunch Cosby supporter, Daniel Horsmanden, who was convinced that the city was under a grievous threat, and was tried in front of the judges that Cosby appointed to replace Morris and his allies. Cosby's opponents within the legal profession, such as William Smith and James Alexander, largely stayed out of the case.

One of the things that brought the accusations to the fore was considerable uneasiness in the colony over the threat of foreign attack, with the outbreak of war against Spain after a quarter-century of peace. Among the principal accusations that emerged in the trials was that the conspiracy was promoted by agents of foreign powers, especially Catholics. From the outset, the authorities focused especially on a group of "Spanish Negroes"—Africans who had been seized from Spanish ships and sold as slaves, despite their claim that they were free people in the service of Spain. As the cycle of fear intensified, some began to accuse various white persons of working on behalf of the "popish" powers. Suspicion fell in particular upon John Ury, a Latin master who was accused of being a Roman Catholic priest. He was condemned and executed.

The conspiracy trials, and the fact that political elites divided over them, suggest the intensity of political affairs in New York. Yet the factions that emerged during the Cosby reign were short-lived. That was largely because the actual differences that separated the parties were modest. Both were led by prominent families seeking power and influence, and some of the party leaders—Morris himself being the most prominent example—opposed the government only so long as they were excluded from its benefits. Morris was appointed governor of New Jersey in 1738 and was as eager to claim executive prerogatives as any of his predecessors. It was extremely difficult to build a permanent opposition to government around such a figure.

With the decline of the Morrisite faction, New York politics was controlled for most of the next two decades by a political alliance of James DeLancey—Cosby appointee and longtime opponent of Alexander and Morris—with David Jones, a Long Islander who served as speaker of the assembly. Both of them made their reputations by opposing Cosby's successors, and they continued to campaign against concentrated power even as they exercised it. Their principal critics were members and associates of the powerful Livingston family, itself allied both personally and politically to Alexander and Morris. Yet the Livingstons, versed in the rhetoric of law as well as Protestant and opposition politics, proved more effective at voicing dissent than obtaining or exercising power, and the DeLancey group attained a substantial period of dominance.

PROPRIETORS AND FACTIONS: PENNSYLVANIA AND NEW JERSEY

Pennsylvania politics appeared considerably more stable than that of New York over the first half of the eighteenth century. Stability did not mean the absence of factional divides. The difference was the presence in the former colony of the Penn family, who were increasingly unpopular proprietors. Whereas New York's leading families alternately vied for the favor of the royal governor and of a wary populace, the constant superintendence of the Penns in the Quaker colony, whose interests seemed increasingly in conflict with those of the population at large, left little room for a competitive proprietary faction. The opposing Quaker Party, composed both of Friends and allies from outside of the Society, dominated Pennsylvania elections and the assembly long after Quakers became a minority in the province.

An important factor in the course of Pennsylvania politics was the nature of Quaker belief. There was no formal authority figure in Quaker meetings. Friends spoke whenever the spirit moved them. They were similarly willing to voice their political opinions, even in the presence of those in authority. They did not defer much to William Penn when he resided in Pennsylvania; they were even less deferential toward his widow or toward a son whose only interest in the colony seemed to be the extraction of profit.

In the early years, William Penn struggled against both Quaker and non-Quaker settlers who opposed what they considered the excesses of proprietary rule. The principal opposition was led by the Quaker lawyer David Lloyd, whom Penn originally recruited to be his attorney general. Lloyd soon embarked on a lengthy career opposing his former patron as spokesman for popular rights. He served as speaker of the assembly for more than a dozen years and worked to build a political base by opposing proprietary prerogatives.

Opposition grew still more intense after Penn suffered a stroke in 1712 that removed him from active administration of the colony and was followed by his death in 1718. There ensued a battle for control of the colony between the families of Penn's two wives: Gulielma Springett, who died in 1694, and the much younger Hannah Callowhill, whom he married the following year and who outlived her husband by eight years. Callowhill's family prevailed, and the colony passed to her sons, John, Thomas, and Richard Penn. Thomas moved to Pennsylvania in 1732 and became the active proprietor.

While Penn's widow administered the colony, the opposition was again led by former Penn family associates, in this case Lloyd and Sir William Keith, who had been appointed lieutenant governor by the proprietary family in 1717. Once in Pennsylvania, Keith sided with the assembly against the proprietor. After being removed from his position by Hannah Penn, Keith continued in the assembly, where he joined Lloyd in opposition.

The arrival of Thomas Penn in 1732 only furthered the alienation of the populace. Penn had left the Society of Friends for the Church of England, and his principal purpose in Pennsylvania was not to further the Quaker experiment but to repair his family's damaged fortune. Whenever the assembly voted to impose taxes on the colony, the proprietor demanded that they exempt his lands. He also sought to enforce his claims to collect quit-rents on other's properties. In so doing, the proprietor set his interests against those of the population at large, and the Quaker Party was able to attract a broad spectrum of popular support in opposing him.

A critical fact of Pennsylvania politics was the new Frame of Government that William Penn was compelled to approve in 1701. Whether by design or inadvertence, the new constitution broke with longstanding British traditions by giving no formal role to the governor's council, leaving the governance of Pennsylvania entirely to a governor and the assembly. Thus the British doctrine of mixed government, favoring balanced rule by representing the three separate branches of society in the government —monarchy, aristocracy, and the people—never quite worked in Pennsylvania. There politics uniquely pitted the two extreme branches—the executive and the populace—without an intermediary. While New Yorkers generally aspired to obtain for themselves the same political privileges that the people claimed within the British political system, Pennsylvanians believed they already had their liberties, which they attributed to the distinct society in which they lived and to their unique constitutional arrangements. Liberty in Pennsylvania meant, in part, the ability of the popular branch of government to confront their governors without intermediaries.[4]

That the governor, unlike his New York and New Jersey counterparts, was an agent of a proprietor rather than of the Crown further emboldened the opposition. This was a culture that still showed great respect toward monarchs and monarchy in general. In New York and New Jersey opposition factions always had to insist on their loyalty to the Crown, employing the traditional distinction between a benevolent king and his corrupt servants. Pennsylvanians, by contrast, could attack both a greedy proprietor and his governors without implying any challenge to the king. By the late colonial period, in the aftermath of the Stamp Act controversy, even as Americans were widely questioning the new British imperial policies toward North America, Pennsylvania leaders such as Benjamin Franklin were at the same time sponsoring a movement to take the province away from the proprietor and make it a royal colony.

Aside from a willingness to oppose proprietary greed, Pennsylvanians did not look for much from their government. The assembly was less interested in writing good laws than in preventing bad ones, and little legislation was passed in Pennsylvania. That was fine with most of the population, who, during the first half of the eighteenth century, enjoyed a prolonged period of economic opportunity in an environment of relative peace. Thus as Irish and German settlers moved into the Pennsylvania backcountry, their interests initially aligned them with those of a Quaker Party favoring low taxes and limited government rather than a proprietor seeking to shift the burden of taxes from his to other people's properties. For decades the proprietary faction was scarcely able to compete with the Quaker Party for political control.

As was the case in other areas of social life, New Jersey's politics were the most complex of all. With Quakers and Anglicans dominating West Jersey, and with a Scottish and Anglican proprietary group in East Jersey that was closely linked to New York, New Jersey exhibited characteristics of both of its neighbors as well as having distinctive aspects of its own. Between 1703 and 1738, New Jersey and New York shared a common royal governor. Yet their situations varied considerably. New Jersey politics was long controlled by an alliance of the two powerful elites based in the former capitals at Burlington and Perth Amboy, who dominated the council and, for substantial periods, the assembly as well. As in New York, their rule would be challenged by other elite families, although far less effectively than in its neighbor. More than in New York, they also faced substantial opposition from less-prominent settler families.

While the West Jersey proprietary had established the most liberal social order in the region, the East Jersey proprietors, mostly of Scots backgrounds, were a very different group. Having surrendered the government of East Jersey to the Crown in 1702, the proprietors retained title to vast tracts of land and maintained enormous influence—more, in fact, than the Penn family was able to exert in their colony after the restoration of the proprietorship. For decades, those proprietors dominated the Governor's Council, and they managed to get their supporters elected members of the assembly from Perth Amboy and the surrounding counties. They were not above manipulating the vote to do that, using their control of the appointments to the offices of county sheriff, but often they did not have to. Their control over so much land, as in New York, gave them considerable influence over the votes of their dependents. And by aligning themselves with the Burlington elite, they formed a powerful interest in the government.

New Jersey was largely insulated from external attack and would remain so even after that was no longer the case with the Quaker colony. New Jersey bordered New York and Pennsylvania, not the Ohio country or New France. Its native population had largely been pacified by the dominance of the Six Nations in the region. Thus New Jersey's leaders were able to concentrate their efforts on expanding their landholdings and defending their titles.

The proprietary group faced substantial opposition from two places. One came from among the proprietors themselves. The most important force in East Jersey was the resident proprietors, mostly Scots, who controlled the local or resident Board of Proprietors. Their opponents were largely nonresidents and non-Scots, who were sometimes referred to as the nonresident proprietors or the "English" proprietors. A larger group of opponents came from among the settler populations of the older towns, especially Newark and Elizabethtown, settled principally by New Englanders in the seventeenth century, who held land claims that conflicted with those of the resident proprietors. Until the middle years of the century, that group possessed a very limited ability to oppose the proprietary faction.

The relative political stability that emerged during the early decades of the eighteenth century broke down during a period of renewed imperial war. The quarter-century of peace between Britain and France that had followed the Treaty of Utrecht (1713) was interrupted first by war with Spain in 1739, followed by King George's War, fought by Britain against both France and Spain. For the next quarter of a century, the British colonies were largely either at war or under threat of war. Those conflicts took a toll on both the prosperity and the security of the colonies, which experienced new disruptions in the political order.

Parties that thrived on peace did not necessarily adapt well to its disappearance. Pennsylvania's Quaker Party of course professed a testimony of peace, while in New York the powerful DeLancey faction drew much of its strength from the most secure areas of the colony: Long Island, New York City, and the lower Hudson Valley. New Jersey, protected by both of its neighbors, was even less exposed. Yet with increasing threats of war and disruption, the dominant faction in each colony began to face renewed opposition—from backcountry populations who lived under threats of attack from the French and their Indian allies, from vocal Protestant groups advocating more aggressive action against the Catholic power in New France, and from common settlers who questioned the military strategies, religious sentiments, and self-interested economic policies of their leaders. Opposition parties appropriated those concerns in a series of new popular appeals for Protestant liberties. What emerged was a popular politics permeated by issues of religion, ethnicity, class, and race. The end result would be disorder and turmoil in each of the colonies.

War broke out between Britain and Spain in 1739. Hostilities began when a Spanish captain in the Caribbean chopped off the ear of his British rival, Robert Jenkins, as a challenge to the British naval presence. The "War of Jenkins' Ear," also referred to as King George's War in North America and as the War of the Austrian Succession in Europe, grew more serious for Britain when France stepped in on the side of its Catholic ally.

Over the next quarter of a century, Britain and France fought two long wars, with an interval between them that often seemed as much an anticipation of later warfare as a period of peace. Middle Colony inhabitants played only a small role in King George's War. They participated in the celebrated capture of the French fort at Louisbourg at the mouth of the St. Lawrence in 1745 and joined with Iroquois warriors at Albany anticipating an attack on New France. They suffered the sack of Schenectady, New York. The war persuaded a number of prominent New Yorkers that it was time to solidify their alliance with the Six Nations. At the same time, many colonists in the region were more concerned with other matters, such as taxes in Pennsylvania, land titles in New York and New Jersey, and religious awakening almost everywhere.

The Seven Years' War—a global war often called the French and Indian War in North America—was another matter. The war began in 1754 and 1755 within the western reaches of the Middle Colonies, and a significant portion of the fighting took place on its frontiers. In that war the fate of Britain's American colonies in general, and the Middle Colonies in particular, was very much at issue.

The war was brought about in part by the continuing expansion of British settlers into western Pennsylvania, implicitly threatening French control of what has become the upper Midwest. To protect their colonies, France built a series of forts along the contested border between Britain's Middle Colonies and New France. The focal point became that point in western Pennsylvania where the Ohio, Allegheny, and Monongahela rivers met, near the site of what is today Pittsburgh. That territory was claimed not only by New France but also by three British colonies: Virginia, Connecticut, and Pennsylvania. There France built the impressive Fort Duquesne. In response, the colony of Virginia sent an expeditionary force headed by a young gentleman named George Washington, age twenty-one, in an attempt to warn the French off and make room for Virginia's land claims—and land speculations—in the area.

The expedition proved disastrous. Washington had little military experience and equally little control over his force, which included not only Virginians but also a group of Indian allies, some of whom had little inclination for a peaceful resolution with the French. The attempted warning turned into a massacre of his French adversaries. The murdered French commander was

Joseph Coulon de Jumonville, brother of Captain Coulon de Villiers, a senior officer. A French army then pursued Washington, who suffered a severe defeat and an embarrassing surrender.

Though neither side wanted war, war is what they got. The focus remained on western Pennsylvania, and in 1755 Britain sent a vast army under General Edward Braddock to attack Fort Duquesne. The result was even worse than Washington's expedition. Braddock's heavily laden army moved slowly, transporting wagons and canon and literally building the road as it went. As they approached the vicinity of the fort, they were surprised and ambushed in the woods. Braddock was killed, and his panicked men fled. With the flight of Braddock's army, Pennsylvania lay unprotected all the way to Philadelphia.

Fortunately for Pennsylvanians, the French army did not pursue. Fort Duquesne was a defensive establishment and lacked sufficient men to undertake an attack of the sort Americans feared. Nonetheless, a wave of terror struck colonials about the course of the war, the security of their homes, and their way of life. Preachers throughout the region expressed the dangers they would face to their lives and their immortal souls if they were overrun by their Catholic enemies. That message was internalized by colonists such as Princeton's Esther Burr, who recorded in her journal the rumor she heard that fifteen hundred French and Indian warriors surrounded the borders of the province waiting to attack, so that "unless the God of Armies undertakes for us, we are lost."[5]

For the remainder of the war, the Middle Colonies, bordering French possessions to the west and to the north, remained hotly contested terrain. Northern New York saw numerous battles at Crown Point and at Forts William, Oswego, and Ticonderoga, with fighting all around its borders. As much as anything else, British victory depended on winning over hostile Indian nations in the Ohio Valley, many of whom started out aligned with New France and had to be wooed to Britain's side. That was accomplished in 1758 at a conference in Easton, Pennsylvania, as British negotiators secured their support through a combination of gifts, the provision of trade goods greater than the French were able to supply, and the promise of no further intrusions on Indian lands. The last of those promises barely outlasted the war, however.

The worst destruction within the region took place in western Pennsylvania, and it was largely Pennsylvania's fault. The colony's relations with its Indian neighbors had deteriorated severely by the middle of the eighteenth century, owing to continuing expansion onto native lands. A focal point of controversy was the notorious "Walking Purchase," which had dispossessed many Lenape or Delaware Indians from their lands and driven them to the western borders of the colony (see chapter 3 above). There is a great deal of ambiguity about the story, although Logan's crafty dealings in recruiting runners rather than walkers was surely not what earlier negotiators, if they did negotiate such a treaty, had intended. The Lenape never forgot what they reasonably considered coercion and fraud, and many remained hostile to the Pennsylvania colony ever after.

The New York frontiers fared better. A critical hub of the war effort was Albany, serving in particular as the center of the crucial diplomatic alliance with the Six Nations. In 1754 representatives of the various colonies met in that city to attempt to establish a centralized colonial authority for war and diplomacy and, more importantly, to work with their allies in the Six Nations. The conference produced a scheme for unifying the colonies, drafted by Benjamin Franklin—the Albany Plan of Union—that was never implemented, having been opposed both by Parliament and by various colonial governments.

The Albany conference was indicative of the fact that the Middle Colonies housed a significant group of provincial imperialists—men who believed that the colonies' futures lay as part of an expansive empire of British liberty. Included in that group were men such as Benjamin Franklin and his Pennsylvania ally Joseph Galloway, along with William Livingston and his partner, William Smith Jr. Also included were a well-connected group of Scots in New York and New Jersey led by James Alexander and Alexander Kennedy. Franklin credited Alexander and Kennedy as key figures in inspiring the conference and the plan of union; Kennedy was also the principal publicist of the day for reaffirming the broken alliance with the Six Nations.[6]

The leading figure in carrying out imperial diplomacy was Sir William Johnson, an Irish-born settler who established an estate at Johnson manor in the Mohawk Valley to the west of Albany. Johnson established close relations with his Mohawk neighbors and was a tireless advocate of providing gift goods to the Six Nations to cement the alliance. In 1755 he was appointed Superintendent of Indian Affairs for the northern colonies. Johnson extended his contacts to his personal life, cohabiting and raising a family with Molly Brandt, sister of the Mohawk chieftain Joseph Brandt.

For all of Johnson's efforts, the Six Nations remained divided. Since the Grand Settlement of 1701, they had striven to remain neutral between Britain and France, or at least to avoid being labeled an overt enemy of either one. It was a delicate balancing act, a masterful use of diplomacy and power. At the outset of the war the Mohawk, the easternmost of the Five Nations, aligned themselves most closely with Britain, while the western nations —in closer proximity to the French and surrounded by their supporters—were more divided. But even the Mohawk were split, with a Catholic Mohawk population that had relocated to villages in the vicinity of Montreal supporting France. One of Johnson's chief tasks was to keep the trade goods flowing, and it was in part the availability of British supplies and the relative cheapness of their goods compared to those of the French that enabled Johnson eventually to gain the Seneca and other western Indians to the British side.

The new era of war altered the workings of politics in the Middle Colonies. During the long decades of peace and the distant rumblings of King George's War, politics in each of the colonies had entered upon a period of relative stability, fueled by conditions of prosperity and security and by a political ideology resistant to the idea of excessive executive power. The Seven Years' War changed much of that. In both New York and Pennsylvania, the dominant faction confronted opposition from rivals promoting a more aggressive military stance and stronger defensive measures, often linked to anti-Catholic rhetoric in a war between Protestant and Catholic imperial powers. New Jersey was a bit of an anomaly here, since the protection its neighbors gave to its borders made external threats less urgent. Nonetheless, all three colonies experienced the dissolution of political stability and the resumption of a more competitive politics, leading to considerable turbulence and still greater appeals by the parties for popular support against the monopolization of power.

The most dramatic effect was in Pennsylvania. Much of the

support for the Quaker Party was a result of the prosperous and peaceful state of the colony, but that changed with the outbreak of war. Quakers in the assembly had long been reluctant to vote funds for aggressive military measures. During peacetime such a position generally appealed to the public because it helped keep taxes low. Even during King George's War, the assembly approved only an initial modest appropriation for war. When the proprietor requested additional funds, the Quaker Party was able to shift public attention from their reluctance to provide necessary military supplies to Penn's unwillingness to pay taxes on proprietary property.

The Seven Years' War was different. Here the need for provincial defense was far more apparent to those living on the frontiers, and requisitions of funds larger and more frequent. With the aid of Benjamin Franklin, the assembly managed to finesse the issue of raising war funds, offering money instead for "the King's use," and the Quaker Party kept control of the assembly. Not all Quakers went along with the compromise, however, and a number of prominent Friends left government rather than continue to administer the war. The result was that after 1755 the majority of the Quaker Party members in the assembly were non-Quakers.

Friends found their influence further reduced after the war. The wartime creation of the "Friendly Association," an organization devoted to promote peace between Pennsylvania and its Indian neighbors, had dramatically increased suspicion of the Quaker commitment to frontier defense. With the conclusion of hostilities, Friends were anxious to retrench their support for military measures. At the same time, hostilities flared between the predominantly Irish and German settler populations on the frontiers and the nearby native peoples, and the Quaker Party would lose the adherence of those settlers and its control of government.

The war years also produced a reconfiguration of politics in New York. The DeLancey faction had drawn much of its support from groups farthest removed from frontier attacks. During King George's War, they successfully balanced modest support for the war effort with a close reign on financing, but that proved more difficult during the greater threats posed by the Seven Years' War. One of the issues was trade with French Montreal, in which some of their merchant supporters engaged. Another was the desire by some for a more aggressive pursuit of the war. The Livingston family, with its principal base on their upper Hudson Valley estate, was among those supporting a more aggressive stance. The Livingstons and their allies were strong promoters of the Albany Conference of 1754, designed to foster active intercolonial cooperation and cementing a military alliance with the Six Nations. The DeLanceys were far less enthusiastic about the conference or its aims. As the war progressed, allies of the Livingstons began to supplant the DeLancey faction within the assembly.

The Livingston's hostility to New France was amplified by their religion. The family and their most prominent associates belonged to staunchly Reformed denominations, those with the strongest anti-Catholic sentiments. In Scotland, the Livingstons had been prominent as orthodox Presbyterians, although in Albany they worshipped in its closest local equivalent, the Dutch Reformed Church. By the mid-eighteenth century many of the family were back in Presbyterian churches, and their politics were very much influenced by their religious affiliations. They and their allies benefited when the war against France brought renewed expressions of anti-Catholic sentiment in the region, with preachers declaring it a war for liberty against popery and spreading fears that French victory would threaten the Protestant religion.

The Livingstons directed their suspicions not only at Catholics but at the Church of England, which Reformed Presbyterians considered to be too close to its Catholic roots and too closely entangled with imperial authority. That was the church to which most of their DeLancey party opponents belonged. In New York that affiliation became an issue in 1752, when the New York Assembly granted a charter for a college in the colony. The Anglican Church offered land for the college, assuming that and its control of the board of trustees would allow it to control the college. They did not anticipate the opposition such a plan would provoke.

The leading figure in opposition to Anglican control of the college was William Livingston, from a minor branch of the Livingston clan. A Yale-trained lawyer living in New York, Livingston had worked in the law offices of James Alexander and

William Smith Sr., and his partner in many of his efforts was Smith's son, William Jr. Never happy with the law, Livingston instead embarked on a career as a publicist and politician.

In 1752 Livingston, with the help of Smith and another associate, John Morin Scott, began to write the *Independent Reflector*,[7] modeled on British literary magazines. The paper began with public-spirited essays and advocating a college for the province, but once the Anglican Church made its offer, the principal theme became opposition to Anglican control. The *Reflector* argued that limiting religious freedom at the college would hinder its usefulness to the province and leave it a backward, unenlightened place, one that would cede growth and prosperity to more liberal neighbors.

Livingston extended his attack on Anglican power in what came to be known as the Episcopate Controversy, the effort by some leading Anglicans, especially in the Middle Colonies, to obtain an Anglican bishop, or episcopate, for North America. In this case, Presbyterians from the Middle Colonies joined with allies from New England in attacking the plan as an effort to privilege the Anglican Church and destroy the positions of the Reformed denominations in the colonies. Livingston himself contributed an important publication to that campaign.[8]

The position of the Anglican Church had been at issue in the Middle Colonies from early on. Especially important was New York, where Anglican governors Benjamin Fletcher and Lord Cornbury had set out to turn the ambiguous Ministry Act of 1692 favoring Protestant ministers into a bona fide Anglican establishment. That effort had effectively collapsed in 1707, with the trial of the Presbyterian minister Francis Makemie, imprisoned by Cornbury for preaching without a license from the governor. The jury found for Makemie.

What underlay the Makemie verdict was the Union of Parliaments of England and Scotland in 1707. An important aspect of the Union had been the securing of the separate religious establishments of the Church of England (Episcopalian) and Church of Scotland (Presbyterian). Makemie therefore was able to argue successfully that he belonged to a church as fully established within the British empire as the Anglican Church. The promoters of the union had thus rather unwittingly managed to disestablish the imperial church. Anglicans would continue to press the case for establishment thereafter, but they would never prevail.

The episcopate debate brought many of the same arguments to the fore that had first surfaced during the college controversy. Anglicans, led by Thomas Bradbury Chandler of Elizabethtown in New Jersey, contended that a bishop was an essential part of an Episcopal religious order. The church required a bishop, for only bishops were allowed to appoint Anglican ministers, and the absence of one required a ministerial candidate to embark on a risky and costly voyage to England. Their opponents countered that creating a bishop by act of Parliament, as Anglicans sought, would privilege the position of that church in violation of the Union settlement and would inexorably entangle that church with civil authority. Indeed, that was the point, as the Church of England contended that its hierarchy was inevitably intertwined with the state, with the king or queen serving as head of both. Their habit of referring to everyone else as dissenters— and not as churches on an equal footing, as the Makemie verdict implied—did much to alienate those outside of the church's communion.[9]

The controversy over the episcopate also affected Presbyterians and other Reformed groups in Pennsylvania and New Jersey and contributed to political disorder. In New York, it led to the electoral loss of David Jones, speaker of the assembly and DeLancey's coalition partner from Long Island, whose constituents were predominantly Presbyterian. In Pennsylvania, it played a large role in the rise of a Presbyterian interest and the eventual defeat of the Quaker Party. And in New Jersey, it combined with other issues to set Presbyterians against Anglican control of the levers of power and, especially, of land.

TURMOIL

Popular politics extended beyond the realm of elections and government. In the decades after 1740, each of the mid-Atlantic colonies experienced a period of intense civil disorder, with crowd activities and violent episodes carried on outside of the political system. The timing of those events varied from colony to colony, as did the issues at stake, from land titles and tenant loyalties to frontier security and race. In each colony an array of crosscurrents came together within contentious and often highly disordered political systems.

The first to experience disorder was New Jersey, which was consumed by a dramatic series of land riots in the decade after 1745. The underlying causes were conflicting land claims, some of which dated back to the first days of the colony. After James had conveyed the territory to Berkeley and Carteret in 1664, but before word had reached New York, Governor Nicolls granted portions of what would become the Jerseys to two groups of migrants of New English origin, who ended up in what would become Elizabethtown and the Monmouth Patent. The Jersey proprietors insisted that the Nicolls patents were invalid and that the settlers would have to renew them under the new proprietary authority, but the townspeople refused. The ownership of those territories would remain at issue for more than a century.

There were other land disputes in New Jersey as well. An even more difficult case involved another set of New Englanders who had settled in Newark. The Newark migrants arrived with a strongly independent streak that derived from their attachment to a radical form of Congregationalism. Settling in New Jersey, they purchased their lands from local Indian nations, maintaining that the land did not belong to the proprietors at all. In addition, there were overlapping land deeds issued by competing groups of proprietors in the Jerseys, and an increasing number of settlers who simply moved onto, or "squatted" on unused lands claimed by proprietors.

The situation festered for many years, with settlers and whole communities living on lands claimed by the proprietors. What set the conflict in motion was the desire of the East Jersey resident proprietors to expand their estates and gain money in the process by enforcing their claims at law. James Alexander—a Scot and an East Jersey proprietor—stood at the center of the effort, compiling the famous *Bill in the Chancery of New Jersey* (1747) to back the proprietary claims. In response to threats from the proprietors and forcible evictions, settlers who lived on those properties began a series of attacks of their own to resist proprietary encroachments, pushing out those tenants who had been settled on contested lands by the proprietors and taking over their properties. Eventually, the townspeople formed committees to correspond with one another and act jointly against the proprietary interest.

As the proprietors lost some of their control on the ground, their power in the assembly also diminished. The East Jersey proprietors had previously been a dominant interest there, but representatives in that body had little desire to antagonize so large and unified a group as the various land claimants and the communities that supported them. Instead, the assembly put forward a series of compromise measures that suggested the emergence of a new balance in politics between the proprietary faction and their opponents among the populace.

The populace itself was divided, however. The proprietors did count on the loyalty of their own subordinates, some of them with ethnic or family connections to the largely Scottish East Jersey proprietors. From that group came most of the tenants that the proprietors installed on disputed farms in place of evicted land claimants. Proprietary politics was thus also often an ethnic politics. Differences also emerged among the various groups of land claimants. For example, the claims of the Elizabethtown folks, who rested their cases on patents from Governor Nicolls, differed greatly from those who claimed their lands on the basis of Indian patents or the mere right of possession. The proprietors took advantage of those divisions to try to create discord among their opponents, settling some of the less-challenging cases in order to separate those claimants from their more radical neighbors.

New York also experienced land disputes, albeit somewhat later than in New Jersey. Underlying it all was the fact that the Hudson Valley housed the largest manorial properties in the region. The events in New York were more diverse than those in its neighbor, involving Dutch settlers, migrants from Ireland, and New Englanders among others. They were also more spread out. In the lower Hudson Valley some rioters based their claims on Indian purchases. Other settlers in the Upper Hudson rested their cases on titles from Massachusetts, which had its own claims to lands east of the Hudson River. And in the territory that later became Vermont, New York, Massachusetts, and New Hampshire all maintained claims.

In New York, the dispute came to a head after mid-century with the efforts of a number of the manor lords to force squatters living on their lands to pay rent or face eviction. Settlers responded at first with a series of legal maneuvers. In the upper Hudson Valley, even inhabitants with no ties to Massachusetts actively sought titles from that colony to use against the authorities in New York. It rarely worked. Still, many settlers resisted efforts to make them pay rent, countering with force of their own, threatening both landowning families and the tenants installed by the manor lords. What emerged was a long series of legal contests replete with violence and counter-violence.

The land disputes in New York posed a serious problem for the influence of the manor lords, especially the Livingstons, one of the most aggressive families and one that also depended heavily on its tenants for political support. During the 1760s, the Livingstons garnered considerable popular support in the colony for their aggressive stance during the Seven Years' War as well as for their vocal defense of religious dissenters in the colony against Anglican claims of supremacy. Their initial opposition to the Stamp Act in 1765 further appealed to groups among the populace.

Their aggressive measures against land claimants on their properties were less popular with the public, however. For the first time, Livingston candidates for the assembly began losing bids for election in their own neighborhoods. Moreover, the family's aggressive land policies served to undermine their reputation as vocal advocates of colonial liberty, a status the Delanceys claimed. Thus the Livingston faction never achieved the dominant position in New York politics that their rivals held.

Renewed imperial conflict had an even more marked political impact in Pennsylvania, which for so long had been protected from the ravages of border warfare. That began to change with the outbreak of the Seven Years' War, as numerous frontier communities suffered attacks, killings, and the capture of settlers by hostile Indian nations. Nor did the conclusion of the war end the troubles. With migrants pressing farther onto Indian lands, and western Indians fearful of what British settlers would do now that they no longer faced threats from the French on the frontier, an alliance of native peoples in 1763 launched the coordinated attack on the frontiers that has come to be known as "Pontiac's Rebellion," named for one of the active chiefs. Much of the resistance was motivated by the dreams and preaching of

Neolin, the "Delaware Prophet," who urged them to resist European ways. Many western inhabitants were killed or captured by angry Indian peoples, and those western communities clamored for support from the British army and the colony. Once again, the Quaker Party was considerably less aggressive in defending the frontiers than western settlers thought necessary.

Some of those settlers decided to act for themselves. At the time, a number of Christian Indian families, mostly friendly to the colonies, were living on Conestoga Manor. Settlers in the area suspected them of providing weapons and supplies to hostile Indians and asked to have them removed, but without effect. Thus in December of 1763, a posse of more than fifty armed men from in and around the towns of Paxtang and Derry attacked the manor and killed the few Indians present at the time. The remainder were taken to the Lancaster workhouse for protection, but two weeks later more than a hundred "Paxton Boys" rode into Lancaster and slaughtered the remaining Indians.

The Paxton uprising embroiled the colony in conflict. Quakers and their eastern allies were appalled. As the Paxton Boys threatened to descend on Philadelphia to remedy their grievances, easterners took up arms. Even a few Quakers joined the move for defense. That led to considerable hostility among religious and ethnic groups. In the presses, Quakers and their allies attacked those responsible as Irish savages and Presbyterian rebels. Benjamin Franklin, in fact, accused the Paxton men of being the true savages in the conflict. Paxton supporters in turn attacked Quakers as hypocrites for posing as pacifists when called upon to defend western settlers but then taking up arms on behalf of their Indian friends. The affair ended in a negotiation outside the city, where Benjamin Franklin persuaded the Paxton men to retreat in exchange for a promise to hear their grievances. But the movement had injected violence into the political order and encouraged the use of ethnic and racial prejudices in political rhetoric.[10]

The result was injurious to the Quaker Party. Presbyterians in the west increasingly lined up against the party, as did the other large group in the region, German-speakers, who hitherto had largely supported the Quaker Party. In the newly competitive elections of 1764, many Germans deserted the Quakers for the Proprietary Party, which took advantage of the situation to promise greater support for frontier defense. The Quaker Party no longer enjoyed the dominance it long had held.

The return of empire and war to a central position in Middle Colony politics disrupted the movement toward stable political relationships that had developed at mid-century and led to periods of volatility and violence. That was accompanied by ever-increasing popular participation in the political process, including that of groups who had hardly been active before. While the nearly universal cry was for political liberty, political leaders increasingly based their appeals for support on the ethnic and religious identities of their constituents. With the advent of war and frontier violence, that appeal was increasingly accompanied by a rhetoric highlighting both anti-Catholicism and racial fear, which came together in attacks upon the supposed savagery of native peoples aligned with New France. Competitive politics, in turn, amplified those appeals. And because popular politics in the region had always been about opposition—to governors, corrupt administrators, or proprietors—it remained a heavily polarized politics, with leading men increasingly employing popular appeals against religious, ethnic, and racial others.

Empire and Revolution

THE SUCCESSFUL CONCLUSION OF the Seven Years' War brought about major changes in the place of the Middle Colonies in British America. At the outset, what may have been the most conspicuous was the unprecedented uniformity of sentiment on the part of mid-Atlantic residents, expressed on all manner of public occasions. Middle Colonists, like others in British America, came to regard themselves as Britons and patriots, their liberty, prosperity, and opportunity secured by the fundamentals of the British Constitution, by an enlightened monarchy, and by the protection of British arms. With the removal of France from Canada and the Ohio region as a result of the Treaty of Paris, the Middle Colonies no longer sat at the juncture of conflicting empires. They now found themselves instead on the western frontier of colonial expansion, a flashpoint for conflicts between settlers and native populations, to be sure, but at a time when the prospects for accommodation seemed, for the moment, brighter than before. Many of the western Indians who had initially sided with France had largely come over to the British side by the end of the war, owing to their recognition of the superiority of British arms over their French rivals and of the ability of British traders to produce gifts and trade goods in quantities and at prices well below what New France had provided.

Expressions of British patriotism during and after the war

came from across the political spectrum. At the College of Philadelphia, President William Smith extolled the virtues of British liberty from an Anglican viewpoint in sermons preached during the war "Chiefly with a View to the Explaining of the Protestant Cause, in the British Colonies." At the rival Presbyterian College of New Jersey in Princeton, President Samuel Davies celebrated the recently deceased George II for a reign uniquely "favourable to liberty, peace, prosperity, commerce, and religion."[1] Mid-Atlantic residents everywhere began to speak of a "westward course of empire," a phrase borrowed from the Irish clergyman and philosopher Bishop George Berkeley, now adapted to suggest the prospect that the American colonies were destined to become the future center of the British world.[2] No one doubted that the capital of that empire would be found in the Middle Colonies, at Philadelphia, on account of its dynamism, its centrality within British America, and its connectedness to the leading currents of Britain's commercial and cultural worlds.

We now know, of course, that the era of peace and harmony—between the colonies and Britain, and within the Middle Colonies—proved to be short-lived. As Middle Colony settlers eagerly moved westward into what they viewed as newly opened lands, any hope of accommodation with the western Indians broke down into frontier warfare and racial massacre. Moreover, the conclusion of the war led not only to patriotic sentiments but to changes in imperial policy such as the Stamp Act that would inspire a new era of colonial resistance to British authority.

Philadelphia would indeed emerge as a major capital city in the years that followed, but not of the British empire. Rather, it would be as a meeting place, first of a Continental Congress defending American liberties, and later of a new American nation. And political sentiment in the Middle Colonies, which had seemed so unified, would split apart in the years leading up to independence. The mid-Atlantic would in fact become the most deeply divided of the major regions of British America, and the movement for independence there would, in general, lag behind that found to the north and to the south. The alteration in the strategic position of the mid-Atlantic, from the crossroads of an empire to a new central place of its own, would expose both some of the rifts and contradictions that had developed in the society and culture of the Middle Colonies and some of what it promised for the future.

The war, and the Treaty of Paris of 1763 that ended it, brought important changes to British diplomacy and imperial policy as well as to the way Middle Colony residents felt about those things. Many of the changes were about money. The war was expensive, much of it paid for by borrowing, and the end of the war left the British treasury in substantial debt. To that was added the cost of administering and securing the new territories on the mid-Atlantic frontier. As imperial authorities viewed the situation, the war had been fought in large part to protect the colonial frontiers, especially in the mid-Atlantic, and it was appropriate to ask lightly taxed colonials to help pay the costs of empire. Thus British officials began drafting plans to extract revenues from the colonies.

Those costs would be further increased if British forces had to keep fighting their Indian neighbors. Peace with native peoples depended in large part on the protection of their lands from encroachments by westward-moving settlers, something British officials had promised to Native Americans at the Easton conference and elsewhere. Thus officials issued the "Proclamation of 1763," which was intended to maintain the separation of settlers and natives by prohibiting settlement beyond a proclamation line roughly coincident with the Appalachian ridge. That was followed by the 1768 Treaty of Fort Stanwix negotiated with the Six Nations, which attempted to reserve those nations' lands at the expense of lands occupied by some of their Indian rivals.

What made enforcement of either the Proclamation or the Treaty so difficult was that the end of hostilities had unleashed a countervailing growth in westward settlement, with the Middle Colonies at the center of the movement. With the accession of the new lands to Britain, both the French threat and the danger that New France would incite its Indian allies against them were removed. The result was a new wave of emigration from Britain, predominantly of farming families seeking agricultural lands far in the backcountry. The result was that the war cost the native peoples of the region far more than it cost the settler population.

The focus of movement into the backcountry differed from what it had been before. For decades, Pennsylvania had been the most desirable location for new migrants. With the increase in population, Pennsylvania lands had become quite expensive, and its frontiers were now distant from markets. New York was a different story. The inland presence of the Six Nations, continual threats from New France, and the monopolization of lands by the manor lords had long retarded growth in that colony beyond the Hudson Valley. But the elimination of New France diminished the threat of attack and left the colony's western Indians with greatly reduced leverage; they no longer held the balance of power between European empires. The new wave of migrants to the mid-Atlantic arrived largely through New York City and traveled into its backcountry, setting that city on a path toward becoming the leading city on the east coast and the principal port of entry for Europeans arriving in North America.

The new migration led directly to growth and expansion in both population and the economy. It also created two kinds of conflicts. One was the competing set of land claims, dating to the proprietary period, that were now brought to a head, especially in rapidly expanding upper New York. The result was the eviction of tenants, rioting, and challenges to local legal authority. The other kind of conflict was renewed frontier fighting growing out of the "Indian Great Awakening" and exemplified in Pontiac's War, which brought together a broad coalition of native peoples dissatisfied with what British victory had left for them. That, in turn, led to settler retaliation in the Paxton uprising and other similar events.

Changes in the imperial situation led to substantial divisions within the political system as well. Whereas in other American regions colonial opposition to British authority was often headed by a unified leadership, in the Middle Colonies one found division and often stalemate. That was in part because preexisting divisions in ethnicity, religion, politics, and class as well as factional rivalries continued to dominate the region. With very few exceptions, the Middle Colonies simply lacked a leadership that drew respect across factional lines. For a time, parties vied with one another for reputations as the spokesmen for popular opposition to unpopular British policies. In New York, Livingstons and DeLanceys both stood for a time as proponents of popular opposition. So also did some leaders of the Quaker Party in Pennsylvania as well as their Presbyterian rivals.

Most of those leaders proved in the end to be reluctant rebels. Societies that had been founded on proprietary power and Restoration hierarchies proved much better at vocalizing rivalries among competing elite groups than in actively resisting established authority. Wealthy and prominent families had much to lose from extended disorder. Much of the leadership in the region adhered to the Church of England, and their loyalty to the Anglican Church was often coupled with loyalty to the state of which it was an integral part. In Pennsylvania, moreover, Quakers generally backed away from any form of resistance that incorporated acts of violence.

Local leaders were reluctant rebels for other reasons too. The Livingston group in New York, for example, was too closely linked to landed proprietorships to advocate a real restructuring of society, a fact that their opponents quickly recognized. Moreover, even those Middle Colony leaders who were most vocal in opposing early British policies demonstrated a marked concern for the Enlightenment principles of balance, order, and constitutionalism. That was especially true of the lawyers, men such as Delaware's John Dickinson, author of the *Letters from a Farmer in Pennsylvania* (1767), which had articulated American opposition to the Townshend Duties and advocated a firm and uncompromising resistance. Yet Dickinson was never able to bring himself to vote for independence and breaking the bonds of the British Constitution, and he absented himself from the Continental Congress for the crucial vote. Even more reluctant was New York's William Smith Jr., ally of the Livingstons and longtime defender of Whig principles. Smith opposed independence, spent the war in exile on the Livingston estate, and continued to propose plans to heal the breach with Britain long after the accomplishment of such an end became wholly impractical. And there were others like them.

With the political leadership reluctant to take Middle Colony protests in a socially disruptive direction, a new group of leaders emerged with more radical ideas. Some were new men who had not been part of the old elite but had assumed prominent roles as Quakers and others dropped out of the political leadership. Examples were Timothy Matlack of Pennsylvania, a "fighting Quaker," and Albany's Abraham Yates, who started life as a tradesman but rose to a prominent position in the law and in public life. Others were new to the region entirely, recent migrants drawn to the mid-Atlantic, and to Philadelphia in particular, by its cosmopolitan character and its increasingly prominent place within the wider world of the Enlightenment. They included Thomas Paine, political writer and author of the radical and enormously influential pamphlet *Common Sense*. Another was John Witherspoon, College of New Jersey president and the only clergyman to sign the Declaration of Independence. Others followed.

What took place in the mid-Atlantic was a revolution in the most literal sense of the word: a revolution, or turning, in the affairs of men (and women). More than in most parts of early America, many who had dominated from above dropped out of the political scene. Some of those who had been below in the political order now had an opportunity to rise above, at least among the white population. Politics was no longer purely a contest between leading families, or at least between long-standing leading families. Some new people assumed leadership positions.

It is thus no surprise that, despite Philadelphia's central role as political capital during the Revolutionary era, political leadership would pass to inhabitants of regions such as New England and the Chesapeake that had more unified elites. It would lodge there for half a century. Mid-Atlantic elites, by contrast, would continue to lead the new nation in commerce and finance, from Robert Morris and Alexander Hamilton, who devised the financial supports for the Revolutionary and national governments, to the merchant and banking leaders who drove economic growth in the new nation.

The events that followed the Seven Years' War had exacerbated many of the social divisions in the Middle Colonies. Political and class divisions were accentuated by the combination of prosperity and poverty emerging from new commercial realities. One of the ironies of the situation is that those divisions, including the most extreme expressions of distinct ethnic, religious, and racial identifications, developed simultaneously with the perceived need to articulate a larger identity of "the American."

In that effort the mid-Atlantic led the way. It was during those years that J. Hector St. John de Crèvecoeur began composing his *Letters from an American Farmer*, asking the famous question,

"What is the American?" The author's answer, as we have seen, was to make diversity itself, a fundamental Middle Colony characteristic, into the American's distinguishing feature. Moreover, the American was immersed in the predominant values of the region—the settler values of economy, expansion, and development—which incorporated the settler population, while leaving aside groups such as Indians and Africans, whose presence left them outside of, or in direct conflict with, the settlement project.

Crèvecoeur's solution highlights some of the ironies in the story of the Middle Colonies. The region emerged out of a contest for empire among diverse European powers and Indian nations, solidified by the complex arrangement of the Covenant Chain centered in upper New York. The stability that provided allowed for the development of a peaceful and prosperous colony next door in Pennsylvania that would attract an abundance of migration and trade to the region and beyond. It was the very conditions of toleration, peace, and prosperity, coupled with a culture of aggressive commercial enterprise, that spurred colonial expansion and westward movement, leading to almost inevitable conflicts between settlers and Indians over the control of territory. Over the long term, that expansion probably precluded any serious chance at maintaining a peaceful coexistence of the sort that the diplomacy of James's government was intended to foster. Instead, it set a course for repeated Indian wars and continual Indian removal. A society founded on diversity served to extend a broad-based and dominant European culture, as modified by the New World environment, well beyond the bounds of the mid-Atlantic and into the American interior.

Notes

PROLOGUE. Region and History

1. The region generally defined as the Middle Colonies includes the four colonies of New York, New Jersey, Pennsylvania, and Delaware, although the smallest of those colonies, Delaware, is sometimes treated along with its larger neighbor, Maryland, as a Chesapeake rather than a mid-Atlantic colony. Here we will include discussions of Delaware when its society functioned within the mid-Atlantic orbit but will pay less attention to its Chesapeake involvements.

2. Joseph A. Conforti, *Saints and Strangers: New England in British North America* (Baltimore: Johns Hopkins University Press, 2006).

3. The question was asked explicitly by the "American Farmer," J. Hector St. John de Crèvecoeur, writing principally from New York while posing as a farmer in Pennsylvania, in his classic *Letters from an American Farmer* (London, 1782).

4. See *Friends and Neighbors: Group Life in America's First Plural Society,* ed. Michael Zuckerman (Philadelphia: Temple University Press, 1982).

ONE. The Origins of the Middle Colonies

1. Donna Merwick, *Possessing Albany, 1630–1710: The Dutch and English Experiences* (New York: Cambridge University Press, 1990).

2. Annette M. Cramer van den Bogaart, "The Life of Teuntje Straatmans: A Dutch Woman's Travels in the Seventeenth Century Atlantic World," *Long Island Historical Journal* 15 (2003): 35–53.

3. Evan Haefeli, "The Revolt of the Long Swede: Transatlantic Hopes and Fears on the Delaware, 1669," *Pennsylvania Magazine of History and Biography* 130 (2006): 173–80.

4. Mildred Murphy DeRiggi, "Quakerism on Long Island: The First

Fifty Years, 1657–1707" (Ph.D. diss., State University of New York at Stony Brook, 1994), 77–101.

TWO. The Duke's Dominions

1. James has been the subject of renewed interest among historians, who continue to debate his motives. In many respects the terms of the argument remain much as they were during James's reign: his sympathizers applaud his unilateral insistence on toleration, which his detractors continue to view as simply a subtle strategy to insinuate Catholicism into the kingdom. While the ultimate answer to that question lies buried with James, it is probably safe to say that, as a devout Catholic, James did aspire to return Britain to the church, but that his immediate preference was to do so voluntarily rather than by force.

2. Quoted in Robert C. Ritchie, *The Duke's Province: A Study of New York Politics and Society, 1664–1691* (Chapel Hill: University of North Carolina Press, 1977), 34.

3. Quoted in Alan Tully, *Forming American Politics: Ideals, Interests, and Institutions in Colonial New York and Pennsylvania* (Baltimore: Johns Hopkins University Press, 1994), 15.

4. Nicolls to Lord Clarendon, 7 April 1666, quoted in Ritchie, *Duke's Province*, 52.

5. Daniel K. Richter, *Facing East from Indian Country: A Native History of Early America* (Cambridge: Harvard University Press, 2001), 129–49.

6. Quoted in Ritchie, *Duke's Province*, 207.

7. Robert Quarry to the Lords of Trade, 16 June 1703, quoted in *Documents Relating to the Colonial History of the State of New Jersey* (Newark, Trenton, etc., 1880–), 2:544.

8. *Colonial History of New Jersey*, 3:198–204; 4:8–10.

THREE. Penn's Proprietary

1. Mary Maples Dunn and Richard S. Dunn, eds., *The Papers of William Penn*, 4 vols. (Philadelphia: University of Pennsylvania Press, 1982), 2:135–238.

2. "Benjamin Furly's Criticism of the Frame of Government," in *Papers of William Penn*, 2:229–38; Ned C. Landsman, " 'Of the Grand Assembly or Parliament': Thomas Rudyard's Critique of an Early Draft of the Frame of Government of Pennsylvania," *Pennsylvania Magazine of History and Biography* 105 (1981): 469–81.

3. "Initial Plans for Philadelphia," in *Papers of William Penn*, 2:118–23.

4. Recent studies have lowered our estimates of the "Great Migration" to New England; see, e.g., Virginia DeJohn Anderson, *New England's Generation: The Great Migration and the Formation of Society and Culture in the Seventeenth Century* (New York: Cambridge, 1992).

5. William Penn to ——, July 1681, quoted in Gary B. Nash, *Quakers*

and Politics: Pennsylvania, 1681–1726 (Princeton: Princeton University Press, 1968), 10.

6. Robert Barclay to William Penn, 19 November 1681, *Papers of William Penn*, 2:132.

7. Penn to Council, 19 August, 1685, quoted in Nash, *Quakers and Politics*, 49.

8. "The Journal of the Reverend George Keith," ed. Edgar L. Pennington, *Historical Magazine of the Protestant Episcopal Church* 15 (1951): 343–487.

FOUR. The Commercial Crossroads
of the British Atlantic

1. Samuel Maverick to the Earl of Clarendon, in New York Historical Society, *Collections* (New York, 1811–), vol. 2 (1869), pp. 1–14, 19–22, quoted in Robert C. Ritchie, *The Duke's Province: A Study of New York Politics and Society, 1664–1691* (Chapel Hill: University of North Carolina Press, 1977), 12.

2. Donna Merwick, *Possessing Albany, 1630–1710: The Dutch and English Experiences* (New York: Cambridge University Press, 1990).

3. Donna Merwick, *The Shame and the Sorrow: Dutch-Amerindian Encounters in New Netherland* (Philadelphia: University of Pennsylvania Press, 2006).

4. James Henretta, "Families and Farms: *Mentalité* in Early America," *William and Mary Quarterly*, 3rd ser., 35 (1978): 3–32.

5. Stephen Wickes, *A History of the Oranges in Essex County, New Jersey from 1666 to 1806* (Newark, 1892), 141–43.

6. James T. Lemon, *The Best Poor Man's Country: A Geographical Study of Early Southeastern Pennsylvania* (Baltimore: Johns Hopkins University Press, 1972). The phrase would be a common one applied to the Middle Colonies.

7. Gottlieb Mittelberger, *Journey to Pennsylvania*, ed. and trans. Oscar Handlin and John Clive (Cambridge, Mass.: Harvard University Press, 1960).

8. Quoted from the Logan Papers in James G. Leyburn, *The Scotch-Irish: A Social History* (Chapel Hill: University of North Carolina Press, 1962), 171.

9. Franklin, *The Autobiography of Benjamin Franklin*, 2nd ed., ed. Leonard Labaree et al. (New Haven: Yale University Press, 2003), 144–45.

10. Gary B. Nash, *Quakers and Politics: Pennsylvania, 1681–1726* (Princeton: Princeton University Press, 1968), 279–80, 325–26.

FIVE. The Crossroads of Cultures

1. J. Hector St. John de Crèvecoeur, *Letters from an American Farmer and Sketches of Eighteenth-Century America,* ed. Albert E. Stone (New York: Penguin Books, 1981; first published 1782), 69–70.

2. Michael Zuckerman, ed., *Friends and Neighbors: Group Life in America's First Plural Society* (Philadelphia: Temple University Press, 1982).

3. A somewhat different use of the term "Protestant pluralism" can be found in Richard W. Pointer, *Protestant Pluralism and the New York Experience: A Study of Eighteenth-Century Religious Diversity* (Bloomington: Indiana University Press, 1988).

4. A. G. Roeber, " 'The Origin of Whatever Is Not English among Us': The Dutch-speaking and the German-speaking Peoples of Colonial British America," in *Strangers within the Realm: Cultural Margins of the First British Empire,* ed. Bernard Bailyn and Philip D. Morgan (Chapel Hill: University of North Carolina Press, 1991), 220–83, esp. 221, 226.

5. John Murrin, "English Rights as Ethnic Aggression: The English Conquest, the charter of Liberties of 1683, and Leisler's Rebellion in New York," *Authority and Resistance in Early New York,* ed. William Pencak and Conrad Edick Wright (New York: New York Historical Society, 1988), 56–94.

6. Firth Haring Fabend, *A Dutch Family in the Middle Colonies, 1660–1800* (New Brunswick, N.J.: Rutgers University Press, 1991), 161–62.

7. David William Voorhees, "The 'Fervent Zeale' of Jacob Leisler," *William and Mary Quarterly,* 3rd ser., 51 (1994): 447–72; Adrian Howe, "The Bayard Treason Trial: Dramatizing Anglo-Dutch Politics in Early Eighteenth-Century New York City," *William and Mary Quarterly,* 3rd ser., 47 (1990): 57–89.

8. Philip Otterness, "The 1709 Palatine Migration and the Formation of German Immigrant Identity in London and New York," *Explorations in Early American Culture, Pennsylvania History* 66 (1999): 8–23.

9. Charles Lodwick, "New York in 1692," *Collections of the New York Historical Society,* 2nd ser., 2 (1849): 244, quoted in Joyce Goodfriend, *Before the Melting Pot: Society and Culture in Colonial New York City, 1664–1730* (Princeton: Princeton University Press, 1992), 3.

10. *Frame of Government* (1682), in *The Papers of William Penn,* ed. Mary Maples Dunn and Richard S. Dunn et al. (Philadelphia: University of Pennsylvania Press, 1981–), 2:212–26.

11. Patrick Griffin, *The People with No Name: Ireland's Ulster Scots, America's Scots Irish, and the Creation of a British Atlantic World, 1689–1764* (Princeton: Princeton University Press, 2001). There is also considerable evidence that "Scots-Irish" communities often contained migrants from Scotland, either because they ventured first to Ulster or because emigrant ships frequently called at both Scottish and Ulster ports.

12. The Irish "New Lights" were trained by liberal and Enlightened professors at Glasgow University. They strongly opposed the church's insistence on doctrinal conformity reflected in the requirement that ministers formally subscribe to the Westminster Confession of Faith. They were a very different group from those called New Lights in New England, who

emerged in the aftermath of the Great Awakening and who will appear in the next chapter.

13. *A Declaration and Remonstrance of the Distressed and Bleeding Frontier Inhabitants of the Province of Pennsylvania* (Philadelphia, 1764), in *The Paxton Papers*, ed. John R. Dunbar (The Hague: Martinus Nijhoff, 1957), 99–110.

14. Howard Miller, "Evangelical Religion and Colonial Princeton," *Schooling and Society*, ed. Lawrence Stone (Baltimore: Johns Hopkins University Press, 1976), 115–45.

15. The best source is *The Independent Reflector, or Weekly Essays on Sundry Important Subjects More particularly adapted to the Province of New-York By William Livingston and Others*, ed. Milton M. Klein (Cambridge Mass., 1963; first published 1754).

16. Thomas Bradbury Chandler, *An Appeal to the Public, in Behalf of the Church of England in America* (New York, 1767).

17. Benjamin Franklin, "Observations Concerning the Increase of Mankind," in *The Papers of Benjamin Franklin,* ed. Leonard W. Labaree et al. (New Haven: Yale University Press, 1961), 4:225–34.

18. Crèvecoeur, *Letters from an American Farmer,* 74–75.

19. Ibid., 68, 75–76.

six. The Crossroads of
Philosophy and Faith

1. Franklin's "Memoirs," which were only subsequently given the name of an autobiography, were written in four installments between 1771 and 1788.

2. Nina Reid-Maroney, *Philadelphia's Enlightenment, 1740–1800: Kingdom of Christ, Empire of Reason* (Westport, Conn.: Greenwood Press, 2001), chap. 2.

3. The term "latitude-men," or Latitudinarian, was originally applied to English ministers during the Restoration era who favored restoring the Anglican Church on broad rather than narrow terms, thereby drawing many former dissenters into the religious establishment.

4. Published in Philadelphia by William Bradford, 1757–1758.

5. Anne H. Wharton, *Salons Colonial and Republican* (Philadelphia: J. B. Lippincott, 1900), 13, quoted in Anne M. Ousterhout, *The Most Learned Woman in America: A Life of Elizabeth Graeme Fergusson* (University Park: Penn State University Press, 2004), xiii.

6. *Milcah Martha Moore's Book: A Commonplace Book from Revolutionary America*, ed. Catherine La Courreye Blecki and Karin A. Wulf (University Park: Penn State University Press, 1997).

7. *The Autobiography of Benjamin Franklin*, ed. Leonard W. Labaree et al., 2nd ed. (New Haven: Yale University Press, 2003), 116–18.

8. Ibid., 150–51.

9. Sara S. Gronim, *Everyday Nature: Knowledge of the Natural World*

in Colonial New York (New Brunswick, N.J.: Rutgers University Press, 2007), 111.

10. *The Journal of Esther Edwards Burr, 1754–1757,* ed. Carol F. Karlsen and Laurie Crumpacker (New Haven: Yale University Press, 1984), 123.

11. Annis Boudinot Stockton to Julia Stockton Rush, 8 April (no year listed), Benjamin Rush Papers, Rosenbach Museum and Library, quoted in *Only for the Eye of a Friend: The Poems of Annis Boudinot Stockton,* ed. Carla Mulford (Charlottesville: University of Virginia Press, 1995), 18.

12. Frank Lambert, "Subscribing for Profits and Piety: The Friendship of Benjamin Franklin and George Whitefield," *William and Mary Quarterly*, 3rd ser., 50 (1993): 529–54.

13. Alison to Ezra Stiles, 24 March 1762, quoted in Reid-Maroney, *Philadelphia's Enlightenment,* 62.

14. Reid-Maroney, *Philadelphia's Enlightenment,* 65.

15. *The Diary of Mary Cooper: Life on a Long Island Farm, 1768–1773* (Oyster Bay: Oyster Bay Historical Society, 1981).

16. John Blair, *The New Creature Delineated. In a Sermon, Delivered in Philadelphia, February 26, 1767* (Philadelphia, 1767), esp. 22–23, 29–30; Blair, *Essays on the Nature, Uses and Subjects of the Sacrament of the New Testament. II. On Regeneration, wherein the Principle of spiritual Life thereby implanted; is particularly considered . . .* (New York, 1771).

17. *Journal of Esther Burr,* 98, 102.

18. "To my Burrissa, 11 April, 1757," in Mulford, *Only for the Eye of a Friend,* 78–79.

19. *Journal of Esther Burr,* 63.

20. Ibid., 257.

21. Ibid., 183.

SEVEN. Politics at the Crossroads

Epigraph quoted in Gary B. Nash, *Quakers and Politics: Pennsylvania, 1681–1726* (Princeton: Princeton University Press, 1968), 49.

1. *The Federalist Papers*, ed. Isaac Kramnick (New York: Penguin, 1987), #10.

2. The essential account remains James Alexander's *A Brief Narrative of the Case and Trial of John Peter Zenger Printer of the New York Weekly Journal* (New York, 1736), ed. Stanley Nider Katz (Cambridge, Mass.: Belknap Press, 1963).

3. They are available in a good modern edition as *Cato's Letters: Or, Essays on Liberty, Civil and Religious, And Other Important Subjects*, ed. Ronald Hamowy, 2 vols. (Indianapolis: Liberty Fund, 1995). On the use of *Cato's Letters* in colonial political disputes, see Heather Elizabeth Barry, "'So Many American Cato's': John Trenchard and Thomas Gordon in Eighteenth-Century British America" (Ph.D. diss., State University of New York at Stony Brook, 2002), esp. chap. 4, and appendix 3.

4. Alan Tully, *Forming American Politics: Ideals, Interests, and Institutions in Colonial New York and Pennsylvania* (Baltimore: Johns Hopkins University Press, 1994), chap. 7.

5. *Journal of Esther Edwards Burr, 1754–1757*, ed. Carol F. Karlsen and Laurie Crumpacker (New Haven: Yale University Press, 1984), 162–63.

6. *The Autobiography of Benjamin Franklin*, ed. Leonard W. Labaree et al., 2nd ed. (New Haven: Yale University Press, 2003), 209–10.

7. *The Independent Reflector: Or Weekly Essays on Sundry Important Subjects More Particularly Adapted to the Province of New-York*, ed. Milton M. Klein (Cambridge, Mass.: Belknap Press, 1963).

8. William Livingston, *A Letter to the Right Reverend Father in God, John, Lord Bishop of Llandaff . . .* (New York, 1768).

9. Thomas Bradbury Chandler, *An Appeal to the Public in Behalf of the Church of England in America* (New York, 1767).

10. Depictions of the Paxton Boys and their opponents can be found in *The Paxton Papers*, ed. John R. Dunbar (The Hague: Martinus Nijhoff, 1957). Franklin's main contribution was *A Narrative of the Late Massacres, in Lancaster County, of a Number of Indians, Friends of This Province*, 55–75.

EPILOGUE. Empire and Revolution

1. William Smith, *Discourses on Several Public Occasions During the War in America* (London: A. Millar, 1759); Samuel Davies, *A Sermon Delivered at Nassau-hall, January 14, 1761: On the Death of His Late Majesty King George II* (New York, 1761).

2. Andrew Burnaby, *Travel Through the Middle Settlements in North-America*, 2nd ed. (London, 1775), 110; George Berkeley, *Verses On the Prospect of Planting Arts and Learning in America*, in *A Miscellany, containing Several Tracts on Various Subjects*. (Dublin: G. Faulkner, 1752), 55–84.

Essay on Sources

There has been no full-length treatment of the Middle Colonies since Thomas Jefferson Wertenbaker's *The Founding of American Civilization: The Middle Colonies* (New York: Charles Scribner's Sons, 1938). Shorter treatments include the chapter on the region by John J. McCusker and Russel R. Menard in *The Economy of British America, 1607–1789* (Chapel Hill: University of North Carolina Press, 1985) and my own chapter in *The Oxford History of the British Empire*, vol. 1, *The Origins of Empire*, ed. Nicholas P. Canny (Oxford: Oxford University Press, 1998). A forthcoming work by Wayne Bodle was not yet available when this book was completed.

The individual colonies of the region have been better served. Each colony was treated in the History of the American Colonies series: John E. Pomfret, *Colonial New Jersey: A History* (New York: Charles Scribner's Sons, 1973); Michael Kammen, *Colonial New York: A History* (White Plains, N.Y.: KTO Press, 1975); Joseph E. Illick, *Colonial Pennsylvania: A History* (New York: Charles Scribner's Sons, 1976); and John A. Munroe, *Colonial Delaware: A History* (Millwood, N.Y.: KTO Press, 1978), and all have received substantial treatment in other works. A good regional study of the mid-Atlantic backcountry is Peter C. Mancall, *Valley of Opportunity: Economic Culture along the Upper Susquehanna, 1700–1800* (Ithaca, N.Y.: Cornell University Press, 1991).

PROLOGUE. Region and History

The use of a regional approach to explore British colonial America has been a popular trend in recent years; major syntheses that have employed a regional focus include Jack P. Greene, *Pursuits of Happiness: The Social Development of Early Modern British Colonies and the Formation of American Culture* (Chapel Hill: University of North Carolina Press, 1988) and David Hackett

Fischer, *Albion's Seed: Four British Folkways in America* (New York: Oxford University Press, 1989). See also the several regional essays in *The Origins of Empire,* ed. Nicholas Canny. Michael Zuckerman has a general discussion of regionalism in *A Companion to Colonial America,* ed. Daniel Vickers (Oxford: Blackwell Publishers, 2003), 311–33.

On the problem of viewing the Middle Colonies as a region, see Robert J. Gough, "The Myth of the 'Middle Colonies': An Analysis of Regionalization in Early America," *Pennsylvania Magazine of History and Biography* 103 (1983): 392–439, and Wayne Bodle, "The 'Myth of the Middle Colonies' Reconsidered: The Process of Regionalization in Early America," in ibid., 113 (1989), 527–48. On the Middle Colonies as precursor to American society, see especially Michael Zuckerman, "Puritans, Cavaliers, and the Motley Middle," in *Friends and Neighbors: Group Life in America's First Plural Society,* ed. Michael Zuckerman (Philadelphia: Temple University Press, 1982), 3–25.

Two major approaches to the study of early America that have become popular in recent years are Atlantic history and continental history. The first, focusing on the development from the early modern period onward of an interconnected world of commerce and communications, is outlined by Bernard Bailyn in *Atlantic History: Concept and Contours* (Cambridge: Harvard University Press, 2005). Also useful for early Americanists is *The British Atlantic World, 1500–1800,* ed. David Armitage and Michael J. Braddick (New York: Palgrave Macmillan, 2002). A work that demonstrates substantial Atlantic connections between the early Middle Colonies and Virginia is April Lee Hatfield, *Atlantic Virginia: Intercolonial Relations in the Seventeenth Century* (Philadelphia: University of Pennsylvania Press, 2004).

Continental history, by contrast, considers early American settlements within the larger world of empires and peoples across the American continent. An influential conceptual study in that field is Richard White, *The Middle Ground: Indians, Empires, and Republics in the Great Lakes Region, 1650–1815* (New York: Cambridge University Press, 1991), which looks at the area just beyond bounds of the Middle Colonies. A major work with much attention to the Middle Colonies is Daniel K. Richter, *Facing East from Indian Country: A Native History of Early America* (Cambridge: Harvard University Press, 2001).

ONE. The Origins of the Middle Colonies

The native peoples of the region have been the subject of considerable attention of late. Especially useful is Daniel K. Richter, *The Ordeal of the Longhouse: The Peoples of the Iroquois League in the Era of European Colonization* (Chapel Hill: University of North Carolina Press, 1992). A newer work is Amy C. Schutt, *Peoples of the River Valleys: The Odyssey of the Delaware Indians* (Philadelphia: University of Pennsylvania Press, 2007).

Dutch New Netherland is surveyed in Oliver A. Rink, *Holland on the*

Hudson: An Economic and Social History of Dutch New York (Ithaca, N.Y.: Cornell University Press, 1986) and Jaap Jacobs, *New Netherland: A Dutch Colony in the Seventeenth Century* (Leiden: Brill, 2005). An examination of Dutch commercial patterns is Donna Merwick, *Possessing Albany, 1630–1710: The Dutch and English Experiences* (New York: Cambridge University Press, 1990). The same author treats Dutch-Indian relations in *The Shame and the Sorrow: Dutch-Amerindian Encounters in New Netherland* (Philadelphia: University of Pennsylvania Press, 2006), which is no compliment to the Dutch. A popular history is Russell Shorto, *The Island at the Center of the World: The Epic Story of Dutch Manhattan and the Forgotten Colony That Shaped America* (New York: Random House, 2004). On the Dutch Golden Age, see Jonathan I. Israel, *The Dutch Republic: Its Rise, Greatness, and Fall, 1477–1806* (Oxford: Clarendon Press, 1995).

TWO. The Duke's Dominions

A look at James Stuart can begin with the volume by John Miller in the English monarchs series, *James II* (New Haven: Yale University Press, 2000). For background on the Restoration, see Gary De Krey, *Restoration and Revolution in Britain: A Political History of the Era of Charles II and the Glorious Revolution* (Palgrave Macmillan: London, 2007) and N. H. Keeble, *The Restoration: England in the 1660s* (Blackwell Publishing: Oxford, 2002). An important new work is Steven Pincus, *1688: The First Modern Revolution* (New Haven: Yale University Press, 2009).

On James's colony, see Robert C. Ritchie, *The Duke's Province: A Study of New York Politics and Society, 1664–1691* (Chapel Hill: University of North Carolina Press, 1977); also John M. Murrin, "English Rights as Ethnic Aggression: The English Conquest, the Charter of Liberties of 1683, and Leisler's Rebellion in New York," in *Authority and Resistance in Early New York,* ed. William Pencak and Conrad Edick Wright (New York: New York Historical Society, 1988), 56–104. Joyce D. Goodfriend, *Before the Melting Pot: Society and Culture in Colonial New York City, 1664–1730* (Princeton: Princeton University Press, 1992) surveys life in that conquered city. The East Jersey venture is explored in Ned C. Landsman, *Scotland and Its First American Colony, 1683–1765* (Princeton: Princeton University Press, 1985).

For an effective argument about the broadening of toleration under James, see Haefeli, "The Creation of American Religious Pluralism: Churches, Colonialism, and Conquest in the Mid-Atlantic, 1628–1688" (Ph.D. diss., Princeton University, 2000). On Governor Andros, see Mary Lou Lustig, *The Imperial Executive in America: Sir Edmund Andros, 1637–1714* (Madison, N.J.: Fairleigh Dickinson University Press, 2002). Jacob Leisler's world is covered in David William Voorhees, "The 'fervent Zeale' of Jacob Leisler," *William and Mary Quarterly,* 3rd ser., 51 (1994): 447–72. Leisler's antagonist, Robert Livingston, is the subject of Lawrence H. Leder, *Robert Livingston, 1654–1728, and the Politics of Colonial New York* (Chapel Hill: University of North Carolina Press, 1961). The aftermath of Leisler's rebellion is discussed in Adrian Howe, "The Bayard Treason Trial: Dramatizing Anglo-Dutch Politics in Early Eighteenth-Century New York City," *William and Mary Quarterly,* 3rd ser., 47 (1990): 57–89; and Randall H. Balmer, *A Perfect Babel of Confusion: Dutch Religion and English Culture in the Middle Colonies* (New York: Oxford University Press, 1989). One of the subsequent governors, the notorious Lord Cornbury, is vigorously defended from charges both of corruption and cross-dressing, and the use of scandal in the politics of the period is analyzed by Patricia U. Bonomi, *The Lord Cornbury Scandal: The Politics of Reputation in British America* (Chapel Hill: University of North Carolina Press, 1998).

On the Covenant Chain, see Francis Jennings, *The Ambiguous Iroquois Empire: The Covenant Chain Confederation of Indian Tribes with English Colonies from Its Beginnings to the Lancaster Treaty of 1744* (New York: W. W. Norton, 1984), Stephen Saunders Webb, *1676: The End of American Independence* (New York: Knopf, 1984), and Daniel K. Richter and James H. Merrell, *Beyond the Covenant Chain: The Iroquois and Their Neighbors in Indian North America, 1600–1800* (Syracuse, N.Y.: Syracuse University Press, 1987).

THREE. Penn's Proprietary

A good short treatment of the life of William Penn is Mary K. Geiter, *William Penn* (Pearson: Essex, 2000). Also essential are *The Papers of William Penn,* ed. Mary Maples Dunn and Richard S. Dunn, 5 vols. (Philadelphia: University of Pennsylvania Press, 1982–1987). Gary B. Nash, *Quakers and Politics: Pennsylvania, 1681–1726* (Princeton: Princeton University Press, 1968) remains important on the colony's early years. Richard T. Vann, "Quakerism: Made in America?" in *The World of William Penn,* ed. Richard S. Dunn and Mary Maples Dunn (Philadelphia: University of Pennsylvania Press, 1986), 157–70, questions the proportion of early settlers who were in fact Quakers. On Quaker childrearing, see Barry Levy, *Quakers and the American Family: British Settlement in the Delaware Valley* (New York: Oxford University Press, 1988). See the works on individual topics below.

FOUR. The Commercial Crossroads
of the British Atlantic

Among the best accounts of economic life in early Philadelphia is *The Autobiography of Benjamin Franklin,* 2nd ed., ed. Leonard Labaree et al. (New Haven: Yale University Press, 2003). Quaker trading is the subject of Frederick B. Tolles, *Meeting House and Counting House: The Quaker Merchants of Colonial Philadelphia, 1682–1763* (Chapel Hill: University of North Carolina Press, 1948). Also see Thomas M. Doerflinger, *A Vigorous Spirit of Enterprise: Merchants and Economic Development in Revolutionary Philadelphia* (Chapel Hill: University of North Carolina Press, 1986). New York merchants are well covered in Cathy Matson, *Merchants and Empire: Trading in Colonial New*

York (Baltimore: Johns Hopkins University Press, 2002); see also Simon Middleton, *From Privileges to Rights: Work and Politics in Colonial New York City* (Philadelphia: University of Pennsylvania Press, 2006).

A special issue of *Early American Studies* (Fall 2006) devoted to "Women's Economies in North America before 1820," was edited by Cathy Matson; see also Joan M. Jensen, *Loosening the Bonds: Mid-Atlantic Farm Women, 1750–1850* (New Haven: Yale University Press, 1986). Adrienne D. Hood, *The Weaver's Craft: Cloth, Commerce, and Industry in Early Pennsylvania* (Philadelphia: University of Pennsylvania Press, 2003) explores weaving in the region. The lower classes are the subject of Billy G. Smith, *The "Lower Sort": Philadelphia's Laboring People, 1750–1800* (Ithaca, N.Y.: Cornell University Press, 1990). See *The Infortunate: The Voyage and Adventures of William Moraley, an Indentured Servant,* ed. Susan E. Klepp and Billy G. Smith (University Park: Penn State University Press, 1992), for the life story of one whose career was far less successful than Franklin's.

German and Irish migration are discussed in Marianne S. Woceck, *Trade in Strangers: The Beginnings of Mass Migration to North America* (University Park: Penn State University Press, 1999); see also Aaron Spencer Fogelman, *Hopeful Journeys: German Immigration, Settlement, and Political Culture in Colonial America, 1717–1775* (Philadelphia: University of Pennsylvania Press, 1996). Rosalind J. Beiler, *Immigrant and Entrepreneur: The Atlantic World of Caspar Wistar, 1650–1750* (University Park: Penn State University Press, 2008) is one among a number of excellent newer works. The principal primary account is Gottlieb Mittelberger, *Journey to Pennsylvania,* ed. Oscar Handlin and John Clive (Cambridge, Mass.: Belknap Press, 1960; first published, 1756). See also *Souls for Sale: Two German Redemptioners come to Revolutionary America,* ed. Susan E. Klepp, Farley Grubb, and Anne Pfaelzer De Ortiz (University Park: Penn State University Press, 2006). The backcountry economy is explored in Mancall, *Valley of Opportunity.*

The dramatic growth in consumption in the eighteenth century is the subject of T. H. Breen, *The Marketplace of Revolution: How Consumer Politics Shaped American Independence* (New York: Oxford University Press, 2004); see also Carole Shammas, *The Pre-industrial Consumer in England and America* (New York: Oxford University Press, 1990). A work that highlights the early commercial history of Easthampton and more is T. H. Breen, *Imagining the Past: East Hampton Histories* (Reading, Mass.: Addison-Wesley, 1989). Bernard Bailyn discusses the two migration streams to North America, especially in the aftermath of the Seven Years' War, in *Voyagers to the West: A Passage in the Peopling of America on the Eve of the Revolution* (New York: Knopf, 1986). Migration to the region in general is covered in Ned C. Landsman, "Migration and Settlement," in *Blackwell Companion to Colonial American History,* ed. Daniel Vickers (Oxford: Blackwell, 2003), 76–98.

Mixed settlements on the frontiers are considered in James Hart Merrell, *Into the American Woods: Negotiators on the Pennsylvania Frontier* (New

York: W. W. Norton, 1999), and Jane T. Merritt, *At the Crossroads: Indians and Empires on a Mid-Atlantic Frontier, 1700–1763* (Chapel Hill: University of North Carolina Press, 2003). The experience of African Americans in the northern colonies is discussed in Ira Berlin, *Many Thousands Gone: The First Two Centuries of Slavery in America* (Cambridge: Harvard University Press, 1998). New York's African and African American community is the subject of Graham Russell Hodges, *Root and Branch: African Americans in New York and East Jersey, 1613–1863* (Chapel Hill: University of North Carolina Press, 1999). See also Gary B. Nash, *Forging Freedom: The Formation of Philadelphia's Black Community, 1720–1840* (Cambridge: Harvard University Press, 1991).

FIVE. The Crossroads of Cultures

While the diversity of the Middle Colony population has often been cited, there have been few comprehensive studies. Among those, see Sally Schwartz, *"A Mixed Multitude": The Struggle for Toleration in Colonial Pennsylvania* (New York: New York University Press, 1987). See also Richard W. Pointer, *Protestant Pluralism and the New York Experience: A Study of Eighteenth-Century Religious Diversity* (Bloomington: Indiana University Press, 1988).

The subject of toleration has been better served. See Thomas J. Curry, *The First Freedoms: Church and State in America to the Passage of the First Amendment* (New York: Oxford University Press, 1986); Andrew R. Murphy *Conscience and Community: Revisiting Toleration and Religious Dissent in Early Modern England and America* (University Park: Penn State University Press, 2001); Chris Beneke, *Beyond Toleration: The Religious Origins of American Pluralism* (New York: Oxford University Press, 2006); and especially the survey by Evan Haefeli, "Toleration and Empire," in a forthcoming volume of the *Oxford History of the British Empire*. The situation in Pennsylvania is the subject of J. William Frost, *A Perfect Freedom: Religious Liberty in Pennsylvania* (New York: Cambridge University Press, 1990). I have discussed the relationship of toleration and tolerance in "Roots, Routes, and Rootedness: Diversity, Migration, and Toleration in mid-Atlantic Pluralism, *Early American Studies* 2 (2004): 267–309.

One group that has received substantial attention recently is the community of German-speakers. On religion, politics, and property among them, see A. Gregg Roeber, *Palatines, Liberty, and Property: Germans Lutherans in Colonial British America* (Baltimore: Johns Hopkins University Press, 1993); Philip Otterness, *Becoming German: The 1709 Palatine Migration to New York* (Ithaca, N.Y.: Cornell University Press, 2004); and Mark Haberlein, *The Practice of Pluralism: Congregational Life and Religious Diversity in Lancaster, Pennsylvania, 1730–1820* (University Park: Penn State University Press, 2009) as well as the works cited for chapter 4. Patrick Griffin, *The People with No Name: Ireland's Ulster Scots, America's Scots Irish, and the Creation of a British Atlantic World, 1689–1764* (Princeton: Princeton University Press, 2001), looks at a people who in fact had many names. New York's African and African American community is the subject of Graham Russell Hodges, *Root and Branch: African Americans in New York and East Jersey, 1613–1863*.

The best source on the King's College controversy is the *Independent Reflector Or Weekly Essays on Sundry Important Subjects More particularly adapted to the Province of New-York By William Livingston and Others,* ed. Milton M. Klein (Cambridge: Harvard University Press, 1963; first published 1754). The long argument over episcopacy is covered most passionately, if not always most reliably, in Carl Bridenbaugh, *Mitre and Sceptre: Transatlantic Faiths, Ideas, Personalities, and Politics, 1689–1775* (New York: Oxford University Press, 1962). There is, finally, no substitute for reading Crèvecoeur's *Letters from an American Farmer and Sketches of Eighteenth-Century America,* ed. Albert E. Stone (New York: Penguin Books, 1981; first published 1782), 69–70.

six. The Crossroads of
Philosophy and Faith

There are many excellent works on Franklin, beginning with *The Autobiography of Benjamin Franklin.* Among the rest, see Edmund S. Morgan, *Benjamin Franklin* (New Haven: Yale University Press, 2002). Franklin's science is explored in Joyce E. Chaplin, *The First Scientific American: Benjamin Franklin and the Pursuit of Genius* (New York: Basic Books, 2006). On science and enlightenment, see Nina Reid-Maroney, *Philadelphia's Enlightenment, 1740–1800: Kingdom of Christ, Empire of Reason* (Westport, Conn.: Greenwood Press, 2001). Science in New York is well covered in Sara S. Gronim, *Everyday Nature: Knowledge of the Natural World in Colonial New York* (New Brunswick, N.J.: Rutgers University Press, 2007); especially important is her chapter on the female biologist Jane Colden. Cadwallader Colden is the subject of a forthcoming work by John Dixon, to be published by Cornell University Press.

The works of other women writers can be pursued in Ann M. Ousterhout, *The Most Learned Woman in America: A Life of Elizabeth Graeme Fergusson* (University Park: Penn State University Press, 2004) and *Only for the Eye of a Friend: The Poems of Annis Boudinot Stockton,* ed. Carla Mulford (Charlottesville: University of Virginia Press, 1995). See also *The Journal of Esther Edwards Burr, 1754–1757,* ed. Carol F. Karlsen and Laurie Crumpacker (New Haven: Yale University Press, 1984) and Susan M. Stabile, *Memory's Daughters: The Material Culture of Remembrance in Eighteenth-Century America* (Ithaca, N.Y.: Cornell University Press, 2003). On the rural enlightenment, see John Fea, *The Way of Improvement Leads Home: Philip Vickers Fithian and the Rural Enlightenment in Early America* (Philadelphia: University of Pennsylvania Press, 2008).

Quaker antislavery is the subject of Jean R. Soderlund, *Quakers and Slavery: A Divided Spirit* (Princeton: Princeton University Press, 1985). For the convoluted history of abolition in Pennsylvania, see Gary B. Nash and Jean R. Soderlund, *Freedom by Degrees: Emancipation in Pennsylvania and Its Aftermath* (New York: Oxford University Press, 1991). On the proliferation of academies and the creation of an "evangelical educational empire," see Howard Miller, *The Revolutionary College: American Presbyterian Higher Education, 1707–1837* (New York: New York University Press, 1976). The relationship of religion to enlightenment is discussed in Ned C. Landsman, *From Colonials to Provincials: American Thought and Culture, 1680–1760* (New York: Twayne Publishers, 1997).

There has been no full-length study of the Great Awakening in the Middle Colonies published in close to a century, but the region is better covered in general works than it used to be, including in two general studies, Thomas S. Kidd, *The Great Awakening: The Roots of Evangelical Christianity in Colonial America* (New Haven: Yale University Press, 2007) and Frank Lambert, *Inventing the Great Awakening* (Princeton: Princeton University Press, 1999). There is good material on the event and its ramifications in Marilyn J. Westerkamp, *Triumph of the Laity: Scots-Irish Piety and the Great Awakening, 1625–1760* (New York: Oxford University Press, 1988); Leigh Eric Schmidt, *Holy Fairs: Scottish Communions and American Revivals in the Early Modern Period* (Princeton: Princeton University Press, 1989); Reid-Maroney, *Philadelphia's Enlightenment*; and John F. Frantz, "The Awakening of Religion among the German Settlers in the Middle Colonies," *William and Mary Quarterly* 22 (1976): 266–88; see also Aaron Spencer Fogelman, *Jesus Is Female: Moravians and Radical Religion in Early America* (Philadelphia: University of Pennsylvania Press, 2007). On the role of religion and the "Indian Great Awakening" in Pontiac's Rebellion, see Gregory Evans Dowd, *A Spirited Resistance: The North American Indian Struggle for Unity, 1745–1815* (Baltimore: Johns Hopkins University Press, 1992).

SEVEN. Politics at the Crossroads

Carl Becker's classic *History of Political Parties in the Province of New York, 1760–1776*, 2nd ed. (Madison: University of Wisconsin Press, 1960) is the starting point for regional politics. The politics of both New York and Pennsylvania are covered in Alan Tully, *Forming American Politics: Ideals, Interests, and Institutions in Colonial New York and Pennsylvania* (Baltimore: Johns Hopkins University Press, 1994). Also see John M. Murrin, "Political Development," in *Colonial British America: Essays in the New History of the Early Modern Era,* ed. Jack P. Greene and J. R. Pole (Baltimore: Johns Hopkins University Press, 1984) as well as Patricia U. Bonomi, *A Factious People: Politics and Society in Colonial New York* (New York: Columbia University Press, 1971) and Gary B. Nash, *Quakers and Politics*. New Jersey politics is the subject of Thomas L. Purvis, *Proprietors, Patronage and Paper Money: Legislative Politics in New Jersey, 1703–1776* (New Brunswick, N.J.: Rutgers University Press, 1986). On royal politics and respect for the king, see

Brendan McConville, *The King's Three Faces: The Rise and Fall of Royal America, 1688–1776* (Chapel Hill: University of North Carolina Press, 2006). An important discussion of the concept of deference in early America, edited by Billy G. Smith and Simon Middleton, is in a special issue of *Early American Studies* 3 (2005); see also Richard R. Beeman, *The Varieties of Political Experience in Eighteenth-Century America* (Philadelphia: University of Pennsylvania Press, 2004).

A very effective discussion of the Zenger trial and the concept of the public, among other things, is Michael Warner, *The Letters of the Republic: Publication and the Public Sphere in Eighteenth-Century America* (Cambridge: Harvard University Press, 1990), chapter 2. On the "Real Whigs" Trenchard and Gordon, see especially Bernard Bailyn, *Ideological Origins of the American Revolution* (Cambridge: Harvard University Press, 1967), followed by many other works. The political dimension of the slave conspiracy trials is discussed in Jill Lepore, *New York Burning: Liberty, Slavery, and Conspiracy in Eighteenth-Century Manhattan* (New York: Alfred A. Knopf, 2005).

Land riots are subjects of Brendan McConville, *Those Daring Disturbers of the Public Peace: The Struggle for Property and Power in Early New Jersey* (Philadelphia: University of Pennsylvania Press, 1999); and Thomas J. Humphrey, *Land and Liberty: Hudson Valley Riots in the Age of Revolution* (DeKalb: Northern Illinois University Press, 2004).

The most comprehensive discussion of the Seven Years' War in America is now Fred Anderson, *Crucible of War: The Seven Years' War and the Fate of Empire in British North America, 1754–1766* (New York: Alfred A. Knopf, 2000), which devotes considerable attention to its western Pennsylvania beginnings. The Albany conference is the subject of Timothy J. Shannon, *Indians and Colonists at the Crossroads of Empire: The Albany Conference of 1754* (Ithaca, N.Y.: Cornell University Press, 1992). Gregory Evans Dowd, *War under Heaven: Pontiac, Indian Nations, and the British Empire* (Baltimore: Johns Hopkins University Press, 2004) and Richter, *Facing East from Indian Country*, look at the changing political situation that confronted native peoples in the region. The Episcopate Controversy and Anglican imperial efforts are the subjects of Carl Bridenbaugh's rather one-sided, *Mitre and Sceptre: Transatlantic Faiths, Ideas, Personalities, and Politics, 1689–1775* (New York: Oxford University Press, 1962). Patricia U. Bonomi, *Under the Cope of Heaven: Religion, Society, and Politics in Colonial America* (New York: Oxford University Press, 1986) is another strong treatment of the relationship of religion and politics.

EPILOGUE. Empire and Revolution

Edmund Sears Morgan, *The Birth of the Republic, 1763–1789*, new edition (Chicago: University of Chicago Press, 1993) remains a useful summary of the political events that followed the conclusion of the Seven Years' War. The Middle Colonies are well treated in Edward Countryman, *A People in*

Revolution: The American Revolution and Political Society in New York, 1760–1790 (Baltimore: Johns Hopkins University Press, 1973); and Gary B. Nash, *Urban Crucible: The Northern Seaports and the Origins of the American Revolution* (Cambridge: Harvard University Press, 1986). See also Judith L. Van Buskirk, *Generous Enemies: Patriots and Loyalists in Revolutionary New York* (Philadelphia: University of Pennsylvania Press, 2002) and *Beyond Philadelphia: The American Revolution in the Pennsylvania Hinterland,* ed. John B. Frantz and William Pencak (University Park: Penn State University Press, 1998). Timothy H. Breen's *Marketplace of Revolution* considers the influence of a rapidly expanding commercial culture on the events leading up to Revolution.

Migration and westward expansion before the Revolution are discussed in Bernard Bailyn, *Voyagers to the West: A Passage in the Peopling of America on the Eve of the Revolution* (New York: Knopf, 1988); its effect on Native Americans in the region appears in Dowd, *A Spirited Resistance*. The lack of an established identity for Americans who suddenly found themselves together in a new nation is the theme of John M. Murrin, "A Roof Without Walls: The Dilemma of American National Identity," in *Beyond Confederation: The Origins of the Constitution and American National Identity,* ed. Richard Beeman, Stephen Botein, and Edward C. Carter II (Chapel Hill: University of North Carolina Press, 1987), 333–48. Interesting treatments of the process of creating new political identities include David Waldstreicher, *In the Midst of Perpetual Fetes: The Making of American Nationalism, 1776–1820* (Chapel Hill: University of North Carolina Press, 1997) and Simon P. Newman, *Parades and the Politics of the Street: Festive Culture in the Early American Republic* (Philadelphia: University of Pennsylvania Press, 1997), both of which devote substantial attention to Philadelphia and the mid-Atlantic. A new work that connects frontier violence to politics and to the emergence of racial identities is Peter Silver, *Our Savage Neighbors: How Indian Wars Transformed Early America* (New York: W. W. Norton, 2007).

Index

Defoe, Daniel, 160
deism, 159
DeLancey, James, 186, 189; and De-
Lancey faction, 192–200
Delaware: lower counties of, 55, 67,
93; as Middle Colony, 9, 215n;
wheat growing and, 109;
Wilmington, 93
Delaware County, 90
Delaware Indians, 9, 13–14, 101,
134; and "walking purchase," 71–
72
Delaware River, 10, 12, 77; Dutch
along, 23, 28; Philadelphia lands
on, 64, 92; and Swedes, 27
Dickinson, John, 212
Disease, among Indian populations,
18–19
diversity, 111–43; on Long Island,
20; of native peoples, 18–19; of
Netherlands, 22, 114; of New
Netherland, 20, 22, 113–16; of
New Sweden, 20; of Pennsylvania,
126–34
Dominion of New England, 47–49
Donegal (Pa.), 129
Dongan, Thomas, 49
doubt, principle of, 146
Drummond, James, 46, 52
Drummond, John, 46, 52
Dubois, Isaac, 160
Duke's Laws, 36
Dutch Reformed Church, 114–16,
138; Dutch college, 178, and
Pinkster, 121; revival within, 163–
64, 167–68; women's roles in, 119,
121
Dutch Revolt, 114
Dutch settlers, 22–26; commercial
style of, 87–88; inheritance
among, 87–88; and language, 118;
and Leisler, 50, 51; women's roles
among, 88–89
Dutch West India Company, 21–22,
80–84, 114–15

Easthampton, 85, 120
East New Jersey, 44–47; conflicts in,
52–53, 68; and Great Awakening,
165–66; manors of, 87, 98–99,
105; and surrender to crown, 53
Easton Conference, 196, 210
economy, 76–110; household, 93–
96; Long Island, 84–86; New
Netherland, 80–84; Pennsylvania,
89–101; Quakers and, 90–92;
women and, 93–96
Edict of Nantes, 34, 49, 119, 123
Edinburgh, 165
education, 178–81; in academies,
178–79; Presbyterian, 132–33;
and Scottish universities, 130,
164–65
Edwards, Jonathan, 162
Elizabethtown, 44, 45, 78, 135, 138;
land riots in, 203
Enlightenment, 145–50; Dutch,
160–61; evangelical, 172–77; New
York, 160–62; and order, 212; and
progress of knowledge, 158, 175;
Quakers and, 147–50; and radicalism, 160; and religion, 159; Scottish, 150–52; tradesmen's, 157–60;
women and, 155–57, 162
Esopus, 23
Essay on Projectors (Defoe), 160
Essays to Do Good (Mather), 160
Establishments, religious, 126
evangelicals, 163–77; Enlightenment
and, 172–77; and nature of conversion, 172–73. *See also* Great
Awakening
Ewing, John, 175
exploration of Middle Colonies, 8–9,
19

faction, 182–93, 211; Delanceys,
192–200; Morrisites, 188–89;
New York, 185–89; Presbyterian,
202; proprietary, 189–92, 206–7
Fairfield County (Conn.), 109–10

families: Dutch, 88, 119; Iroquois, 15–16; linear, 85; and marriage, 119; Quaker, 65–66; Scots and Irish, 99; and tribalism, 85–86, 119, 120

Fenwick, John, 40, 45

Fenwick's Colony, 45, 60

Fergusson, Elizabeth Graeme, 155–57, 176

Finns, 27

first purchasers (of Pennsylvania), 64, 68

Fithian, Philip Vickers, 176

Five Nations, 9, 14–19, 133–34; alliance with Dutch, 25; and covenant chain, 41–44; diplomacy of, 198; and "Grand Settlement," 53–54; Hiawatha legend among, 14; Iroquois League, 14–17; and longhouses, 15–16; treaty-making among, 42–43; and "walking purchase," 71–72; women of, 15–16

Fletcher, Benjamin, 51, 201

Forks of the Delaware, 102–3, 171

forts: Casimir, 27; Christina, 27, 81; Duquesne, 195–96; Nassau, 81; Orange, 18, 21, 23, 81; Oswego, 196; Stanwix, 210; Ticonderoga, 196; William, 196

Fox, George, 58, 69, 147

Frame of Government of the Province Pennsylvania in America, 62–64, 126; rejection of, 67–68; third *Frame of Government,* 73, 191

France: exploration of mid-Atlantic by, 19; and fur trade, 25; trading posts of, 17–18; wars with, 194–98

Franklin, Benjamin, 92–93, 103; and Albany plan, 197; and American Enlightenment, 145, 157–60; and American Philosophical Society, 153; *Autobiography,* 92–93, 103, 145, 157; Essay on Population, 141; *General Magazine,* 155; and

movement for royal governor, 192; and Paxton rioters, 130–31, 141; and slavery, 178; and William Smith, 152; and George Whitefield, 166–67, 176–77

Freehold (N.J.), 165–66

Free Society of Traders, 91–92

Frelinhuysen, Theodorus, 163–64

Friendly Association, 199

Fundamentall Constitutions of Pennsylvania, 62, 125–26

Furley, Benjamin, 63, 127

fur trade, 17–18, 110; Dutch and, 37–38, 76–77; France and, 25; Swedes and, 27

Galloway, Joseph, 197

Gardiner, Lion, 29, 85, 89

Gardiner, Mary, 89

Gardiner's Island, 29, 85

German Reformed Church, 128, 133, 170

German-speakers: migration of, 65, 96–98, 126–27; and Palatines, 97, 120–21, 127; and Quaker Party, 206–7

Germantown, 65

Glasgow, 130; Enlightenment, 165; university, 130, 168

Glorious Revolution, 48–49

Godfrey, Thomas, 152, 158

Gordon, Thomas, 187–88

Graeme Park, 155–57, 176

Graham, James, 40

Grand Settlement of 1701, 53–54

Gravesend, 59

Great Awakening, 163–72; divisions caused by, 167–68; legacy of, 172–73; New Side and Old Side in, 168–70; Quakers and, 168. *See also* Whitefield, George

Great Lakes, 10–12, 77

Green, Enoch, 176

Gustavus Adolphus (Gustav II Adolf), 26

London, 91, 127; Yearly Meeting of, 178
Long Island: economy of, 84–86; families, 85–86; Great Awakening in, 167–68, 171; and Leisler, 50, 120; missions in, 171; New England settlements on, 28–30, 36, 38, 84–86, 120; radicalism of, 29, 39; and wampum trade, 28; women, 85–86
Long Island Sound, 13, 28, 120
Long Swede, Revolt of, 28
Louis XIV, 34
Louisbourg, 195
lower counties. *See* Delaware
Lutherans, 116, 117, 128, 133, 170
Lynn (Mass.), 28–29

Madison, James, 180; and *The Federalist,* 182
Mahicans, 17
Makemie, Francis, 201–2
manors, 78, 86–87: East Jersey, 46, 87, 98–99; on Long Island, 29, 85; New York, 38, 86–87; Pennsylvania, 63
maritime trades, 84–85, 105, 108
Maryland, 67
Massachusetts, 54
Mather, Cotton, 160
Matlack, Timothy, 212
Maverick, Samuel, 76
McDougall, Alexander, 160
Melfort, Lord (John Drummond), 46, 52
Mennonites, 127, 128, 133
merchants: after conquest, 86; Dutch, in New York, 37, 80–84, 117–18; in New York City, 38–39; Quaker, 91–92; Scots and Irish, 96, 137
Methodists, 133
métis, 102
Middle Colonies: agriculture of, 10; and American values, 214; definition of, 9–10; divisions within,

209–10; and extension of boundaries, 109–10, 213–14; as region, 1–7, 9–12; topography of, 10–12
Middlesex County (N.J.), 53
migration: chain migration, 127–28; German, 96–98; of native peoples, 14; Quaker, 64–66; Scots, 135–38; as subject of publication, 129; Ulster, 98–101, 129–33, 218n; to western New York, 210–11; to western Pennsylvania, 195, 210–11
Milborne, Jacob, 50–51, 119
mills, textile, 93
mines, 96. *See also* iron plantations
Ministry Act, 123
Minuet, Peter, 8, 27
missionaries, 101–3, 133, 171
Mittelberger, Gottlieb, 97, 129
mixed settlements, 101–3
Mohawk River, 12; Five Nations and, 14; valley of, 102, 109, 120–21
Mohawks, 41–42; Catholic, 198. *See also* Five Nations
monarchy, support for, 191–92
Monmouth Patent, 45, 78, 203
Montauk Indians, 29
Montour, Madame, 102
Montreal, 18, 25, 199–200
Moody, Deborah, 59
Moore, Milcah Martha, 157
moral philosophy, 133, 148–50, 179–80
moral reform, 177–78
moral sense, 149
Moravians, 101, 102, 128, 133, 170, 173
Morris, Lewis, 186, 188–89
Morris, Robert, 213
Muhlenberg, Henry Melchior, 170
Muslims, 115, 122

native peoples: agriculture among, 13–14; chieftains among, 13–14; diversity of, 134; and Great

Awakening, 171–72; and "Indian Great Awakening," 172; migrations of, 14; racial characterizations of, 133–34; of region, 12–19. *See also* Delaware Indians; Five Nations; Montauk Indians; *and* Susquehannocks

natural philosophy, 153, 158–59

natural religion, 146, 169

Neolin, 171–72, 205–6

Neshaminy, 164

Netherlands: commercial landscape of, 22; competition with England, 26; diversity of population of, 22, 114; Dutch war for independence in, 21, 114; exploration of Middle Colonies by, 19; "Golden Age" of, 22; Quakers from, 65; wars with England, 26

New Amsterdam, 23, 80–81: population of, 20; slave trade in, 84; surrender of, 32; trade of, 23; tradesmen in, 81

Newark (Del.) academy, 155, 169

Newark (N.J.), 44, 78, 93, 135, 138; land riots, 203

New Brunswick, 163–64

Newcastle (Del.), 100

New Jersey, 44–47; assembly of, 204; central corridor of, 93, 98–99, 136–37, 138; Concessions and Agreements of, 44; Dutch settlement in, 44–45; New England settlements in, 44–45; politics in, 192–93; Presbyterians in, 138; religion in, 134–40; Seven Years' War in, 198; shares governor with New York, 54; and southern Jersey Enlightenment, 176

New Lights: Irish, 130, 165, 169, 218n; New English, 218–19n

New London (Conn.), 173

New Londonderry (Pa.), 179

New Netherland, 21–26; commercial landscape of, 23–24; diversity of, 20, 22, 113–16; in Dutch empire, 20–21; economy of, 80–86; Indian relations of, 25–26; and New Netherland Company, 21; population of, 20, 86

New Sweden, 20–21, 26–27

Newton, Isaac, 145–46

New York (city), 38–39, 79; African community in, 121; Anglicization of Dutch in, 121; and Great Awakening, 167–68; and slave conspiracy trials, 106–8, 188–89

New York (colony): as diplomatic center, 43–44; duke and, 33–41; factious politics of, 185–89; group pluralism in, 117–22; increased immigration to, 210–11; origins of, 32–33; population of, 87; Seven Years' war and, 196–98; shares governor with New Jersey, 54

New-York Weekly Journal, 186

Nicholson, Francis, 49

Nicolls, Richard, 32, 36, 39–40, 203

Nicolls Patent, 45, 203

Nottingham, 179

Occum, Samson, 171

Ohio Country, 101, 110, 134; and Seven Years' War, 195–97

Orange, House of, 72. *See also* William of Orange

Oyster Bay, 29, 30, 168, 171

Paine, Thomas, 146, 213

Palatines, 97, 120–21, 127, 128

Pamela (Richardson), 174

Paterson, William, 180

patriotism (British), 208–9

patroonships, 26, 81–82

Paxtang, 130

Paxton Boys, 130–31, 141, 205–7

Penn, William (admiral), 55, 62

Penn, William (proprietor), 33, 55–59; *Case of West Jersey Stated,* 60; and Catholics, 126; and duke of York, 55–57; loses charter, 72–73;

Penn, William (proprietor) (*cont.*)
on religious liberty, 58–59; and the
Society of Friends, 57–59
Penn family: as proprietors, 190;
Richard, 190; Thomas, 73, 190–
91; William, Jr., 73, 190
Pennsylvania, 55–75; Charter for,
60–62; contested proprietorship
of, 73; diversity within, 126–34;
expense of western lands in, 210–
11; German-speakers in, 126–29;
government of, 191; Indian relations of, 72; land policy of, 63; legislation in, 192; movement for
royal governor in, 192; politics of
war in, 198–99, 205–7; population
of, 75, 103; Seven Years' War in,
197
Pequea, 179
Pequots, confederacy of, 28
Pequot War, 13
Perth, Earl of (James Drummond),
46, 52
Perth Amboy, 10, 135; elite of, 192–
93
Philadelphia, 63–64, 79; as American
capital, 209; as Enlightenment city,
147; as "green country town," 64;
literary culture in, 152–58; merchants and migration to, 127; plan
for, 92; population of, 75; Presbyterian church in, 167; as projected
British capital, 209
Pietists, 128, 163–64, 170
Pinkster, 121
pluralism, 111–43; group, 117–22;
Protestant, 113–16, 218n
Pontiac's Rebellion, 205–6
popular politics, 184–93, 202–7,
211
population: of Five Nations, 17–18;
of New Amsterdam, 20; of New
Jersey, 45; of New Netherland, 20,
86; of New Sweden, 20, 27; of
New York, 87, 211; of Pennsylvania, 75, 92, 103, 211

poverty, 104–6; and risk, 104; and
tenancy, 105; and working poor,
105–8
preachers: evangelical, 173–74;
Quaker, 91, 148; and Seven Years'
War, 196; women, 148
Presbyterians: and education, 132–
33; and Great Awakening, 168–
70; New Jersey, 138; and proprietary party, 202, 206–7; Reformed, 133; reunification, 172–
73; and Scottish Enlightenment,
151; seceder, 130, 133, 142; from
Ulster, 99–100, 129–33, 167
Priestley, Joseph, 146
Prince, Sarah, 174–76
Proclamation of 1763, 210
proprietors, 184–85, 193. *See also*
Scots proprietors
Protestantism: and Enlightenment,
149; and liberties of Protestants,
194
provisioning trade, 76–77

Quaker Party, 183, 192, 194, 198–99,
202; Germans and, 199; and Pax-
ton rioters, 206–7
Quakers. *See* Society of Friends
Quarry, Robert, 52
Quebec, 18, 110
Queen's College (N.J.), 178
Quietism, 56, 148
quitrents, 64, 68

Raritan Indians, 30
redemptioners, 97–98
region: in early America, 2–3, 215n;
and extension of Middle Colony
region, 109–10, 213–14; and subregions, 3
Reid, John, 161
Religious establishments, 126
Rensselaerswyck, 21, 26, 38, 81–82
resident proprietors, 52–53. *See also*
Scots proprietors
Restoration, 34–35; colonies of, 56–

economic goals of, 80; fall of, 47–48; "Glorious Revolution," 48–49; as king, 32–33, 47–48; as Lord High Admiral, 33–34; and New York politics, 185–86; and William Penn, 33, 61–62; and Pennsylvania charter, 61; and the prerogative, 34–35; as proprietor, 33–36; relations of, with Dutch, 33–34

Zenger, John Peter, 186–88
Zinzendorf, Nicholas, 170, 173